The Crucifixion of Jesus

Frontispiece: One of the oldest known representations of the crucifixion. Wooden doors of the church of Santa Sabina, Rome, 422–32.

THE CRUCIFIXION OF JESUS

HISTORY, MYTH, FAITH

GERARD S. SLOYAN

Fortress Press/Minneapolis

THE CRUCIFIXION OF JESUS
History, Myth, Faith

Cover graphic: "It Is Finished," by Sandra Bowden, painter and print maker, living in Clifton Park, N.Y. Used by permission of the artist.
Cover design: Ann Elliot Artz

Library of Congress Cataloging-in-Publication data

Sloyan, Gerard Stephen, 1919–
    The crucifixion of Jesus : history, myth, faith / Gerard S.
Sloyan.
        p.   cm.
    Includes bibliographical references and index.
    ISBN 0-8006-2930-2 (hard).—ISBN 0-8006-2886-1 (pbk.)
    1. Jesus Christ—Crucifixion.   2. Jesus Christ—Passion—Role of
Jews.   3. Satisfaction for sin.   4. Crosses—Cult.   I. Title.
BT453.S635   1995
232.96'3—dc20   95-2480
                                                                           CIP

The paper used in this publication meets the minimum requirements of American National Standard for Information Sciences—Permanence of Paper for Printed Library Materials, ANSI Z329.48-1984.

Manufactured in the United States   AF 1-2886 (paper)/1-2930 (cloth)

99   98   97   96   95   1   2   3   4   5   6   7   8   9   10

Contents

List of Illustrations

Frontispiece: One of the oldest known representations of the crucifixion. Wooden doors of the church of Santa Sabina, Rome, 422–32.

Plate 1: Face of Christ at Center of Cross. Ravenna: S. Apollinaire in Classe (6th c.).

Plate 2: The Crucifixion (detail). Duccio, Italian, 14th c.

Plate 3: Crucifixion. Lucas Cranach the Elder, German, 16th c.

Plate 4: Christ Expiring on the Cross. Theodor Boyermanns, Flemish, 17th c. Metropolitan Museum of Art, New York. Religious News Service Photo.

Plate 5: Crucifixion Icon. School of Novgorad. Russian Museum, Leningrad.

Plate 6: Crucifix, c. 1650. Michodean, Mexico. Denver Art Museum.

Plate 7: Crucifixion. Sadao Watanabe, Japanese, 20th c.

Plate 8: Le Crucifix (1943). Marc Chagall. Vatican Museum.

Plate 9: Headpiece to "Apparition": Christ on the Cross (1939). Georges Rouault.

Plate 10: 7 Last Words. Sandra Bowden. Mixed media.

Preface

A word of thanks is in order to Temple University which underwrote an academic course of lectures spread over two semesters that formed the basis of various chapters in this book; likewise to the intrepid Ms. Nadia Kraychenko of the word-processing center of its College of Arts and Sciences. Later the same day of each presentation to a graduate seminar, I was hosted by the faculty-student colloquium of Temple University's department of religion (in the first and last instances), then by the Lutheran Theological Seminary of Philadelphia, LaSalle University, St. Joseph's University, Villanova University, and St. Charles Borromeo Seminary. A Temple colleague in the chair of the department at the time, Dr. Robert B. Wright, made the arrangements through the Philadelphia Consortium of Religious Studies, which he brought into being.

I am very grateful to John T. Render, C.P., of Louisville, Kentucky, for his sharing of images from his extensive archive of depictions of the crucifixion. They enrich and enliven the book, and I appreciate his generosity.

Gratitude must also be expressed to the Institute for Ecumenical and Cultural Research of St. John's University, Collegeville, Minnesota, where the original research was done, whose director is Dr. Patrick A. Henry, and to the staff of the University's Alcuin Library, especially Carol Johnson and Stefanie Weisgram, O.S.B. As in all my scholarly endeavors, this one could not have been brought to completion without the active assistance of my sisters Virginia Sloyan and Sister Stephanie, R.S.M.

Abbreviations

ACW	Ancient Christian Writers
ANF	Ante-Nicene Fathers
CChr	Corpus Christianorum
CSEL	Corpus scriptorum ecclesiasticorum latinorum
DACL	*Dictionnaire d'archéologie chrétienne et de liturgie*
DS	Denzinger-Schönmetzer, *Enchiridion symbolorum*
GCS	Griechischen christlichen Schriftsteller
HTR	*Harvard Theological Review*
IEJ	*Israel Exploration Journal*
LCL	Loeb Classical Library
MT	Masoretic text
PG	J. Migne, *Patrum graecorum*
PL	J. Migne, *Patrum latinorum*
SC	Sources chrétiennes

Citations without a series or alternative publication data given are from the Loeb Classical Library.

Introduction

Jesus of Nazareth in Galilee died on a cross at the hands of Roman justice, probably in the year 30 of the Common Era. Hundreds of thousands were subjected to this cruel punishment before and after him. Yet one is hard-pressed to provide the name of another victim of crucifixion—apart from his companions in life Peter and Andrew—to whom Christian legend has attributed the same fate. Jesus emerges from those myriads of nameless slaves, brigands, and insurgents as "the Crucified."

Others are remembered for the way they died. That is not unusual: Socrates, Jewish and Christian and Muslim martyrs both by name and nameless, the dead of the Nazi Holocaust and other genocides whose sole crime was their peoplehood. Many of these deaths were preceded by the most shameful indignities and tortures. The death of Jesus was hardly unique in its ignominy. He did not, according to the Gospels, survive long on the cross. No carrion birds soared low over his carcass, his lifeblood seeping out to signal imminent death, as commonly happened to those left to die by this form of execution. Millions of innocent victims of political warfare have been subjected to greater tortures than he, as Amnesty International and similar agencies document from month to month. Why, then, is he remembered as if he, uniquely, had died as an innocent victim and in this fashion?

For two reasons, chiefly. The violent deaths of history's great ones—among whom he must be reckoned—are usually a matter of swift dispatch. Few meet their end in as sordid and demeaning a fashion as this, marked by details their devotees then celebrate. Far more important are the cosmic effects attributed to the death of Jesus, to which its actual circumstances are subordinate.

The circumstances are not subordinate for everyone. They have been made the subject of what can only be called a Christian piety of pain. In this development—it is not primitive in the church, not even early—the lacerations of his flesh by flogging, the nails in his hands and feet and the spear that pierced his side, the helmet of spines that indented his skull, and the mocking and spitting became paramount. From the early Middle Ages onward, God's love for a sinful humanity came to be gauged by the amount of pain Jesus endured on behalf of those who, by their sins, deserved it.

The chief actual sufferers from Jesus' death by crucifixion have been, paradoxically, not Christians but Jesus' fellow Jews. From an early period—the mid-second century can be documented—the apparent complicity in his death of the priestly leadership of the Jerusalem Temple with the Roman prefect of Palestine was extrapolated by Christians to the whole city, the whole land, and before long the whole people. Jews have suffered untold indignities at the hands of Christians, even to their liquidation, as a result of the way Jesus died. So much is this the case that the image of a cross bearing Jesus' body, a crucifix, is taken by Jews as being, far from the sign of the redemption of the human race that it is for Christians, a reproach intended for them for killing God's Son. For this deed Christians devised the term *deicide,* the murder of deity. Efforts of the latter half of this century to convince Jews that no such symbolism is intended by the crucifix have been largely unavailing. The misconception of this symbol by Christians themselves has been such—even though a reproach to Jews is no part of it—that as many centuries may be required to convey what Christians mean by it as went into its perception as a symbol of oppression.

The four Gospels present Jesus' crucifixion in close conjunction with his upraising from the dead. This joining of the two is as much theological as chronological. When Christians conceive his death and resurrection correctly it is as one mystery of faith, not two. Paul is the earliest expositor of the meaning of his death we know of, although he may have been preceded by compilers of passion narratives like the one used by Mark or the framers of statements like the one found in Romans 3:24c–25a: "Christ Jesus, whom God put forward as a sacrifice of atonement by his blood, effective through faith." In seven letters that are certainly Paul's, spanning the years 50–57 C.E., he never uses the phrase "death and resurrection." It is clear, however, that his use of the terms "death," "cross," "death on the cross," or "word of the cross" always implies resurrection, often in a phrase that occurs nearby. In the same way, his use of "resurrection," "glory," or "splendor of the Father" when referring to Christ is a way of including the death in shame that preceded it.

Luke, whose Gospel and Acts of the Apostles together constitute one quarter of the New Testament, creates uneasiness in Christians of a particular theological persuasion by treating the crucifixion of Christ as the necessary precondition of his resurrection. For it is Christ's resurrection that Luke holds to be the cause of human "remission of sins" (his characteristic phrase). This uneasiness is explained by the reformers' having overcome the reign of what was thought to be a *theologia gloriae* ("theology of glory")—Christians triumphant with Christ over sin and death—by a return to the New Testament *theologia crucis* ("theology of the cross"). The triumphalist outlook of the Renaissance papacy was not what the Augustinian hermit

Martin Luther had in mind. That came later. The evidence is scanty that schoolmen like Thomas Aquinas and Bonaventure, whom Luther thought ill of and gave no evidence of having known intimately, had replaced the man of Calvary with a figure of heavenly glory. Theologians like them had kept the two together fairly successfully, in a way their fourteenth- and fifteenth-century successors, whom Luther knew much better, had not. What he meant when he first employed the phrase *theologia crucis* was an emphasis on the cross as the only true theology. Anything other than that was a mis-conceived *theologia gloriae*. The result was an intensified popular preaching of faith in the cross, a devotion already in place. The reformers' special con-tribution was a reminder of the Pauline teaching that it is faith that justifies sinners, making them just with God's justice, rather than any trust in human deeds apart from the divine gift and impulse. But faith in Christ's resurrec-tion as likewise a saving deed of God was not notably restored.

The unity of cross and resurrection as the one paschal (i.e., Passover) mys-tery that the liturgies and the teachings of the years 100–600 conceived it to be had been sundered for almost a thousand years when the reformers came on the scene. They achieved the goal of restoring much of Pauline thought to the West but not all. Christ's death on the cross, believed in by grace through faith, was rightly but only partially perceived as Paul's view of the cause of fallen humanity's restoration. The Easter mystery, gloriously trum-peted in hymnody and chorale, remained by and large a separate matter, a deed of God that vindicated the Innocent Sufferer but not a justifying action for humanity on a par with the cross. Luther thought that the Catholic iden-tification of believers with the risen Christ was too facile, preceded as it was by deeds of penance but with little true repentance. It was this that he and his followers set out to repair. Still, repentance could itself be a human "work." It was effective only if it were seen as a faith-inspired response to God's deed of the cross.

The Eastern churches have a better record of keeping the two events to-gether as a single mystery, chiefly through their celebration of the Divine Liturgy. This sacrificial meal was never for them simply a memory of a deed of God once done, but always a memorial, a living symbol re-presenting Jesus' self-offering to God. It was more than that. The Holy Liturgy was always the piety of the East, not just its public prayer. The Catholic West had allowed the two to come apart, possessing the same eucharistic faith as the East but not making it the people's piety or instruction. Not even the biblical Word as preached in the power of the Spirit succeeded in bringing the two events together. It was only the early liturgies, of which the procla-mation of Scripture was an integral part, that could keep crucifixion and resurrection together in the popular mind for the unity they are. But the Western liturgy was celebrated in a tongue increasingly incomprehensible to the people, and the preaching that accompanied it was often not in its spirit.

A remarkable essay in theology by two Anglican priests, Sir Edwyn Clement Hoskyns and Francis Noel Davey, was published posthumously by Methodist editor Gordon S. Wakefield.[1] The book's early paragraphs set out the authors' intention of letting those who wrote the New Testament speak for themselves, presenting *their* theology however unsystematized and unselfconscious. The fundamental assumption any student of these writings has to make, the authors say, is that, as they left the hands of the first-century writers, they seemed to them to make sense. The peculiar sense made by the New Testament terms for crucifixion and resurrection is in such a delicate, dialectical balance that the two authors were afraid to betray it by entitling their book *Crucifixion and Resurrection,* hence the hyphen, *Crucifixion-Resurrection.* They feared that the conjunction *and* might do harm to the total interdependence of the two concepts, confirming the false impression that either could be considered in isolation or that the one was but an addendum to the other.

When the *risen* Christ is displayed iconographically on crosses in the sanctuaries of churches of the Catholic tradition of the West, Jews tend to be puzzled but pleased by the substitution. Some Christians are displeased by what they take to be a deemphasis of Jesus' redemptive death, while other Christians deplore any imaged representation at all. Such glorified Christs on the cross are, of course, an attempt to say that crucifixion-resurrection is the one mystery of faith.

Clearly the discussion up to this point has been theological, assuming as it does that crucifixion-resurrection is a mystery believed in with the faith of the church. Many persons keenly interested in the way Jesus died do not profess such faith. They are not kept from an inquiry into the question by that fact. Some say that adherents of a religion are those most incapable of a dispassionate exploration of its core. People who maintain this view tend to be nonadherents or former adherents of the religion under discussion. They think that religions are best examined nonreligiously, that is, historically or sociologically, aesthetically or economically. This approach can result in the examination of an aspect of a religion but not that about it which is irreducibly religious.

Indeed, many who explore a religion linguistically, archaeologically, socially, or however it may be are convinced that their concern is not an aspect but the entire phenomenon. For them what is called "religion" is reductively a matter of social behavior or tribal mores. Not many respectable scholars of particular religions fall in that category. The examiners of religions (in the plural) or religion as a "human phenomenon" frequently do.

For anyone who takes Judaism or Islam, Christianity or Hinduism or Buddhism seriously, it is all but impossible to explore dispassionately the

1. *Crucifixion-Resurrection: The Pattern of the Theology and Ethics of the New Testament* (London: SPCK, 1981).

central matter that constitutes it. Whether one is committed, noncommitted, or committed against the subject, dispassion does not describe the scholarly search. Passion connotes undergoing something, being gripped by something. It need not be one's feelings or emotions. Intellectual passion is real and it is very strong. In scholarly explorations of the crucifixion of Jesus—as considered separately from his resurrection by both religious believers and nonbelievers in it—it is impossible to discover dispassion, either intellectually conceived or as it touches the whole person. Too many claims have been made for this death, too many lives have been lost both in witness to its meaning and as a tragically misguided conclusion from its meaning, for this dispassion to be possible.

Is the cross the symbol of a necrophilic cult, as it seems to be? Does it accept suffering willingly while millions go convinced, religiously or otherwise, that life's main purpose should be to avoid suffering? Many have the conviction that pain should not be piously reflected on but eliminated, whether by meditative transcendence or physical or mental cure. Does faith in the cross relieve the burden of sin or does it create guilt for sins? All such questions prove inescapable for those who study Jesus' *death* and the effects it has had, whether they were reared in a religious tradition or a religious vacuum.

Compounding this is an all but universal interest in the *life* of the man Jesus by anyone who has heard of him. Jews are an exception because his followers have caused them so much anguish. They have long ago classified him as a teacher of the late Second Temple period who is of little interest to them. Any persons who have come to know his teaching intimately, although not as believers, can be puzzled at the emphasis put on his death when it seems to them that his life is what matters. How can one see his life, teaching, and example on the one hand, and his death and resurrection on the other, as a single fabric? The evangelists did not seem to integrate them successfully, nor Paul nor the Epistle to the Hebrews nor Revelation. All left to the later church the problem of relating Jesus' teaching career to the tragic events of his last few days. Outsiders to Christianity perceive the problem. Those within frequently do not.

It is possible, of course, to bracket all theological consideration of the death of Jesus and attend to it as an event in human history. This way lies open to the historically sophisticated, whether believers in Jesus' death as a religious mystery or not. They cannot lay their faith or unfaith, their prejudices, or their passions completely aside. What they can do is follow the canons of modern historiography developed since the Enlightenment, more especially since 1800. It is essential, at the same time, that they be aware of the canons of ancient historiography. To dismiss these conventions impatiently, expressing regret that the four evangelists wrote more in the spirit of Homer, Herodotus, and the Deuteronomist than Tacitus and Josephus (themselves "ancients," although in a different mold), is to find the history in the Gospels and other New Testament books questionable.

Matthew, Mark, Luke, John, Paul, John of Patmos, and the anonymous others meant to write history in the fashion of biblical historians. The resurrection of Jesus from the dead was witnessed by no one, they say. They report that once he was raised he appeared in an altered, glorified state and to believers only. The writers make no claim that this new life of his was history in the ordinary sense; rather the opposite.[2] But when it came to his apprehension by the temple authorities or the Roman soldiery in an olive orchard by night, his appearance before religious and civil authority ending in capital sentence, and his being submitted to the tortures attendant on crucifixion, a historical account was undoubtedly intended.

The Gospel narratives were based on a sum of historical reminiscences. These had been elaborated with the passage of time, but then so is all ancient history. History in the Gospels is not a bald factual chronicle. It encompasses an imputation of motives and states of mind, although only John of the four presents Jesus' thoughts and intentions. In this the Gospels resemble all ancient history and much of modern.

In brief, the circumstances of Jesus' death are open to inquiry because a number of ancient documents originating in a community sympathetic to him recorded them. No cross-reference with other writings is possible until mentions in pagan polemical literature and the Talmud begin to occur. There is nothing unusual in this. We do not possess primitive testimony to any religion from outside it, only from within. An old challenge asks why no mention of Jesus' execution exists in imperial records if it were so important. This challenge rests on a number of assumptions, some of them false and the rest doubtful: that *any* correspondence from Pilate to Rome is extant; that he thought the victim important enough to report his death by name; that as a prefect of the equestrian order he would have been expected to send forward an account of all the insurgent colonials he sent to the stake and crossbeam.

The place to begin this inquiry appears to be the only narrative account we have of Jesus' last days, the Gospels. Paul frequently mentions, a quarter of a century after the event, that Jesus died this way, but he provides no particulars. As background to the trial and crucifixion accounts, a summary of what is known of Roman and Jewish justice is in order; more than that, of who was condemned to crucifixion in the ancient world and on what charges. The risen-life narratives need to be reported on but not with the same detail as the trial and crucifixion accounts, since data of the same his-

2. Gerald G. O'Collins makes the point successfully when he argues that, although the "resurrection is a real bodily event involving the person of Jesus of Nazareth," the resurrection of Jesus "is not an event *in* space and time and hence should not be called historical" since "we should require an historical event to be something significant that is known to have happened in our space-time continuum." See his "Is the Resurrection an 'Historical Event'?" *Heythrop Journal* 8 (1967): 381–87; quotations from pp. 381, 384.

torical order are not in question. This inquiry into history will be the subject of chapter 1 here.

A second aspect of the overall study will be the interpretation put on Jesus' death by those who believed in his resurrection. Luke's volume two, entitled much later "the Acts of the Apostles," purports to convey the way Jesus' disciples understood these events a short seven weeks after they occurred. The public proclamation of him as dead and risen that, as Acts maintains, the action of the Spirit made possible proves to be a set of apologetic arguments that had been crafted over the course of decades. These were framed on the basis of the Septuagint Greek translation of the Bible, which only some diaspora pilgrims in a Jerusalem crowd would have been at home in. The speeches of Peter in early Acts clearly come from a much later time. There is a great variety of theological understandings of the meaning of crucifixion-resurrection to be found in the New Testament, not just the Lukan theological history written in the late first century. It is important to try to discover what underlay the decision—evidently taken very early—to find virtue in Jesus' ignominious death. One needs to ask, What is the likeliest explanation of the disciples' decision not simply to acknowledge that their champion had been condemned as an enemy of the state but to boast of his shameful end? What led them to claim for it the power, if not to reverse world history, at least to steer it in an entirely new direction; to make reparation for all disordered human behavior and enable the entire race to live a new, Godlike existence? The origins of the death of Jesus as "saving" and the several ways in which this belief has been expressed theologically should come next in order.

The third part of this study will review the variety of understandings Christians of the centuries have derived from or placed upon the biblical data. It is put that way and not "the New Testament data" because the Scriptures of the Jews were taken to be a *prophetic* record of the career of Jesus as much as the New Testament was a *retrospective* one. The first Christian "testament" was employed in this project equally with the second. Much of this work of identifying the meaning of Jesus' death has been done, as numerous histories of Christian doctrine disclose. Some of these are tendentious, as one would expect. The authors of such works, like those in the Christian gnostic tradition, hold positions that they do not see reflected in what became the orthodox theologies (called "soteriologies," a word that describes theories of salvation) of the centuries.

A fourth portion of the study will do what has been far less commonly done than the first three. It will try to track the various Christian pieties that have surrounded the crucifixion, especially those that treat it in relative isolation from the resurrection. One needs to ask whether these pieties have induced a morbid acceptance of suffering, even a seeking it out in emulation of Christ's sufferings. If the latter, is that a good thing or a bad, or is it a mixture of the two? A further question is whether the present temper of the times makes the suffering Christ an attractive figure to some believers but repellent to others. If such is the case, is there any correlation between dire poverty or powerlessness and attraction to a suffering Jesus, or is economic status no part of the formula? The gnostic denial of Jesus' humanity, after all, was philosophically based, being the province of intellectuals who looked pityingly on those who, unlike themselves, were immersed in matter. The Monophysite position, which held the total absorption of human nature by deity, although allied to gnosis, was one that proved very popular with the landless peasants of Egypt and Syria. They looked to liberation from suffering far more than to identification with it. One needs to ask, Which modern groups and classes are most heartened by a suffering, crucified Jesus, and for which has he the least appeal?

Another aspect of the dying Savior figure central to Christianity is the impact it makes on non-Christians who are not Jews. The Islamic world venerates 'Īsā, son of Maryam, as the last and greatest of prophets before Muhammad, but has learned from the Holy Qur 'an that he did not die on the cross. Another man was substituted in his place. The views of the peoples of the Far East of a suffering Christ figure need to be examined, even if only a small minority of the learned among them and those exposed to missionary activity have heard of Jesus. Would the image of the Crucified tend to attract or to repel the Buddhist and the Hindu masses if it were presented as the symbol of a compassionate God?

What impact does a dying and rising Christ make on a Western intellectual community devoid of Christian or Jewish influence if such can be identified? On a psychological and psychiatric community? Not least importantly, on artists in every medium who have been variously uplifted, seared, scarred, graced by their near or far acquaintance with the mystery of the cross?

Finally, worthy of discussion are a few contemporary soteriologies of note, which see humanity's condition improved through faith in the person and teaching of Jesus more than in faith in his vicarious death-resurrection. Such, too, are some contemporary theologies of salvation rooted in the experience of repression according to race, class, and gender. Some of these one can readily acknowledge as falling within the Christian tradition, but others are clearly outside it.

In sum, the death of Jesus will be examined in itself; in the interpretation of its significance by those who first reckoned it a religious mystery and later by scoffers at such an absurd conceit; in its theological and iconographic development; and in the pieties, impieties, and perplexities that have always attended it.

CHAPTER ONE

Crucifixion and Why Jesus Was Sentenced to It

There seems to be little reason to doubt that Jesus of Nazareth died in the way ascribed to him, namely, as the recipient of the Roman sentence of death by crucifixion. Nineteenth- and early twentieth-century denials that he ever existed, popular among some rationalists, or that "Jesus" was simply an ideal figure representing the suffering innocent Jew who embodied every biblical virtue, were shown for what they were by Anglican Archbishop Richard Whateley's serious spoof of the last century. He established in his paper *Historic Doubts relative to Napoleon Buonaparte* (1819) that Napoleon never existed. The pseudoscholarship of the early twentieth century calling in question the historical reality of Jesus was an ingenious attempt to argue a preconceived position. The gospel portrait of Jesus' words and deeds does in part derive from a variety of biblical narratives and biblical wisdom. D. F. Strauss took Christian Europe by surprise in demonstrating this in his *Das Leben Jesu* ("The Life of Jesus," 1834–35), but he never denied that a real figure of history was the basis for the Gospel portraits of Jesus, which drew heavily on biblical imagery. Indeed, he thought he was doing a work of constructive rather than destructive theology and was stunned by the response of academic Germany to his contribution. A century of attempts to reconstruct the actual words and deeds of Jesus, culminating in the work of Johannes Weiss and Albert Schweitzer, followed Strauss's book, and was popularly termed "the search for the historical Jesus."[1]

1. John P. Meier makes some helpful distinctions among the terms used in "life-of-Jesus" research since the days of H. S. Reimarus (1694–1768). Sorting out the confused terminology that followed on Martin Kähler's 1892 distinction between the historical (*historisch*) and the historic (*geschichtlich*), which even Kähler did not observe with strict rigor, Meier comes down on these distinctions: the "real Jesus" (the man who did and said certain things in life), the "historical Jesus" (a modern, hypothetical reconstruction of his career), and the "earthly Jesus" (the Gospel picture, however partial and theologically colored, of Jesus during his life on earth). The last term can be ambiguous because it can be, and is, also used "with different nuances, of both the real Jesus and the historical Jesus." For "the Jesus known in faith, the presently reigning Lord of the Church," Meier opts for "the risen Jesus." See his "The Historical Jesus: Rethinking Some Concepts," *Theological Studies* 51 (1990): 3–24; cf. "The Real Jesus and the Historical Jesus," chap. 1 of *A Marginal Jew: Rethinking the Historical Jesus*, vol. 1 (New York:

There is no need here to recall the extra-Christian testimonies to the Christian movement of the late first and early second centuries. Tacitus (d. ca. 120), Suetonius (d. after 122), and the younger Pliny (d. ca. 113) had no special stake in the phenomenon. They simply recorded it.[2] Any deviation from Roman *pietas*—respect for the gods of Rome, the state, and the family—was likely to be labeled benighted or superstitious, especially one originating in Jewish Palestine. The reference to Jesus by the Jewish historian Josephus (d. after 93; he took the name of his patrons of the imperial family, hence the usual designation of it as the *testimonium Flavianum*) was certainly edited in a faith direction by a Christian hand.[3] Its substrate, however, is no more to be impugned than his brief accounts of John the Baptist and James of Jerusalem.[4] Josephus was totally "neutral on the side of Judaism"

Doubleday, 1991), 21–40). The quotations are from pp. 19, 21 of "The Historical Jesus." He thinks that very few "real" persons are available to us from the ancient world, neither Hillel, Shammai, Jesus, nor Peter, and he names Marcus Aurelius as an exception because of his introspective self-disclosures.

2. Tacitus *Annals* 15.44 (ET, John Jackson; LCL, Cambridge, Mass. and London, 1951; 4.282) records that Christus "suffered the extreme penalty" (*supplicio adfectus erat*) under Tiberius. (The citations from the ancient world to follow in this book are all taken from the LCL unless otherwise noted.) For Suetonius, see *Lives of the Caesars* under "The Deified Claudius," 25.4 (ET, J. C. Rolfe, 1914; 2.52), which speaks of his persecution of followers of Chrestus; and "Nero," 16.2 (ibid., 2.110), who inflicted *supplicia* on the Christians, "a class of people given to new and mischievous superstitions"; Pliny the Younger *Letters* 10.96.1–10 (ET, A. N. Sherwin-White, *The Letters of Pliny* [Oxford: Clarendon Press, 1966], 691–710) calls the practice of Christians who sang hymns to Christ as to a god a form of madness (*amentia*) and a perverse and extravagant superstition, the latter a word used by his friend Tacitus ad loc. with the adjective "pernicious" (*exitiabilis*) added. Tacitus writes in that place that Nero made Christians the culprits for the fire of Rome, repeating with Suetonius the rumor that it had been set by the emperor's order.

3. "About this time there lived Jesus, a wise man, *if one indeed ought to call him a man.* For he was one who [was of good conduct and known to be virtuous] *wrought surprising feats and was a teacher of such people as accept the truth gladly.* He won over many Jews and many of the Greeks. *He was the Messiah.* When Pilate, *upon hearing him accused by men of the highest standing among us,* had condemned him to be crucified, those who had in the first place come to love him did not give up their affection for him. [They reported that] on the third day he appeared to them restored to life, *for* [he was perhaps the Messiah concerning whom] *the prophets of God had prophesied these and countless other marvelous things about him. And the progeny* [tò phýlon] *of Christians, so called after him, has still to this day not disappeared"* (Josephus *Jewish Antiquities* 18.63–64) (ET, Louis H. Feldman, 1965; 9.48–51). The passage interrupts the flow of accounts of uprisings in 62–65 C.E., yet much of its vocabulary is Josephan. The italicized phrases are those not found in the Arabic version left by a 10th-century bishop, Agapius of Hierapolis, while those in brackets are to be found there. See Shlomo Pines, *An Arabic Version of the Testimonium Flavianum and Its Implications* (Jerusalem: Israel Academy of Sciences and Humanities, 1971). Drawing on the researches of C. Martin, A.-M. Dubarle, L. H. Feldman, and others, Meier proposed his own reconstruction of the text as Josephus may have written it: "At this time there appeared Jesus, a wise man. For he was a doer of startling deeds, a teacher of people who received the truth with pleasure. And he gained a following both among many Jews and among many of Greek origin. And when Pilate, because of an accusation made by the leading man among us, condemned him to the cross, those who had loved him previously did not cease to do so. And up until this very day the tribe of Christians (named after him) has not yet died out" (*Marginal Jew*, 62).

4. For John the Baptist see Josephus *Antiquities* 18.116–19 (9.80–84). The twenty-four lines in Greek are a straightforward narrative explaining that John, called the Baptist, practiced an immersion (*báptisin*) that was a "consecration of the body implying that the soul was already thoroughly cleansed by right behavior, . . . not to gain pardon for . . . sins." Herod (Antipas) is

so long as the subject he discussed was Jewish. In the case of Jesus, he tells nothing of how he ended, nor does he seem to have heard of the resurrection tradition.

Setting aside for the present the causes that may have led to Jesus' death, it should be helpful to review the kind of death it was. He was a young man, probably in his thirties, in 30 C.E. (the most reliable death date), and presumably healthy. He was likely a small man, as the skeletons of many Semites of the ancient world suggest. The Gospels say that Pontius Pilate, the Roman prefect of Judaea, had Jesus scourged before handing him over to be crucified. After this the soldiers clothed him in purple, wove a crown of thorns for him, and mocked him as "King of the Jews." This is better rendered "of Judaea"; *tōn Ioudaíōn* allows both meanings but was the normal way to designate a place rather than its people. In the Gospel of Mark, probably the first of the four to be written, striking Jesus' head with a reed and spitting on him preceded the mock homage.[5] John has all the scourging and mocking details of Mark but not the spitting.[6] He inserts them in the middle of the extended dialogue he composes between Pilate and Jesus at the praetorium or armed garrison (18:28—19:16), as activities of the (Roman) soldiers. The two principals are inside the building; unspecified Judaeans ("hostile Jews"?) except for "the chief priests and the [temple] guards" are outside in the courtyard. At the end of the inserted material that constitutes the lengthy dialogue, they respond to Pilate's invitation, "Behold, the man!" with the outcry, uttered twice, "Crucify him."[7]

The Markan passion narrative, as it is called, has little detail beyond what is contained in the third of the three predictions of Jesus' death placed on his lips: "The Son of man will be handed over to the chief priests and the scribes, and they will condemn him to death and hand him over to the Gentiles, who will mock him, spit upon him, scourge him, and put him to death, but after three days he will rise."[8] No eyewitness testimony to Jesus' movements on his last day alive need have been required for the Gospel report of

---

described as having brought him in chains to the fortress Machaerus on suspicion that John's eloquence would lead to sedition. This detail does not occur in the Gospels, just as there is no mention in Josephus of Herod's incestuous marriage to Herodias or the beheading of John, the details that they feature. For James of Jerusalem, see *Antiquities* 20.197–203 (ET, 9.494–97), which describes the stoning of "James the brother of Jesus" (in 62 C.E.) for having "transgressed the law," at the direction of the high priest Ananos (Ḥanan or Annas the Younger), an act for which King Agrippa deposed him.

5. See Mark 15:15–19. Matthew at 27:28–29 edits Mark by making it a scarlet military cloak and first placing the reed in Jesus' right hand, scepterlike; Luke uniquely, at 23:7–11, has Pilate send Jesus to Herod (Antipas), there to receive this contemptuous treatment from him and his soldiers while the chief priests and scribes stand by accusingly.

6. See John 19:1–5b. For a careful exploration of these and other details, see Raymond E. Brown, S.S., *The Death of the Messiah: From Gethsemane to the Grave*, A Commentary on the Passion Narratives of the Four Gospels, 2 vols. (New York: Doubleday, 1994).

7. See v. 6.

8. Mark 10:33–34. The other predictions of his death, less detailed, are in 8:31 and 9:31. Matthew retains them at 16:21; 17:22–23; 20:18–19; Luke at 9:22, 24; 18:31–33. John has no such prophecies by Jesus.

occurrences that led up to his death. The knowledge that he died by crucifixion would have been enough. The evangelists probably did not know
which soldiery, Roman or Jewish, visited what cruelties on Jesus, although
those on whose reminiscences they drew may have known. The writers of
the Gospels possessed the general remembrance that temple and imperial
armed forces had acted on orders, the first to harass, then the latter to execute Jesus. That would be all they would need to know in order to tell of
Herod Antipas and Pilate, mutual antagonists brought together briefly over
a common enemy. For, whatever Jesus' alleged crimes, he was at least guilty
of having infused hope of political liberty in an oppressed populace, a fact
that would have posed a threat to the occupying power and its priestly col-
laborators. Pilate's death sentence is reported as delivered diffidently, but
it was he alone who delivered it. The Gospel writers chose to feature the
temple priesthood's initiation of the action against Jesus rather than its final
execution, for reasons that need to be explored.

The Ancient View of Crucifixion

Minucius Felix was a Christian apologist who wrote a dialogue some time
around 200 C.E. entitled *Octavius*.[9] In it a pagan named Caecilius accuses
Christians of every sort of superstition destructive of true religion. Among
them are eating babies and copulating randomly in the dark.[10] Another of
their follies is the worship of one who has been crucified. They get the kind
of altars proper to the abandoned wretches they are because their rites center
on a man punished for his crime. He received the direst penalty (*summo
supplicio*) on the bestial crossbeams of wood.[11] The word *supplicium* used
here is often coupled with *servile,* designating it a slaves' punishment, the
class who most often received it.

The Christian Octavius acknowledges that the mode of Jesus' death was
a scandal even for those who first believed in him, but he meets the charge
obliquely rather than head on. Omitting any pursuit of the way Jesus met
his fate, he says in the apologetic fashion employed by Hellenistic Jews in
the wisdom literature of the Bible that the pagans do worse by venerating
wooden gods. They hold in honor signs of victory such as banners and stan-
dards that are cruciform and made of wood; perhaps the wooden god of
their worship was even at one time "part of a gallows [*infelicis stipitis por-
tio*]!"[12] Important here is the avoidance of the real problem, the death of

9. Minucius Felix, *Octavius,* ed. C. Halm; CSEL 2 (Vienna, 1867), 3–56 (ET, *The Octavius
of Marcus Minūcius Felix,* G. W. Clarke; New York and Paramus, N. J., 1974).
10. See *Octavius* 8–12 for a lurid catalog of supposed Christian practices, which at 13.5
are described as "doting [*anilis*] superstition."
11. Ibid., 9.4; the phrase is *crucis ligna feralia.* See 29.2 for the charge that Christians
worship a criminal (*hominem noxium*) and his cross.
12. Ibid., 29.7; quotation from 23.11 (Clarke, 24.6).

one claimed to be God's own Son on a tree of shame (an *arbor* or *lignum turpe, infelix, infame*). Cicero (d. 43 B.C.E.) called crucifixion the most horrendous torture (*crudelissimum taeterimumque supplicium*).[13] Small wonder that in Minucius Felix's treatise written almost two centuries after the fact, calculated to persuade pagans that the one God of the Christians was the God of the philosophers, the author should sidestep the criminal's death that Jesus died, a man for whom divine honors were being claimed.

The Christian Presentation of Jesus' Mode of Death

The earliest believers in him had no such compunction. As we shall later see, they made a special point of his shameful ending. Why they should have done this rather than suppress it or make apology for it as later Christian philosophers did is not immediately apparent. Jesus' earliest followers, all of them Jews, proclaimed this tortured death among Jews, who might have been open to a particular tale of cruelty at the hands of the Roman oppressor. But Jesus' crucifixion was never presented on those terms. If anything, Roman responsibility was deemphasized in favor of Jewish. Was there, perhaps, some biblical symbolism attached to a death in this fashion that the prophet Jesus was seen to fulfill? There is myriad evidence of God's concern for the suffering just one in Israel (including Joseph thrown into a cistern, Gen. 37:24; Elijah harassed by Ahab and Jezebel, 1 Kings 16–19; and Jeremiah flogged and put in stocks, Jer. 20:2), but as to death by crucifixion, the scanty biblical evidence goes in quite the opposite direction. In a chapter of Deuteronomy that deals variously with expiatory rites over the corpse in an untraced murder, marriage to women taken captives in war, the rights of the firstborn son even if borne by a despised wife, and the capital charge against an incorrigible son, this passage occurs:

> If a man guilty of a capital offense is put to death and his corpse hung on a tree, it shall not remain on the tree overnight. You shall bury it the same day; otherwise, since God's curse rests on him who hangs on a tree, you will defile the land which the LORD, your God, is giving you as your inheritance.[14]

13. M. Tullius Cicero *Against Verres* 2.5.64 (ET, L. H. G. Greenwood, 1935; 2.650–51). Paragraphs 65 and 66 contain a description of the way one crucifixion was carried out.

14. Deut. 21:22–23. Some interpret the phrase "hung on a tree" to mean impaled on a stake. The Israelite punishment of dropping a heavy stone on the victim or something like it is obviously understood to be the proper means of execution (see *M. Sanh.* 6.4), although how widely it was practiced is not known. The treatment of corpses recommended in Deuteronomy was a warning to others, as in Josh. 8:9; 10:26. The Philistines nailed Saul's headless body to the wall of Beth-shan (1 Sam. 31:10), which may have been equivalent to what the Jews proscribed as "hanging on the wood" (Deut. 21:22–23).

This biblical sanction against allowing a corpse to hang more than one day, together with the accursed state of the one so hung (whatever exactly that meant), probably mirrors and at the same time accounts for the failure of Jews to employ this cruel form of torture. The resort to crucifixion among them for high treason in the Hasmonean period and a puzzling exception of its use in the Mishnah (ca. 180 C.E.) will be dealt with below. But, for the moment, one can see why the claim for a messiah who was crucified would be thoroughly repulsive to the Jewish ear. Paul calls the cross a scandal (in translations, commonly, "stumbling block") to Jews and an absurdity to Gentiles. He does this in writing to the once pagan but now believing communities of Corinth (1 Cor. 1:23) and the highlands of the province of Galatia (Gal. 5:11). Paul makes capital of Jesus' presumably accursed condition in the latter epistle by posing the paradox that his "becoming a curse for us" extended "the blessing of Abraham to the Gentiles through Christ Jesus."[15] More of that later; the point for now is that one might have expected the earliest believers in Jesus to avoid or at least soft-pedal the fact that Jesus died as a convicted felon.

They did quite otherwise. They wrote at length not simply that it happened and hence was bound to be remembered, but, for a reason that seemed good to them, they identified this unqualified evil as somehow a good. Christian apologists like Lactantius (d. ca. 320) and Arnobius (d. ca. 330) would puzzle over why God had not proposed an honorable (*honestum*) kind of death for Jesus, but there it was. He died on what the ancient world invariably called in Greek the "criminal wood," as also later in Latin (*mala crux*). The anonymous Epistle (actually a treatise) to the Hebrews unblinkingly calls the cross a sign of "shame" (*aischýnēs*), saying that Jesus endured it for the sake of the joy that lay before him.[16]

The Torture of Crucifixion

The origins of crucifixion are hard to trace. Not only Jews but Greeks, Romans, and those that both of them denoted barbarians considered it an obscene form of punishment. It is commonly called Persian or Medean in its origins, probably because Herodotus (d. after 44 B.C.E.) frequently has these peoples employing it. He generally uses one verb for crucifying living men (*anaskolopízein*) and another for corpses (*anastaurízein*), a distinction later lost.[17] The Homeric mythic tradition does not mention it. From the full range

15. Gal. 3:13–14.
16. See Heb. 12:2.
17. For exhaustive detail on how and by whom crucifixion was administered in the ancient world see Martin Hengel, *Crucifixion,* trans. John Bowden (London: SCM; Philadelphia: Fortress Press, 1977), a revised and enlarged version of the author's "*Mors turpissima crucis:* Die Kreuzigung in der antiken Welt und die 'Torheit' des 'Wortes vom Kreuz,'" *Rechtfertigung:*

of texts it is impossible to be sure whether impaling corpses on a stake (*skó-lops* or *staurós*) or hanging the condemned up to die is in question. Again, whether the victims were affixed by nails or lashed with thongs is not clear in individual citations, any more than whether an upright stake alone or a crossbeam also was used. The only detailed account of a crucifixion Herodotus supplies is the administration of the punishment by the Athenian general Xanthippus to the satrap (*hýparchos*) Artaÿctes for what are called religious offenses: "They nailed him to planks and hanged him aloft; and as for his son, they stoned him to death before his father's eyes."[18]

Detailed descriptions come only from Roman times. Seneca (d. 65 C.E.) refers to a variety of postures and different kinds of tortures on crosses: some victims are thrust head downward, others have a stake impale their genitals (*obscena*), still others have their arms outstretched on a crossbeam.[19] The Jewish historian Josephus, writing of the Jewish War of the late 60s, is explicit about Jews captured by the Romans who were first flogged, tortured before they died, and then crucified before the city wall. The pity he reports that Titus, father of Josephus's imperial patron Vespasian, felt for them did not keep Titus from letting his troops dispatch as many as five hundred in a day: "The soldiers, out of the rage and hatred they bore the prisoners, nailed those they caught, in different postures, to the crosses for the sport of it, and their number was so great that there was not enough room for the crosses and not enough crosses for the bodies."[20] Josephus calls it "the most wretched of deaths." He tells of the surrender of the fortress Machaerus on the east shore of the Dead Sea when the Romans threatened a Jewish prisoner with crucifixion.[21]

An especially grim description of this punishment, meted out to murderers, highwaymen, and other gross offenders, is the following from a didactic poem: "Punished with limbs outstretched, they see the stake as their fate; they are fastened, nailed to it with sharpest spikes, an ugly meal for birds of prey and grim scraps for dogs."[22]

Much later in Latin speech "*Crux!*" became a curse, to indicate the way the speaker thought the one accursed should end. Other epithets among the

---

Festschrift für Ernst Käsemann zum 70. Geburtstag, ed. J. Friedrich, et al. (Tübingen: Mohr; Göttingen: Vandenhoeck und Ruprecht, 1976), 125–84. Some of the same data from the ancient world are found in Urbanus Holzmeister, S. I., *Crux Domini atque Crucifixio; quomodo ex Archaeologia Romana illustrantur* (Rome: Pontificium Institutum Biblicum, 1934), 32, reprinted from *Verbum Domini* 14 (1934): 149–55, 241–49, 257–63.

18. Herodotus 9.120 (ET, A. D. Godley, 1924; 4.298). See also 1.128, where Astyages the Median impaled (*aneskolópise*) the Magians (*mágoi*), interpreters of dreams, who had persuaded him to let Cyrus go free.

19. Seneca *To Marcia on Consolation* 20.3 (ET, John W. Basore, 1935; 2.68).

20. Josephus *Jewish War* 5.451 (ET, H. St. J. Thackeray, 1928; 3.340).

21. Ibid., 7.202–3 (3.563).

22. Pseudo-Manetho *Apotelesmatica* 4.198ff., as cited by Hengel, *Crucifixion*, 9, n. 20 (translation adapted).

lower classes found in Plautus, Terence, and Petronius are "Crossbar Char-lie" (*Patibulatus*) and "Food for Crows" (*Corvorum Cibaria*).[23]

This obscene form of execution seems to go back well before the Persian wars to use in Assyria (by King Ninus against Pharnus of Media), India, Numidia, and especially Carthage (Hamilcar meting it out and Hannibal receiving it in turn).[24] From which of the colonial peoples Rome took it over cannot be determined. Characteristically, the historians of Greece and Rome ascribe it to barbarians capable of such cruelty, not unlike the ascription of the use of poison gas to other nations in the modern world—only the enemy would stoop to this in our day. It is not acknowledged that "civilized" peoples would manufacture it surreptitiously for sale to any buyer.

The Romans attributed crucifixion to the Greeks and the Thracians, even while themselves resorting to it. Plato (d. 348/347 B.C.E.) had referred to it in the following exchange of Polus with Socrates, calculated to make the philosopher choose between the just man condemned to death and the suc-cessful plotter who survives to a long life of tyranny. The former, "if . . . caught . . . is put to the rack and castrated, his eyes burned out, and after . . . seeing inflicted on his wife and children a number of grievous torments . . . he is finally crucified or burnt in a coat of pitch."[25] Glaucon in the *Re-public* apologizes for his harsh language as he puts a similar dilemma: "The just man will have to endure the lash, the rack, chains, the branding-iron in his eyes, and finally, after every extremity of suffering, he will be crucified [lit., impaled; split wide open]."[26] Demosthenes (d. 322 B.C.E.) knew about being "nailed up" as the worst form of execution.[27] The "nailing to planks" written of only by Herodotus (see text at n. 18 above) had its cognate in the victim's being affixed to a *týmpanon* of planks by rings or hooks for public display or torture, sometimes execution.[28]

Flogging usually preceded crucifixion among the Romans, as with the Carthaginians. It weakened the victims to such a degree that their time on

23. Sources given in Hengel, *Crucifixion*, 9–10, nn. 21–23. A brief chapter there (pp. 11–14) describes Prometheus's mythic crucifixion as it is dealt with by the satirist Lucian in his mockery of the gods, *Prometheus* (ET, A. M. Harmon, 1915; 2.242–45), and the account in the *History* of Diodorus of Sicily (d. after 36 B.C.E.) of the crucifixion of Lycurgus by the god Dionysius (3.65.5–6; ET, C. H. Oldfather, 1935; 2.298–301). The cruel punishment that had grown familiar to the Greeks from the Persian and Macedonian wars was retrojected onto the myths that in earlier days did not speak of it. Lucian, incidentally, makes a jab against the Christians in his *Passing of Peregrinus* 13, 11 (ET, 5.14–15, 12–13): "They worship that cruci-fied sophist and live according to his laws. . . . The man who was crucified in Palestine because he introduced this new cult into the world."

24. On Assyria see Diodorus 2.1.10 (ET, 1.352) and especially James B. Pritchard, *The An-cient Near East in Pictures*, 2d. ed. (Princeton: Princeton University Press, 1969), plates 362, 368, 373. On India see Diodorus 2.18.1 (Oldfather, 2.408). On Carthage see ibid., 25.5.2 (ET, Francis R. Walton, 1957; 11.148); 26.23.1; Caesar *The African War* 66 (ET, A. G. Way, 1957; 248).

25. *Gorgias* 473C (ET, W. R. M. Lamb, 1925; 5.349).

26. *The Republic* 361E–362A (ET, Paul Shorey, 1937; 1.125).

27. *Oration* 21 (*Against Meidias*) 105 (ET, J. H. Vince, 1935; 74).

28. See Hengel, *Crucifixion*, 70–71, for data on this pillorying by Greeks, which he calls "not far short of an execution."

the cross was shortened.[29] Lashes of a whip are assumed, but sometimes *hrábdoi* (in Latin, *virgae*), "rods," are mentioned, bringing the torture closer to a cudgeling, depending on their thickness.[30] This was the normal Roman punishment for deserters, later transferred to those guilty of uprising against the state (*seditio*) and high treason (*perduellio*). The punishment *crux* will be named first among the three most severe (*summa supplicia*), following Cicero's usage of the term for "supreme penalty." Nailing was the commonest form of affixing a body to a tree trunk or crossbar, with lashing by bonds done only in addition.[31] The evidence for a peg or saddle (*sedile*) on the stake to support the body at the crotch, thus extending life and torment, is elusive. Seneca says: "You may nail me up and set my seat upon the piercing cross" (*Suffigas licet et acutam sessuro crucem subdas*) and speaks of "weighing down upon one's wound" (*vulnus suum premere*); H. Fulda supplies extensive documentation on the subject.[32] If the victims were generally supported on crosses by such a seat, the custom of leg breaking or *crurifragium* mentioned in John 19:32-33 would be accounted for. Deprived of the rigidity supplied by the lower limbs, the abdominal cavity would sag, bringing on death by asphyxiation.

The record of history on crucifixion as a torture, with all its ugly refinements, is such that one is led to conclude that Jesus' execution was carried out with relative dispatch. As the Gospels describe it in economical prose, it was a matter of inquiry and sentence shortly after sunrise and death by midafternoon. The torments that preceded Jesus' death are given in much greater detail than the death itself. In John's Gospel the actual crucifixion is described in thirty-six Greek words excluding articles and enclitics (19:17-18), while the dicing for his garments by soldiers that follows shortly requires fifty-seven (vv. 23-24).

Ernest Hemingway's short story "Death on Friday" catches the spirit of the Gospel accounts better than many a book-length treatise, whether of devotion or archaeological history. In it, in a Jerusalem tavern on the night

29. Titus Livius *History* 22.13.9 (ET, B. O. Foster, 1929; 5.244); cf. 28.37.3. At times the flogging preceded execution by some other means. Antigonus, the last Jewish king in the Hasmonean line (d. 38 B.C.E.), was beheaded after humiliating flagellation, "the only king to endure this at Roman hands." Dio Cassius 49.22.6 (ET, Earnest Cary, 1917; 386, 388).

30. See Suetonius "Nero" 49.2 (ET, 2.178); Dio Cassius 2.6; 1.68.

31. See J. W. Hewitt, "The Use of Nails in Crucifixion," *HTR* 25 (1932): 29-45; cf. Philo *On Dreams* 2.213 (ET, F. H. Colson and G. H. Whitaker, 5.538); Plutarch *Morals* 499D (ET, W. C. Helmbold, 6.370); Lucan *The Civil War* 6.543-49 (ET, J. D. Duff, 344-45); Seneca "On the Happy Life" 19.3 (ET, John W. Basore, 2.48). Several of these speak of "nailing up" a victim and Lucan of the "nails that pierced the hands [*Insertum manibus*]." A crucified man was found in Jerusalem with a nail still in his heel-bone. See N. Haas, "Anthropological Observations on the Skeletal Remains from Giv'at ha-Mivtar," *IEJ* 20 (1970): 38-59. On the use of nails see also Josef Blinzler, *The Trial of Jesus*, trans. I. and F. McHugh (ET of 2d ed.; Westminster, Md.: Newman, 1959), 250, 264-65.

32. Seneca Epistle 101, "On the Futility of Planning Ahead," 12 (ET, Richard H. Gummere, 1925; 3.164-65); H. Fulda, *Das Kreuz und die Kreuzigung: Eine antiquarische Untersuchung* . . . (Breslau, 1878), a work not available to me.

Jesus died, one of the Roman soldiers who had carried out the sentence can only keep repeating drunkenly: "He looked pretty good out there this afternoon." That is basically the message of the evangelists. They have some interest in the details of the event but not much. It is of less interest to them who did it and how than what was done and why. Even then, their interest in the human "what" and "why" is muted alongside the marvelous result that came of it. Their much greater concern is what God made of it by raising Jesus up and why this should have been done; in other words, what the death can mean for any who are able to see the hand of God in it.

Who Was Crucified and Why

What types of persons were subjected to this cruel ending in the ancient world, and to whom was it seldom or never administered? The short answer to the first is: the slaves and lower classes; soldiers, even in command positions (but not generals); the violently rebellious and the treasonous. As to the second, citizens of the Greek city-states and of the Roman state were usually done away with more briskly, seldom by crucifixion. Poisoning, stabbing, and beheading were the favored methods. Scipio the Elder crucified Roman citizen deserters returned by the Carthaginians in the Second Punic War, as that conflict dragged on (218–201 B.C.E.), to maintain military discipline.[33] P. Gavius, the man whom Verres had had crucified in Sicily with his face to the Italian mainland, was charged with being a spy for the rebel slaves of Spartacus.[34] But in general the *honestiores,* the highborn, did not die that way. It was considered too cruel and, not least, too demeaning for the upper classes. Administered to any but slaves or those who threatened the existing social order, it would be an admission that the minority citizen class could be capable of such bestial conduct. It was admissible to crucify the subhuman but not admissible that the human could act subhumanly. Hence the widespread suppression of the fact that such executions were widespread. The historians tended to deplore the practice as an atrocity perpetrated by others than themselves, the civilized. Cicero could call the torture a plague[35] and Varro and Seneca denounce it, but they regretted it as a necessity of life to cope with the criminal classes. Neither philosophers, playwrights, nor poets engaged in any serious attempt to stamp it out. Like

33. Titus Livius *History* 30.43.13 (ET, Frank Gardner Moore, 1949; 8.532) and 29.18.14, where the citizen soldiers were subjected to *servilibusque . . . suppliciis* ("the punishments of slaves") and were forbidden burial (ET, 278).

34. See n. 13 above.

35. Cicero's successful defense of Rabirius, whom Julius Caesar wished to eliminate, gives a more graphic description of the horrors of crucifixion than in his oration against Verres. See "In Defence of Rabirius" 4.13 (Cicero, *The Speeches;* ET, H. Grose Hodge, 1927; 464), which includes the charge to the executioner: "Lictor, go bind his hands. . . . Veil his head, hang him to the tree of shame [*arbori infelici*]."

American slaveholding in the last century, it was deemed an acceptable social evil.

Josephus was both a Jewish patriot and an apologist for Roman behavior
in his Palestinian homeland. Just before the passage cited above (in the text
at n. 20), he defends Titus by saying that the commander hoped that the
gruesome sight of the corpses of those of Jerusalem who attempted flight
would move the ones within the walled city to surrender. Josephus's vocabulary is interesting here. The besieged Jerusalemites he describes as common
folk among the poor, while those leading the resistance within are rebels or
insurgents (*stasiastaí*) abetted by brigands (*lēstaí*) outside the city. Besides
the action of Titus in 69, Josephus tells of other mass crucifixions by the
Romans in Judaea, notably that of two thousand by Quintilius Varus, legate
of Syria, as he put down a Jewish revolt in 4 B.C.E., the year Herod the
Great died.[36] Ventidius Cumanus, who was procurator in 48–52 C.E., took
a number of prisoners, presumably of both sides, in a Samaritan-Galilean
dispute at Passover tide—the last one he experienced in Palestine. Stepping
in over Cumanus, the legate of Syria Quadratus, upon appeal by the Samaritans, had all the prisoners crucified.[37]

A deed that triggered the Jewish War involved the uncommonly cruel Judaean prefect Florus Gessius, who in Nero's twelfth year (66 C.E.) raided the
temple treasury on a pretext of fiscal exigency. After the confrontation that
ensued he ordered his troops to sack the upper market area of the city and
root out the dwellers in its narrow streets. Many of these "peaceable citizens" were apprehended and, once brought before him, scourged and crucified. Josephus, whose penchant for exaggeration is well known, puts that
day's victims at thirty-six hundred, including the unheard-of indignity of
crucifying Jews who had been awarded the rank of *eques*, "knighthood,"
by Rome.[38]

Those four occurrences over a seventy-year period tell several things
about Roman-Jewish relations. For one, the empire's functionaries posted to
areas like Judaea acted swiftly and cruelly to crush the seeds of rebellion.
The Roman talent for governance by accommodation was clearly subordi-
nated to the sword. Second, decreeing crucifixion for rebellious Jews on the
wide scale was Rome's way of saying that it considered this proud people no
better than a slave population. Third, the Jewish resentment of Roman high-

36. *Jewish War* 2.75 (ET, H. St. J. Thackeray, 1967; 2.350); cf. *Antiquities* 17.295 (ET, 8.508).

37. *War* 2.241 (ET, 2.241); cf. *Antiquities* 20.129 (ET, 9.456), which specifies that both Samaritans and Jews were crucified, a matter left ambiguous in the account in *War* ("all"); Tacitus speaks of Jews' being put to death on this occasion for the effrontery of slaying Roman soldiers (*Annals* 12.54). Cumanus was sent off to Caesar to explain himself and was subse-
quently exiled. His successor Felix promptly apprehended a Jewish guerrilla leader named Eleazar and crucified him and his followers, punishing in an unspecified manner an "incalcul-
able number" of others. See *War* 2.253.

38. *War* 2.305–8.

handedness must have been fierce. Only the destruction of the city and its temple could have deferred any further attempt at revolt, which came sixty-five years later under Bar Kokhba in Hadrian's time.

The Roman Crucifixion of Jesus
and the New Testament

Two self-evident conclusions follow from the above truisms as they apply to Jesus of Nazareth. One is that Pilate must have become convinced, perhaps in very short order, that Jesus and the two men crucified with him constituted a serious threat to the peace of the empire. The other is that there is little likelihood that Jesus' disputes with other religious teachers, or even the charge that he spoke blasphemously, was the immediate cause of his death. The fears that the temple priests had of his influence over the populace were reductively political, since the power over the people they feared to lose was a matter of tithes and taxes, not a religious influence or one of spirit. They knew they could count on a swift reprisal by Roman authority if they only couched their account of the "plot" of Jesus and his followers in the right terms.

If any of this theorizing is true—and the assumptions of fact underlying it have not yet been examined here—it is hard to know why those Jews who first proclaimed him Israel's crucified and risen Messiah, his disciples in his lifetime, did not appeal to Jewish sympathy for him as one more victim of the Roman state. The Jewish populace knew the empire's multitudinous cruelties all too well. So far as we know, Jesus' disciples never made such an appeal—even though Jewish sympathy for him on these grounds would have been overwhelming. Why did his followers go another route and name as the reasons for his death the jealousy of the learned class and the plotting of the hated priesthood, which had to make its point with the Gentile oppressor if he were to be eliminated? Or did they?

The possibilities, here again, are two: that the Gospels and the book of Acts do not present responsibility for Jesus' death as it was conveyed primitively, by oral accounts in the Aramaic language; or that they do, but that the hatred of the common folk for the high priesthood, which acted as Rome's fiscal agent against them, was even greater than for the ultimate oppressor, distant Rome. It needs to be repeated that Jewish familiarity with crucifixion as a Roman punishment was so intimate and detailed that the muted report of Jesus' subjection to it in the New Testament is a mystery. Did the claim of many associates to have seen him risen from the dead relativize the ignominy of the execution utterly? Or were other, stronger forces at work, such as theological reflection, to put a quite different interpretation on the death than ordinary recollection and resentment would have done?

All this we need to speculate on from the scanty data that the New Testament provides.

Did the Jews Crucify?

Before moving to the problems provided by the Gospel accounts of Jesus' appearance before Jewish and Roman authority, one must attend to a final question concerning crucifixion: Did Jews of the first centuries B.C.E. and C.E. ever themselves resort to this form of capital punishment? If they did not, Pilate's reported statement in John's Gospel at 19:6 is an absurdity. There he is quoted as saying: "Take him yourselves and crucify him. I find no guilt in him." Mark and Matthew have Pilate "delivering Jesus over to be crucified," presumably to the Roman legionaries, but Luke is ambiguous. He speaks of Pilate as summoning "the chief priests, the rulers, and the people" (23:13); and, after telling them he finds Jesus guilty of no capital crime and proposing a flogging to placate them, he "handed Jesus over to them to deal with as they wished" (vv. 22, 25). What "them" does Luke have in mind?

There is much not known about how Roman justice was administered in the provinces, so it is unwise to declare apodictically what could or could not have happened. But, reserving the historical credibility of the various Gospels for a later discussion, one can ask now whether any evidence exists that Jews, who had so often been the victims of crucifixion, ever administered it. If the answer is, "No, not under any circumstances," then John's Gospel attributes to Pilate a sneering directive impossible of fulfillment. A complete imponderable is how much mob action a Roman official like Pilate might have turned his back on. In a violent society—and first-century Palestine, like the scene of all repressed peoples in their own societies, was one—much violence occurs apart from that authored by the chief violator, the government. Yet a record of mob violence known of beforehand and allowed to take its course is an unlikely situation. Pilate's activities at any Passover season, when Jerusalem was a tinderbox, would have been in the direction of curbing mob action, not fomenting it. Any execution of Jews would almost certainly take place under cover of legality and for an alleged civil cause. The charge of sedition or seditious intent was, short of murder, the one conceivable cause.

To the question, then, about Jews as capable of crucifying, whether under Mosaic law or in any circumstances: Josephus reports of Alexander Jannaeus (104–78 B.C.E.) that he crucified eight hundred Jewish allies of Demetrius III, king of Syria, who took up arms against him.[39] Yigael Yadin maintains that the Qumran commentary on Nahum 2:12–14 from Cave 4 and the more recently deciphered Temple Scroll refer to this incident when they

---

39. *War* 1.97, 113; cf. *Antiquities* 13.380, 410–11.

speak of the punishment for an informer or traitor and for one who deserts his people for the Gentiles.[40] The punishment is being hanged on a tree to die. Traditional talmudic wisdom is that any reference to this mode of torture goes in the other direction, interpreting Deuteronomy 21:22–23 to mean that a criminal is first put to death and then his corpse hanged.[41] Yadin thinks that the twice-occurring phrase "you shall hang him [the traitor; the one who curses his people] on a tree and he shall die" means that the victim shall die as a result of the hanging. He reconstructs the corrupt phrase of the text, "from of old," to read "*thus was it done* from of old." The actions of a Jewish tyrant are not, of course, to be thought of as normal Jewish practice. The question for the moment is: Did it ever routinely happen? Interestingly, Josephus does not report Herod the Great as having carried out any crucifixions.

Extremely puzzling is the mishnaic passage (late second century C.E.) which says that on one occasion Simeon ben Shetah hanged eighty women in Ashkelon, the only city in Palestine the Hasmoneans did not sack.[42] It goes on to report that the sages opposed the hanging of women and that only the blasphemer and the idolater were hanged. Then comes the traditional Jewish understanding:

> How did they hang a man? They put a beam into the ground and a piece of wood jutted from it. The two hands [of the body] were brought together and [in this fashion] it was hanged. Rabbi Jose says: The beam was made to lean against a wall and one hanged the corpse on it as butchers do.[43]

The appropriate biblical text is then quoted that forbids leaving the body overnight and requires burial the same day. But the Mishnah uses an apodictic form, not the casuistic as in Deuteronomy ("If a man . . ."), and the quotation stops short of 21:23b, which assigns a reason for the requirement to cut the corpse of the accursed one down: "otherwise . . . you will defile the land which the LORD, your God, is giving you as an inheritance."

"All that have been stoned must be hanged," the same passage says. There is an elaborate description of how the huge stone is to be dropped from twice the height of a man; if the first has failed to kill, the stone is dropped a second time as the victim lies supine. Whether this form of execution was a memory of ancient practice at the time of the writing more than it was a current reality is hard to say. Our present interest, however, centers on the Jewish technique of hanging the victim after death rather than before: "A man is hanged with his back to the gallows and a woman with her face

40. Y. Yadin, "*Pesher Nahum* (4QpNahum) Reconsidered," *IEJ* 21 (1971): 1–12; against his view see J. M. Baumgarten, "Does *tlh* in the Temple Scroll Refer to Crucifixion?" *JBL* 91 (1972): 472–81.

41. See the *baraita* in *b. Sanh.* 46b.

42. In *m. Sanh.* 6.4; see *y. Sanh.* 23c.

43. *m. Sanh.* 6.4.

toward the gallows."[44] This cannot be the *stipes* or upright stake in the ground but must be either the *furca,* a V-shaped rack for carts when it was not used for this ugly purpose, or the infamous *tau,* the crossbeam on a stake in the form of a T. Yadin thinks the latter type of cross is attested by the iron spike found in a man's heels, which were nailed together and he hanged alive, upside down, with his knees over the crossbar.[45]

In light of the lateness and uniqueness of the testimony to hanging (crucifixion?) in the Mishnah, it is improbable that this mode of display (execution?) had any currency in Jewish life as a legal punishment. What an incited Jewish mob might have resorted to is impossible to say. In the absence of any Jewish evidence that Jews were regularly inflicting a punishment that had so often been inflicted on them, or any Gospel evidence that a Roman prefect had turned his power of capital sentence over to them in a case of sedition—the charge the Gospel of Luke implies the priesthood brought against Jesus (23:1)—it makes no sense to say that the Jewish authorities crucified him. If that was the way he ended, Roman power must have done it. As to Pilate's taunt in John's Gospel (19:6), if it is historical it need not have been uttered in sarcasm but perhaps in ignorance of Jewish legal custom. He would simply have been giving the implied permission, "If you have some religious reason to eliminate him, go ahead." Pilate would then have indicated Rome's way of doing things on a civil charge, namely, crucifying.

It it more likely, however, that the phrase on Pilate's lips was a calculated Johannine irony. This evangelist frequently has the characters in his drama say more or other than they realize. He makes them unconscious speakers of the truth. If this is the case here, Pilate is telling the priestly inciters to do what they cannot do because of the inhibition of Mosaic precept but what in fact they manage to achieve: Jesus' death by crucifixion.

Why Was Jesus Sentenced to Death?

This brings us directly to the question of the causes that brought about Jesus' death. The four Gospels, products of the mid- to late first century, provide the most details of what led up to it and the event itself. The "passion narratives" are not, however, the earliest extant indication that he died in that manner. The distinction probably belongs to a saying of Jesus found in slightly different forms in several places in the first three Gospels. Mark gives it as, "If anyone wishes to come after me he must deny himself, take up his cross, and follow me" (8:34). Matthew has the identical wording except that

44. Ibid.
45. Y. Yadin, "Epigraphy and Crucifixion," *IEJ* 23 (1973): 18–22. N. Haas, a medical doctor in Israel, has a different theory, namely, that the feet were nailed onto a cleat of olive wood as the victim hung upright (*IEJ* 20 [1970]: 38–59). He assumes in this article the use of the *sediculum* or saddle between the buttocks.

he uses the ordinary verb for "come" rather than "follow" or "come after" (16:24). Luke employs the same verb as Matthew but in a different form and adds the phrase "daily" (9:23). Another version of the same saying in parallel occurs in Luke 14:27 and Matthew 19:38, where the wordings differ notably. In Matthew the saying reads, "Whoever does not take up his cross and follow after me is not worthy of me," while Luke uses the word for "carry" and ends with "cannot be my disciple." Without entering into the question of which is likely to be the more primitive form, it is safe to say that the logion existed in early collections of Jesus' sayings that were circulating in the 50s and conceivably the 40s.

The above saying does not elaborate on how Jesus went to the cross. Knowledge of his ending is simply assumed among believers in him. In the hortatory aphorism—almost certainly devised by an early community rather than spoken by Jesus before he died—the punishment is shorn of its horrors and made a figure of self-abnegation and willing acceptance of suffering. Crucifixion's teeth have been removed. The sentence has become for followers of Jesus what it was for him: not unspeakable torment but acquiescence to the inevitable, freely willed.

Paul speaks often of the death of Jesus (Rom. 5:10; 6:3), at times using the shorthand term "cross" (1 Cor. 1:17, 18; Phil. 2:8; Gal. 5:11; 6:12). Once only does he assign responsibility for it and then it is to the people of Judaea, not to Rome. This occurs in the first-written of his extant letters, 1 Thessalonians (probably in 50), at 2:14b–16. Paul is exhorting the believers in Christ in that large Macedonian city, whom he describes as former idol worshipers (1:9), to persevere in faith despite harassment from their "fellow countrymen" (2:14). The pertinent passage follows:

> For you suffer the same things from your own fellow countrymen [symphy-letōn] as they did from the Judaeans [Ioudaíōn, related to the quality of Christian faith in Ioudaía, which Paul commends, earlier in the verse], who killed both the Lord Jesus and the prophets and persecuted us; they do not please God, and are opposed to everyone, trying to prevent us from addressing the pagans that they may be saved, unto the constant filling up of the measure of their sins. But the wrath of God will come upon them at the end [or, has come upon them at last; the verb is aorist, i.e., timeless].

It has been argued since the mid-nineteenth century that vv. 14–16 in whole or part were an addition to Paul's text by a later, probably Gentile, hand.[46] The sentiment provides an uncommonly bitter ending for the prayer

---

46. For a listing of those who favor and disfavor the opinion that this passage contains interpolated features, see my *Jesus on Trial: The Development of the Passion Narratives and Their Historical and Ecumenical Implications* (Philadelphia: Fortress Press, 1973), 4–5, n. 4. An article sustaining authenticity is Otto Michel's "Fragen zu 1 Thessaloniker 2:14–16: Antijüdische Polemik bei Paulus," in *Antijudaismus im Neuen Testament? Exegetische und systematische Beiträge*, ed. W. P. Eckert, N. P. Levinson, and M. Stöhr (Munich: Kaiser, 1967). Oppos-

of thanksgiving to God that begins at v. 13 (flanked by those of 1:2–10 and 3:9–13). More than that, Paul nowhere else attributes the death of Jesus to anyone, although he often indicates the antipathy of some fellow Jews to his preaching, both those who believe in Jesus and those who do not. Whether the passage is authentic is perhaps less important than the occurrence of a phrase in this piece of occasional correspondence written twenty years after Jesus' crucifixion that takes for granted the recipients' conviction that God has "destined us . . . to gain salvation through our Lord Jesus Christ, who died for us" (5:9–10a). That shows not simply that Jesus' death was to the forefront of Paul's thoughts when he first brought the gospel to Thessalonica but that he had spoken of it as an event that achieved salvation (i.e., deliverance from God's wrath on the last day). A theology of redemption based on Jesus' death, without the details that surrounded it, was already in place. The doubtful character of those verses disputed as Paul's stems not from his incapacity to resort to the apocalyptic language of end-time expectation but from his not having his own Jewish people or the Jews of Judaea as a target in his other extant letters.

The Development of the Passion Narratives

Coming to the Gospels, one asks first about their historical dependability. This is no place for a full review of contemporary thought on the kind of writing they are and how they probably came into existence.[47] The range of opinions goes from that of those Christians who hold it as a dogma (a word they would not use) that the divine inspiration of these writings assures the believer that no detail reported by an evangelist can have happened otherwise than as described, to the view of equally devout believers who think that the evangelists possessed few facts about Jesus' last hours besides knowing that Pontius Pilate, encouraged by the antipathy of the temple priesthood, condemned him to be crucified at Passover time because he constituted a threat to the Roman state. Every sort of opinion in between has been entertained. The narrower range among noninerrantists is between the maximalist view that Jesus' early disciples took pains after his death to garner all the information they could, passing it along as a body of authentic reminiscence, and the minimalist position that some details are marked by such verisimilitude that they should be credited, while the palpably legendary and theological elements must be identified as such.

ing it is Birger A. Pearson, "1 Thessalonians 2:13–16: A Deutero-Pauline Interpretation," *HTR* 64 (1971): 79–94, who cites Baur, Holtzmann, and A. Ritschl as of the same opinion.

47. See Luke T. Johnson, "Jesus in the Memory of the Church," chap. 6 of *The Writings of the New Testament: An Interpretation* (Philadelphia: Fortress Press, 1986), 114–41; Norman Perrin, *Rediscovering the Teaching of Jesus* (New York: Harper and Row, 1967); Vincent Taylor, *The Formation of the Gospel Tradition* (London: Macmillan, 1957).

Until recently the method of approach to the Gospels generally and the passion narratives in particular has been to examine all four for their historicity, checking the details in each against those in the others, and then the four globally against Roman and Jewish history and legislation in the Mishnah and Talmuds (codified two and three/four centuries later, respectively). A method favored since the ascendancy of the Rudolf Bultmann (d. 1976) school, around 1920, has been to try to discover the *tradition* that lies behind each Gospel. This body of primary data, whatever may have been its state of development when it served as the core narrative of a Gospel, was followed by subsequent *editing(s)*, bringing the tradition to its present state.

The method was easy to apply in the cases of Matthew and Luke because their authors had Mark before them and probably a collection of Jesus' sayings (known as Q), which they quoted almost verbatim. Discovering the basic Mark before its author engaged in his editorial activity is obviously not an easy task, and learning what John's sources were, besides the details of the passion he seems to have had in common with Mark and Luke, is nearly impossible. A more fruitful recent avenue of approach has been to view all four evangelists for what they are, storytelling authors each in his own right. This requires a look at the narrative of the last days of Jesus in each Gospel vertically, that is, as the plotted culmination of the narrative, rather than horizontally, by comparing the Gospels primarily with each other.

The important thing the evangelist, who acted as a narrator or storyteller, had to do was choose from among the materials available to him and arrange them creatively in such a way as to produce the maximum impact on the hearer. That last word is especially important, for the Gospels were constructed in the first instance to be memorized by itinerant evangelists, then recited and *heard,* not *read,* normally by people who already believed in what was being announced. The writers had proclaimed portions of their "gospel" aloud hundreds of times before they set themselves to writing it down on parchment as a work of spoken rhetoric. The discipline of "form criticism," as it is called—a hypothesizing on the actual circumstances in the early church that led to the telling of this miracle story or that parable in the form in which it appears in a Gospel—has been of great help in reconstructing the composition process of the smaller units within each Gospel. "Source criticism," the tracking of what came from where, mentioned above, has made a similar contribution. Its chief pitfall is that it tends to assign every scrap of Gospel material to a written source even though the culture that produced it was primarily oral.

The breakthrough in modern Gospel study on historical terms came less than a quarter of a century ago with the recognition that no Gospel writer thought of himself as a collector, compiler, or editor. Each was above all an author. We have on our hands four works of literature by men of genius who possessed hundreds of sayings, anecdotes, and tales in a theologically developed form, however primitive, which they wove into four quite distinct narratives that were fresh compositions. They addressed themselves to hearers who already believed in Jesus of Nazareth—that he was mighty in word and work; that he had proclaimed the word of God from Israel's Scriptures as a restorer of Israel's faith in all its pristine power; and that his was a special view to the final consummation of God's world in an age to come.

The Historical Core of Jesus' Last Hours and the Gospels

Jesus had engaged in many disputes with the learned and in their course earned the enmity of some, but such was not his downfall. It is quite clear that his religious opinions fell within the allowable limits of dispute in the Israel of his day. The opposition of the power class in Jerusalem is what brought about his dissolution. The current high priest Caiaphas and his power broker father-in-law Annas, heartily despised by the people as agents of the Caesars acting through the prefects since the death of Herod the Great, seem to have brought on Jesus' execution. The Galilean evidently spoke against the temple consistently: not the institution of blood sacrifice, any more than the prophets had done, but its perversion by irreligious men who worshiped chiefly at the shrine of their continued exercise of power. The Gospel evidence is that it was they who managed to silence him by playing on the fears of a cruel Roman functionary that he might have a potential uprising on his hands.

The clear possibility exists that the hard core of reminiscence about Jesus' last day or days that survived is contained in the succinct summary of Luke 23:1:

> Then the whole assembly of them arose and brought him before Pilate. They brought charges against him, saying, "We found this man leading our people astray; he opposes the payment of taxes to Caesar and maintains that he is the Messiah, a king."

All the remaining details in the Gospels could have been elaborations of that remembered fact. Even as it stands, the statement is an interweaving of the theological and the political. "Leading astray" had the religious connotation for Jews of deceiving the people over the absolute oneness of God. It could also have overtones of sedition on the lips of Jewish men of power who opposed revolt. The opposition to paying taxes to the occupying power was a clear distortion of Jesus' watchword on the absolute claim of God over the human, a power that he nonetheless acknowledged.[48] The charge that Jesus declared himself Israel's king of the final age—something the first

48. See Mark 12:17; Matt. 22:21; Luke 20:25.

layer of Gospel material says he took pains to avoid—could only have been heard by Roman ears as the seizure of power that several predecessors of Jesus ("messianic pretenders") had made it. On balance, it seems correct to maintain that the disciples of Jesus after his resurrection reconstructed the events of that Friday on the basis of the fact that Roman justice disposed of him, after successful priestly efforts to counter his mounting popularity by delating him on a charge of sedition.

That means that each evangelist culminated his narrative with a recon-structed account of Jesus' apprehension by military power; a Jewish hear-ing—Luke has two, adding to that before the high priest and Council one with the Galilean tetrarch, Herod Antipas[49]—and a Roman trial; and the normal cruelties that accompanied crucifixion. Eyewitness testimony to Je-sus' successive adventures on the way to death would have had to be that of the women at the cross because of the Gospels' insistence that his male dis-ciples, but for one anonymous one, were nowhere on the scene after the arrest in the garden. The Cyrenean native drafted into service, Simon, would be another exception (Mark 15:21). Peter's threefold denial that he knew Jesus, like the disciples' flight, is probably an authentic reminiscence, on the theory that nothing so damaging to the early leadership would have been passed along if it were not regrettably true.

Basic Elements of Mark's Passion Story

An example of the effect of the narrative technique on subsequent genera-tions is Mark's account of Peter's betrayal. Granted its historical basis—Peter as the cowardly denier of his teacher and best friend—Mark uses the device of interpolation or inclusion to tell it. In this narrative device a story is begun and another is told within it, as the closure of the first story coming at the end of the second makes clear. Mark employs it seven times. In six of them the account that forms the brackets is illumined by the narrative that is bracketed. Among the best known of these is the exception, the cure of the hemorrhaging woman (5:25–34) told within the story of the resuscitation of Jairus's daughter (5:22–24, 35–43). Here the "meat" of the sandwich does not shed any particular light on the "bread." There are only the matching details of a girl of twelve years and a woman who had received help from doctors for twelve years. The mysterious parabolic act of the prophecy of the fig tree (11:12–14) is bracketed between two identical phrases describing entry into Jerusalem and its temple area (vv. 11, 15). In conjunction with Jesus' cryptic utterance on faith and faithlessness (vv. 20–25), the prophecy of fruitlessness (v. 14) itself serves to bracket the driving out of the sellers and buyers with its quotation from the prophet (v. 17 = Isa. 56:7).

49. See Luke 23:6–12.

Similarly, in the story of Peter's denial, he is first shown warming himself at the fire in the high priest's courtyard (Mark 14:54), while "all the chief priests, the elders, and the scribes" assemble to do justice (v. 53). He is then later depicted as three times denying vehemently that he knows Jesus (vv. 66–72). In between these brackets that show a cowardly disciple is the story of the courageous Jesus (vv. 55–65). He gives testimony to the truth of who he is (v. 62) against the lying testimony of witnesses (v. 56), while Peter, outside, will lie as brazenly as those witnesses.

All this is part of the plot of Mark's story. He has as a major theme the necessity under which followers of Jesus labor to suffer as he did despite injustices if they are to have any part in his victory over death. Peter is proposed as the cautionary example of a trust betrayed (Judas too, 14:10–11, 43–46). Mark's lesson to his contemporaries is that no tree in the forest is so tall that it cannot fall, no friendship with Jesus so assured that it cannot be betrayed. For purposes of fulfilling Jesus' prophecy of the cock's crowing twice to signal the betrayal (14:30), Mark needs to have the denials occur some time before dawn, when cocks crow. But for purposes of juxtaposing the conduct of Jesus' enemies with that of his false friend, the chief priests and the entire Sanhedrin have to be meeting at night too. This interpolation technique of storytelling has resulted in the so-called night trial of Jesus before Jewish authority. Mark remedies the situation somewhat by having the Sanhedrin "convene" (or "take counsel") early the next morning (15:1), having had them judge him deserving of death the night before (14:64).

Departures from Mark in the Other Gospels

Matthew, however, who follows Mark carefully without at times recognizing the way Mark is framing his narrative, has the arresting party lead Jesus from Gethsemane directly to where Caiaphas and the scribes and elders are assembled (Matt. 26:57). John does the same, compounding matters by doing as Mark does but adding an Annas-to-Caiaphas move to the nighttime story (John 18:24 in the middle of the sequence 18:15–27). Luke seems alerted to the improbability of an assembly of the Sanhedrin by night and solves it by having Jesus led to the high priest's house for custody, where the denials take place by firelight and the guards torment Jesus (Luke 22:54–65). He is brought before the Sanhedrin only "when day came" (v. 66). Despite these correctives, the memory of a judgment of condemnation by the highest body in Israel in totally illegal circumstances has been firmly fixed in Christian memory. By the second century in the Greco-Roman world these believers were interpreting symbolic narrative as history. They had lost the Semitic skill of spotting a story crafted in biblical style. Christians have been misreading their own holy books ever since, often making Jews pay the price of their incomprehension.

The account of the trial of Jesus by Pilate in John will serve as a second example of dramatic narrative that has become confused with mere fact (John 18:28—19:22). Using the irony of which he is supremely capable, this evangelist takes the cause of Jesus' crucifixion placarded above his head and explores it from the standpoint of faith in him versus the unfaith of "the world." In John the placard (*títlos*—a term with which the ancient world's accounts of crucifixions are familiar) reads "Jesus the Nazorean, the king of Judaea [a possible reading: of the Jews]" (19:19).[50] Only John tells of its wording in Hebrew, Latin, and Greek and of Pilate's adamantine stand against changing it to read that Jesus claimed to be such. Whatever the significance of the title in the minds of the executioners—and its recording in all four Gospels says something about its authenticity—John decides to make capital of it with an essay in drama form on authority as confused with coercive power. Jesus has supreme authority under God and in that sense is a king. He is summoned for judgment—and himself passes judgment on his judge. None of Jesus' disciples is likely to have witnessed such a colloquy (despite John's claim at 18:15 that "the other disciple" than Peter was known to the high priest). It is a pure construct, a tidy playlet: one of numerous such in this Gospel. John is theologizing the scanty history he possesses and means to do so.

The other evangelists do the same, if not so overtly. They have a story to tell of a huge injustice wrought against a supremely just one who is just with the justice of God. They know who the characters in their story are, real and perhaps devised. Barabbas (lit., "son of the father," a name unknown in Jewish usage) may be one of the latter. He is portrayed as the guilty insurrectionist set free while the innocent Jesus dies on the same charge. The centurion of Mark 15:39 who pierced Jesus' side with his lance may be another. Mark needed someone for plot purposes to give testimony at the end that Jesus was indeed Son of God. He chose a pagan to give Jesus the coup de grâce while at the same time uttering a statement of faith.

Four different authors wrote four passion plays, each one employing his play as penultimate in the career of Jesus. The last act of the play is Jesus' having risen from the dead. All but Mark provide a series of appearances of Jesus to his friends, in a context of faith in him as risen.

As Mark tells his story "the Pharisees with the Herodians" mount a plot against Jesus early in his public career (3:6). While the house of Herod had lost power in Judaea in 6 C.E. with the displacement of Archelaus, son of Herod the Great, by a succession of Roman prefects beginning with Coponius, Herod Antipas still ruled in Jesus' home province of Galilee and in Perea partly across the Jordan. There is no telling the resentment and scheming of the politically disaffected hangers-on of the house of Herod, but Mark puts them in strange company with the Pharisees. Those purists about law obser-

---

50. Cf. Mark 15:26; Matt. 27:37; Luke 23:38. The wording varies slightly in each case.

vance had religious interests from which the political were never absent.[51] Their opposition to Jesus, however, found early in Mark, survives in all four Gospels in the form chiefly of his debates with the learned. The first three Gospels call these observants "the scribes and the Pharisees" or something similar, while for John they are "the Judaeans" or "Jews" (a term with hostile connotations in 37 of its 71 occurrences) or "Pharisees."

This terminology creates the problem of whether Jesus went to his death as a result of incurring the hatred of the Jewish observant and learned class. The polemic he is reported engaging in, most bitterly in John but also in the first three Gospels, might lead one to think so. In fact, his claim to forgive sins in his own name and the titles "Messiah" and "Son of the Blessed" acknowledged by him and "Son of man" put on his lips as early as the writing of Mark (14:61–62) result in the charge of blasphemy (v. 64). By a Torah standard, he was never guilty of blasphemy in any recorded utterance. In fact, as has been said, none of the interpretations of the law attributed to him in the Gospels falls outside the range of acceptable rabbinic opinions from whatever we can know of them in his time. Most of the data on the question are from a later date. In brief, nothing in the Gospel record leads up to a charge of blasphemy for claiming any of the prerogatives of God, let alone full equality with God. Yet the Gospels leave the distinct impression that his teaching led to threatening opposition to him which culminated in his execution. If the punishment of crucifixion was as harsh as the pagan accounts of it indicate, what could Jesus be thought to have done to send him to such an ignominious death?

A Tentative Judgment on Motives

The answer can only lie in the fear of Pilate that Jesus was spearheading a movement of the liberation of Jews from Roman rule. He was perfectly justified in such suspicions. He may have witnessed mass demonstrations in Jesus' favor in the few short days before his attention was brought to Jesus as the potential leader of an uprising. Something, someone, convinced Pilate that Jesus was so dangerous that he had to go to the stake. If he was perceived as a threat to Jewish power as well as to Roman power, as seems to be the case, the two in concert would have wished to eliminate him. A temple priesthood fearful that a Jew was acting against the empire: that was the perfect formula for moving against one whose chief threat was to the twofold industry of temple sacrifice and collusion over collecting taxes.

If there is anything to these speculations, why did not the evangelists express the cause of Jesus' death more straightforwardly? Why did they leave

51. For the evidence on the Pharisees' thoroughgoing political as well as religious concern, see Anthony J. Saldarini, *Pharisees, Scribes and Sadducees in Palestinian Society: A Sociological Approach* (Wilmington, Del.: Michael Glazier, 1988), 79–106.

future generations to work it out as a historical puzzle? Some say that the Gospel writers adopted an apologetic stance, trying to protect their infant communities against Roman reprisal, in memory viewing the temple and its priests as a paper tiger, now that it was destroyed. But against this view is the total disregard of Roman sensibilities represented by Jesus' contemptuous treatment of Pilate in John. The serious apologist before the empire would never have let that pass.

A much more likely explanation is that all sorts of polemical exchange over what it meant to be an observant Jew had taken place in the diaspora, where the Gospels were written, after the Gentiles sacked Jerusalem. This argumentation is probably much more reflected in the Gospels than any that took place in Jesus' lifetime. Believers in his resurrection had had fifty years or more to make claims for his status vis-à-vis the God of Israel. The Johannine community was making claims of his full possession of deity.

This would tend to put religious questions in the foreground and historical, political ones in the background. The Gospels were written not as works of history but as existential documents of faith for their time. Engagement with the civil powers or with the now powerless temple priesthood would have been part of fading memory.

When all the problems that attend the Gospel accounts of Jesus' sentencing to death have been faced, one major one remains. It is not whether the Jewish authorities crucified him on a count of blasphemy (they almost certainly had the power to execute on a religious charge, but they did not crucify) or why the historical traditions that developed theologically into the four Gospel accounts ended in a deemphasis on Roman responsibility and an emphasis on priestly complicity. No, the main problem is what convinced Pilate that this teacher, of whom perhaps he had never heard, should be eliminated in the company of two nameless others, without any follow-up made to apprehend his companions. Why submit Jesus to a torture reserved for slaves, highwaymen, traitors, and plotters or active insurgents without tracking down the plot of which he was a part? Since Jesus clearly fell into none of the first three categories, what could have convinced Pilate that he belonged in the fourth? Jesus' punishment seems wildly disproportionate to his crime, even if it were only an alleged crime.

One possibility that the earliest believers in Jesus could not have known of, hence not reported on, is that his popularity with crowds especially in Galilee had caused him to be under Roman surveillance for some time. This could result in picking him off as the leader of a movement at the optimum time, namely, the chief pilgrimage feast, as a way to dissuade all Jews from entertaining any ideas of revolt. Such a hypothesis would further mean that the earliest traditions the evangelists inherited were quite wrong in speculating that the temple priests had a leading part in the affair. The priesthood may have had no part or only a minor one.

Another possibility is that Jesus was condemned to death by a suspicious Roman functionary in a case of mistaken identity. The suggestion is not so absurd as it sounds. His crucifixion as one of three to die in this way invites it. Many an innocent person has been put to death after a court process that took the alleged criminal for someone else.

Crediting the Gospels with a more accurate memory of the basic facts, the major remaining possibilities are two: that Jesus' entry into the city had been hailed by a handful of admirers of his deeds amidst a larger crowd of Galileans, who settled on him as representing their liberationist cause. The other possibility is the one the Gospels hint at most strongly: the judicial council of seventy(-two?) over which the high priest presided took the initial steps to be rid of Jesus because his antitemple declarations and behavior were taken to be an attack on the religion of Israel itself. The council engineered Jesus' death by using the prefect Pilate as their unwitting tool, this man who normally manipulated others. Both centers of power had the overwhelming will to stay in power, the one political, the other religio-political. Such people make hasty alliances and act harshly to put down any perceived threat. The clearest memory that the earliest believers in Jesus had—however devoid they were of hard facts—was that throne and altar had acted together against a common enemy: not so much Jesus' person as Jesus as the cause of a possible change in the temple priesthood's fortunes. He only represented it. It would have been Pilate's discovery that Jesus aspired to kingship on terms he did not comprehend that would have settled the matter in his mind.

How Mark's Trial and Passion Account Was Framed

A reconstruction that does no violence to the kind of writing the Gospels are might go as follows. The believers in Jesus' resurrection retained the basic memory that he had been executed brutally amidst the hubbub of a pilgrimage feast. The city had been crowded to overflowing; the temple traffic in commerce was carefully controlled as always; there were lost children everywhere. A diversion outside the city walls was promised: some criminals, in Jewish parlance, "hung up alive" (there was no word in their language for "crucify" or "crucifixion"). Who were the condemned and what had they done? There was little solid information on this point. There never was. The question of who was responsible was not raised. For an oppressed people there is only one answer—the government or the army, which come to the same thing. Those who witnessed the gruesome show would have been either angry or silently admiring, depending on where they stood on the condemned men or on Roman "justice." Most onlookers had no way of telling if the victims were plunderers of the poor or patriots. There would have been rumors about the charge against them but nothing confirmable on the spot: the placards over the victims' heads were often lies, and one was utterly cryptic, "Jesus of Nazareth, King of Judaea."

So many were disposed of in this way. But on the occasion of the feast! Had the pagans no sense of the "piety" they kept boasting of as a Roman virtue? The word might have spread among the crowd looking on in guilty horror: "One of them is different, the just one from the north. We have heard stories of his teaching and his deeds. Why would they want to kill *him?*"

"That is just the kind they can't stand," the answer might have come. "He reminds them of the rotten show they are running. The Romans, the temple priests. It's all the same crowd." But others might have said: "He threatened to destroy the temple of the LORD. I heard him say it."

Those who heard the initial "witnesses to the resurrection" proclaim Jesus as crucified and risen—and that became the technical term for the large apostolic company to whom Jesus appeared in his new, altered state (Acts 1:22)—would have heard Jesus' death always referred to as something God allowed to overtake him. Questions like, "Could any Jews have sought the destruction of a fellow Jew under the occupation?" or, "Was it not the pagans who finished him off in their fashion?" do not seem to have arisen in the Christian circles whose record we have. That either the temple priesthood or the Roman prefect was capable of ruthless action they would have taken for granted. The earliest promulgation of Jesus' death and resurrection was almost certainly as a deed of God, given the absence of any details in the earliest extant proclamation (*kērygma*). It was told in the form in which it appears in Paul's first letter to Corinth (15:3) as "what was handed on." He transmitted it roughly a quarter century after the event in this unadorned phrase: "that Christ died for our sins in accordance with the scriptures." Paul at the same time reminded his congregation of former pagans and a few Jews that he had thus first presented it.

This word about Jesus' death in the Jewish diaspora was given no apologetic cast. It did not assign blame; it was not even described as an execution. The message was probably conveyed to an entire first generation of believers in this form, both within and outside Palestine. In the homeland, however, details would have been ferreted out by Jesus' friends whose belief in his resurrection had rehabilitated them from the shame of their abandonment of him. These fragments of remembrance may or may not have taken the form of a sequential narrative. The memory of the previous night in Gethsemane would, of course, have remained. So would that of Peter's denying that he knew Jesus, of Jesus' having appeared before some arm of Jewish justice, and of the Roman arraignment that sealed his fate. None of these reminiscences can be assumed to have been transmitted in their bald, factual condition. As they reach us in the Gospels they are laced through with typologies, that is, the fulfillment of biblical "types" or figures in Jesus, the perfect antitype. The Hebrew Scriptures employ this internal technique frequently. It seems to have marked the earliest form in which the account of Jesus' sufferings and death was passed along.

There would have been this elaboration from the start, as is the case in ancient historiography generally when facts are in short supply and there is deep commitment to a person or cause. The basic facts were never in doubt: arrest by Roman soldiery or the temple police (a fully paramilitary force) or both; detention and questioning by the temple priesthood, magnified in the telling to the full Sanhedrin; an appearance before the Roman prefect Pilate; and sentence to death on a charge of sedition. When these fragments were first woven into a story is not known. The material is Palestinian. It is impossible to tell if there first emerged an Aramaic narrative or a Greek one from multiple, Aramaic-derived Greek sources. Many maintain that the first evangelist to write, Mark, constructed the first trial and passion story. Others say he had one at hand that he edited. Those who favor the latter theory, like the Czech Jewish scholar of the New Testament, Paul Winter, posit a skeletal account close to the historically probable, to which Mark has made historically improbable additions.[52] But this theorizing entertains the confidence of form criticism that reconstructions of the original text are achievable by eliminating everything that is judged a subsequent editing ("redaction," to use the term that became popular in German scholarship). It assumes the priority of basically historical "tradition" to which theological and apologetic interpretation has been applied. Indeed, the two may well have been interwoven in the earliest pre-Markan form of a collection of vignettes.

Another puzzle is what sources if any Luke and John had, Luke to bring his account into line with historical probabilities and John, whose narrative resembles Luke's in some details, to add materials unknown to the Mark-Matthew tradition.

Looking at Mark closely we find Jesus entering Jerusalem as a pilgrim accompanied by shouts of popular acclaim. It was traditional Jewish practice to recite Psalm 118 to welcome new arrivals (v. 26; cf. Mark 11:9b). Adding to it a phrase from the dynastic oracle of 2 Samuel was not traditional. Only a pre- or post-Easter conviction that Jesus was Messiah could account for this. In the Markan form it is given as: "Blessed is the kingdom of our father David *that is to come*" (Mark 11:10a from 2 Sam. 7:16), with the italicized words a paraphrase of "kingdom . . . and throne that shall stand firm forever." If the reminiscence is authentic, Jesus could be perceived from these shouts to have plans for a political insurgency. David's throne in Judaea, after all, was the one the Hasmonean dynasty and the now displaced

52. Paul Winter, *On the Trial of Jesus,* 2d ed. (rev. and ed. T. A. Burkill and G. Vermes; Berlin and New York: de Gruyter, 1974), 44 and passim.

Herodian house claimed, even though neither derived from David genealogically. No action is reported against Jesus on this occasion, however, despite all the words that swirled about his head.

The next event is a deed that was directed at the heart of the temple, which had as its business blood sacrifice to YHWH (Mark 11:15, 17). Mark plants in the center of Jesus' action against the money changers a reminder of his scruple about an oral precept against defiling the sacred space: "He did not permit anyone to carry anything through the temple area" (v. 16). That later editorial addition was meant to establish Jesus' sensitivity to purity laws, as if to say that his opposition to cultic purity was not in question. The overturning of the tables was unmistakably a symbolic act that constituted lèse-majesté against divinity itself in the eyes of the temple's priestly custodians. Mark retained a recollection of this act that looked to the temple's future destruction and restoration. It was known to John from another source (John 2:13–22). The challenge of "the chief priests, the scribes, and the elders" that questioned his authority to do "these things" can refer only to his attack on a daily supply of birds and beasts for sacrifice to be purchased with temple coinage (Mark 11:27–29). The intervening challenges in Mark by Pharisees, Herodians, Sadducees, and scribes (see 12:13, 18, 28) is an echo of Jesus' differences with the communities of learning and his voluntarily forfeited political power that Mark has featured throughout. They would have been at one with the temple priests in the shock and outrage that led to his downfall, although on the basis of different perceptions of Jesus' threat to their power.

The plot of the priests and their learned associates skilled in the law begins at 14:1: "The chief priests and the scribes were seeking a way to arrest him by treachery and put him to death." Mark adds a scruple about fear of a riot if it were attempted in the week of Passover (v. 2). His narrative clue in 3:6, which involves a partial set of the same plotters, Pharisees and Herodians (see also 12:13), is a device preparing the reader for the totality of the known opposition. A series of vignettes interrupts the story of the arrest. It includes Judas's plan to betray, the final supper, and Jesus' prayer in the company of his disciples on the Mount of Olives. Judas's conspiring is with the priests, hence it is they from whom the apprehending party comes (v. 43). It is "the high priest and all the chief priests and elders and scribes" (v. 53) before whom Mark says he is led.

To maintain that John's mention of a battalion (*speîra*) and a tribune (*chilíarchos*) in the arresting party proves that it was a Roman operation is not very helpful since John has earlier mentioned Judas as "getting a band [*speîran*] from the chief priests and guards [*hypērétas*] from the Pharisees" (18:3). One cannot pick one's villains on the basis of what is inherently probable when the Gospel writers seem to be reporting on two agencies of violence working in concert. Mark's indefinite "*crowd* with swords and clubs" (14:43), a noun in which Matthew (26:47) and Luke (22:47) follow him, may best cover their and our ignorance of the event. When, one may ask, was military discipline ever preserved on a mission such as this?

Jesus' Temple Predictions as the Cause of His Undoing

Whatever Mark's sources may have contained about a Jewish hearing, the challenge to Jesus about his views of the temple is supported by two things: his recent demonstration against it (Mark 11:15–19) and the multiple appearance of his "temple sayings" in the Gospels and Acts of the Apostles. These indicate that he had authored some such predictive and perhaps threatening utterance as: "Do you see this great edifice? There will not be left a stone upon a stone that will not come hurtling down" (Mark 13:2; parallels in Matt. 24:2; Luke 21:6).[53] This was the Jesus whose glorified body became for believers the new temple, replacing the old. Jesus' dire prediction was altered to read, under the influence of his resurrection: "[If you] destroy this temple, in three days I will raise it up" (John 2:19; parallels in Mark 15:29; Matt. 26:61; in Mark 14:58, "made with hands . . . another not made with hands") and in John 4:21: "The hour is coming when you [Samaritans] will worship the Father neither on this mountain nor in Jerusalem."

Mark in his passion story portrays as liars the witnesses to what Jesus has said (14:57), and their testimony does not agree (v. 56). But that is because for Mark Jesus alone is the truth. We surely have in his account the kernel of the Jewish leadership's case against him. Before this they had identified him as prophesying the destruction of the still uncompleted edifice (John 2:20). The faith of the Markan church in Jesus as the Christ and Son of God is put on Jesus' lips when he is questioned (Mark 14:61–62; cf. 1:1). Neither claim—if, as is unlikely, he made both with an affirmative "I am"—nor the prophecy that the Son of man coming with the clouds of heaven will be seated at the right hand of the Power would merit the charge of blasphemy with which the high priest responded. The biblical conditions for blaspheming are not fulfilled either here or in the healing of the paralytic (2:7). Exodus 20:7 gives the basic prohibition against reviling God. (One should note that Hebrew has no precise word for "blaspheme" or "blasphemy.") This is followed up by the punishment of the whole community's stoning to death anyone who *curses* the name of YHWH (Lev. 24:11). Employment of the Name seems essential. Yet Isaiah 37:6 has the commander of the Syrian troops represent his king in saying that the LORD will not save Judah, as King Hezekiah maintains the LORD will do (36:15, 18); the prophet responds by telling the servants of the king that such an utterance "reviles God."

53. E. P. Sanders has collected evidence that would indicate that Jesus' statements and symbolic gesture of destruction were related to an end-time hope of the period for a "new Jerusalem." See *Jesus and Judaism* (Philadelphia: Fortress Press, 1985), 77–91.

When the Septuagint translation uses any word of the *blasphēm-* family it renders a variety of Hebrew verbs that mean curse, taunt, speak ill of, belittle, or defame God (thus 2 Kings [LXX 4 Kingdoms] 19:4, 6, 22). Even destruction of what God has ordained can be called blasphemy (1 Macc. 2:6; 2 Macc. 8:4). This wide range of usage means that "blasphemy" fittingly describes any utterance that is taken to threaten God's uniqueness or majesty.[54] Yet the claim to be God's son or God's anointed king (Mark 14:61) would not be taken in Jesus' day to constitute blasphemy (v. 64). When the high priest asks if Jesus thinks he is such a one he is told: "I am." Surely this reflects the polemic in which the Markan church has been engaged, where this twofold claim for Jesus is taken to connote much more and hence is blasphemous in the wider sense. An encroachment on the divine majesty is understood by the larger Jewish community later in the century as it hears the titles claimed for Jesus (see John 10:33 for an even greater understanding). Mark's account of the priestly hearing reflects the decades of polemic that have gone before.

Would the heated postresurrection exchange between Jewish believers in Jesus and Jewish disbelievers in him be the only explanation of how "blasphemy" got into Mark's Gospel? Scarcely. Its wide range of meaning among Greek-speaking Jews would qualify Jesus' declaration in his lifetime that the temple was to come down as an attack on the God whose house it was. Jesus himself rejected swearing "By heaven!" "By the earth!" and "By Jerusalem!" as thinly veiled avoidances of the divine name (see Matt. 5:34–35). Surely an attack on the temple could be construed as an attack on the person of YHWH. The temple sayings attributed to Jesus in their nontheologized, pre-Easter form were not the predictions of a man of foresight that the temple *would* be destroyed. They were prophetic declarations that God would bring it down, replacing it with a new one of the final age. Jesus is not to be placed in the company of the writing prophets, whom Christian theologians of recent centuries mistakenly classified as promoters of a "purer" religion than one of blood sacrifice. He belongs in their company as one who foresaw a sacrifice befitting the final age to replace the one the high priesthood was presiding over.

Jesus' teaching on proper interpretations of law observance may have elicited annoyance, anger, even violent response from teachers who thought otherwise. It was not such as to bring on a plot to kill him. A careful comparison of what he taught with rabbinic teaching of a later age, critically scrutinized, reveals no major differences, only minor ones of emphasis and opinion. Yet intimations of the will to eliminate him are pervasive in the Gospels. They cannot be traced exclusively to death threats against his disciples of a later time. Violent exchanges over his antitemple stance would explain best the survival of these exchanges in the Gospel tradition (see John 8:59; 10:31;

---

54. For a good discussion of this term and its compass, see E. P. Sanders, *Jewish Law from Jesus to the Mishnah: Five Studies* (Philadelphia: Trinity Press International, 1990), 57–67.

11:53). They are theologized as a result of later christological debates, to be sure, but their primitive form is not hard to identify: "This temple which is God's house will be, should be destroyed." This is not an evangelist of the 60s or 70s C.E. making Jesus a predicter of the future after the event. It is the work of a recorder of his earthly career in a tradition that has never forgotten the utterances of one who threatened destruction of the temple, embarrassing as they may be to record. This would account for the reported threats on his life in a way that his teaching would not, except insofar as his teaching was integral to the prophecy spoken in God's name.

If Jesus' words and his symbolic deed against the temple were sufficient to arouse the desire of the priests and elders to be rid of him, the empire's suspicion of his complicity in rebellion would even more surely bring about his summoning on charges. Much has been made in recent writing of his associations with revolutionary types such as Judas son of Simon the *Iscariot,* taken to be cognate with the Greek loanword from Latin, *sikários,* a dagger wielder; his disciple Simon *hò zēlōtēs* (elsewhere *hò kananaîos*), understood to be a member of a guerrilla band; Simon *Baryona,* an Aramaic word for bandit or gangster; and the designation for James and John, *Boanērgés,* "sons of thunder."[55] The philology is doubtful in three cases and it is by now established that "zealot" meant simply *that* in a religious sense until the late 60s, when it was first attached to bands of insurrectionists.

If the above tags described five of Jesus' companions—the last two given as *his* designation of them—we might have expected the Gospels, having retained this much, to suggest something of their activities. No scrap of anti-Roman action is hinted at. Implicit in some of Jesus' parables, however, is a reminder of the gross injustices under which Jesus' peasant hearers labored. Many of them had lost their land as debtors because of the heavy taxes imposed by Rome and collected by Jewish land agents. The whole fiscal system was ultimately administered by the high priests, but the peasant farmers tended not to know this. They took their wrath out on the large owners or their overseers whose sharecropping tenants they were, land their fathers and grandfathers had forfeited.[56] The distinct possibility exists that Jesus became a popular figure of a quite different sort than he intended, as witnessed by the fragment in John that says he knew "they were going to come and carry him off to make him king" (John 6:15). He is described in the remainder of that verse as having withdrawn again "to the mountain alone," but it is a scene that could have been played out more than once and culminated in the way the crowds hailed him on his entry into Jerusalem.

His constant references to kings and the kingdom in his teaching were to YHWH, Israel's only king, and the full dominion this Sovereign hoped to exercise over all Jewish hearts. No futurist scheme need have been intended:

55. See, respectively, Mark 3:19 and John 6:71; Mark 3:18 and Matt. 10:4; Matt. 16:17; Mark 3:17.

56. See Richard Horsley, *Jesus and the Spiral of Violence* (Minneapolis: Fortress Press, 1993).

a sway expected by Jesus only at "the end of days." "Kingship" or "reign" was a "now" word in Jesus' intention, and not in John's Gospel only. However religiously he intended it, it could not but be heard politically as well. For Jews there was no distinction between the two. Life under their God was for them a totality. If Jesus was a restorationist, and all the Gospel evidence is that he meant to be, he would have spoken of the kingship of YHWH but been heard to mean the kingship of David.

Such being the case with Jewish hearers, how could the following utterance reach the Roman ear without connoting an active seizure of power: "Amen, I say to you, there are some standing here who will not taste death until they see that the kingdom of God has come in power" (Mark 9:1)? Why, both Jewish and Roman authority would have wondered, would large crowds have been assembling in Galilee to hear this man if not with a view to an uprising? This was not a question put by imperial and Sadducee paranoia alone. It could equally have been asked by Jewish hope.

It is scarcely believable that the army of occupation, made up of troops from the other colonies and not Roman legionaries proper, had heard nothing of Jesus' popular acceptance. The question is not, however, What did Pilate know and when did he know it? It is, What prompted him to take the act of condemning Jesus to death that he did? The Gospels provide an answer, namely, condemnation by a Jewish court that triggered Jesus' remanding to Roman justice. Such, at least, is the Mark-Matthew tradition. Luke mutes the Sanhedrin's judgment of condemnation (see 22:71), and John has the chief priests handing Jesus over to Pilate (18:35) but without a clear charge, only that he must be a malefactor (it is literal: *kakòn poiōn*, a "doer of evil") or they would not have done it (v. 30).

The Ambiguous Passion Accounts and Their Emergent Theme

It is impossible to conclude from the Gospels what sequence of events brought Jesus to the cross. It is likely that the evangelists did not know it with any precision and opted to place the blame in a way that is not easy to decipher. Ambiguity is the hallmark of all four accounts. What the writers seemed to know was that Jewish and Roman authorities wanted him out of the way and achieved it in some fashion, concerning which the four had no single clear tradition. The situation is complicated by their conviction that Jesus' death was by no means simply a human drama. God was behind it at every stage, not simply as permitting it but decreeing that it should have ended as it did.

The conventional wisdom has been to maintain that Pilate is portrayed sympathetically and his ultimate responsibility as the hanging judge downplayed for apologetic reasons. The Jesus movement was, if not courting imperial favor, at least trying to avoid political censure. This was especially true of Mark's narrative, the argument goes. He compiled his Gospel in Rome and there played the apologist for his coreligionists. Those who favor this line fail to explain why Mark left so much Roman brutality in his account that he could wisely have omitted, including Pilate's part in the affair. The exchange between Jesus and Pilate in John is completely oblivious to giving offense to Rome. The apologia, if such it was, was evidently not very well carried off. Another consideration regarding this theory is that it assumes that the materials that went into the Gospels were written by and for Gentiles with no attention paid to Jewish sensibilities, only to Roman. Whatever one chooses as the first layer of tradition, however, it contains something to offend everybody, just as the Gospels do in their final form. The evangelists were convinced that a terrible injustice had been done to an innocent man and they were not at pains to protect anyone's sensitivities on that score.

We cannot penetrate even a little bit the historical uncertainties that attend the trial and passion accounts unless we face squarely the reasons the Gospels were written. They were narratives composed from the standpoint of faith to nourish and increase faith. Their primary intention was to keep alive in those who heard them their earlier commitment to the God of Israel who had acted on their behalf in Jesus, God's Anointed. At their baptism the people for whom the Gospels were written—a mixture of Jews and non-Jews in a unique religious venture—had heard fragments of what Jesus had taught but mostly that he had died and risen "for their sins." The literary evangelists were four out of a company of hundreds—by the end of the century, thousands—of oral evangelists. All had a single purpose: to *in*form but only in aid of forming and, in the case of sinners or those who had lapsed in faith, *re*forming in Christ. Bringing about a difference in the lives of already believing hearers was paramount for them. The evangelists both oral and in writing would have been pleased if any pagans heard their message, but they did not write with them chiefly in mind. They did not write for the larger Jewish community either, happy as they would have been if any stopped to listen. They wrote for the company of believers, going into detail about Jesus' last hours to excite sympathy for him but, much more, to elicit revulsion at the thought that they, the baptized, might respond to God's overtures as the characters in the story had done. Thus Simon Peter and the others who shrank from Jesus' need to suffer if he were to enter into his glory (see Mark 8:33 and parallels) were presented as a powerful disincentive to those "glory now" believers who populated all the local churches.

That same Peter and Judas Iscariot were central figures in the passion narratives, more so than the high priest or Pilate. They, along with Peter's two sleeping companions in Gethsemane and the other male disciples who fled, were presented as examples of infidelity in a time of crisis. Believers in Jesus would have to make similar hard choices between him and the disruption of their lives that fidelity could cause. The women at the cross who looked on from a distance (see Mark 15:40–41; John 19:25–27) are depicted in their persevering love purposefully, even as were the women who did not deliver the message that Jesus had risen, "for they were afraid" (Mark 16:8). The other Gospels portray the latter group as acting quite differently (Matt. 28:8–10; cf. John 20:11–18), likewise for the evangelists' purposes. Thus it is that faulting the Gospel writers for conflicting details as if they had "got it wrong" is to miss what they were up to in getting it right. As modern reporters, they were a flat failure. As ancient dramatists they were more than a little successful; in assigning human responsibility for Jesus' death, in light of subsequent history they were tragically successful.

Remembering the purposes of the evangelists and their sources, we need to recall first that the conduct of the Roman soldiery and temple guard was of no consequence to them. These men normally acted in brutal fashion and were so depicted. The Sanhedrin, the high priest, and Pilate, similarly, are cardboard figures who act predictably, namely, as functionaries who put the self-serving cause they are dedicated to above justice to an individual.

There is an important difference, however, in the evangelists' treatment of the two power centers, Roman and Judaean. The narratives coming out of Palestine take repressive Roman behavior for granted. The prefects had acted in no other way since they began to govern in Judaea from 6 C.E., even though they had been imposed in response to a Jewish plea that their coreligionist, the tetrarch Archelaus, be removed. Dispassionate cruelty triggered by fear of the repressed population they presided over was the hallmark of this hegemony. With the high priest and the council of seventy matters were otherwise. This at least was so in the popular Palestinian mind. The Sanhedrin was despised by the Jewish populace generally, despite the presence in that body of some who were pious and just, because of their collaboration with the oppressor. The high priests were thought of as "bought men" because they were appointed and continued in office at the good pleasure of the Caesar. Whereas the Roman functionary Pilate was not expected to act on Jesus' case in any but a predictable way, something vastly different was expected of the priests because of their sacred office. Any view of their part in Jesus' death coming out of Palestine, especially by his partisans, was bound to be colored by the view of them already held by fellow Jews.

The evangelists and their predecessors are not to be thought of as a body known in their day as "the Christians" acting in opposition to a body known as "the Jews." Jesus' devotees in Palestine in the mid-first century were Jewish messianists of eschatological outlook. In Samaria and the near diaspora (modern Lebanon, west Syria, the coastlands of Gaza) they were a mixed population of Jews and non-Jews. The same was almost certainly true of the communities Paul founded around the Levant and of those of whose origins we know nothing, such as in Alexandria and Rome. We know little from Paul's letters of the particulars of Jesus' career, only that he taught, died on a cross, and was raised up. If the basic content of the Gospels was on its way to formation outside the Jewish heartland by 60—a fair assumption—we can assume that the betrayal, as it was perceived to be, of God's just one, Jesus, by the highest religious authority in Judaea would still have rankled. There were, besides, the ongoing debates between the Jesus Jews, with their admixture of Samaritan and gentile believers, and the bulk of Jews, undoubtedly far more law-observant in their ethnic homogeneity than this new band claiming to be Israel. The resultant polemic undoubtedly made its way into the Gospels by means of exchanges reported as having taken place in Jesus' lifetime. An even greater opposition to his followers than the one based on "how to live Jewish" would have been grounded in the memory that Jewish authority had repudiated him for cause. For believers in him he was the one great Jew who should have been accepted.

It is no wonder, then, that the heinousness of the Sanhedrin's action grew in the minds of Jesus' followers. They who should have believed had not, while the Roman prefect, of whom nothing was expected, had been able to ask, "What evil has he done?" (Mark 15:14) and say, "I have found him guilty of no capital crime" (Luke 23:22). The two opposed views of Jesus before his judges were not historical in the ordinary sense. Believers in Jesus probably did not possess enough hard facts for that kind of history writing. They worked up four dramatizations on a biblical model, saying that the enemies of God were of his own people while the despised gentile had acted more nobly. In any event, this emphasis on the part played by the priests and "the whole people" (Matt. 27:25) and the portrayal of Pilate as the vacillating protagonist of Jesus has led to terrible consequences for Jews. It is, however, anachronistic to speak of the "anti-Semitism of the New Testament." "Anti-Judaism" would be a correct second-century term. In the late first century it was the case of a Jewish minority striking out verbally against the Jewish majority for its "anti-Christianism"—to underscore the absurdity of the other term. The warfare was infra-Jewish. It is by now vain to wish it had remained that way. There are much more bitter statements in the Dead Sea Scrolls against the Jerusalem temple priesthood than those found in the Gospels, but the Qumranites died out *as Jews*. A better example that ended in religious coexistence might be the anti-Samaritanism of the rabbis of the Mishnah. There one finds a verbal violence that, mercifully, led to no worse consequence than mutual ostracism because it was played out on a small scale. The Christian-Jewish antipathy might have remained one more example of religion's sorry history of hurling mutual bans but for the Constantinian settlement. That changed everything.

Conclusion

Jesus was executed by a Roman punishment meted out to malefactors of the worst type and to political insurgents, real or suspected. Pilate's motive for sentencing Jesus, if indeed Jesus was subjected to a formal trial, is not known. The highest Jewish religious authority appears to have been interested in stilling his voice—exactly why can only be surmised. Neither the four evangelists (including the book of Acts, Luke's volume two) nor the sources they drew on knew what went on when Jesus appeared before Judaean and Roman justice. How the Jewish court system worked in Jerusalem at the time is not known; Josephus's descriptions are conflicting and the much later Mishnah provides an idealization. The rough justice of imperial legates in the provinces relative to Roman public law is another unknown. The tendency of prefects (later "procurators") to use the Jewish pilgrimage feasts as the optimum time for punishing incipient rebellion for exemplary purposes *is* known. Jesus was a self-declared restorer of the religion of Israel. He did not hesitate to speak of God's plan for the world's final age, in which he and his "twelve" would have a part—he a major one and they a minor. His religious language was that of Israel's future reign and of God's kingship. He spoke and acted against the temple symbolically, saying it would be replaced as part of Israel's restoration. This would have been enough to incur the wrath of the temple priesthood. A fear of sedition in any movement that appeared to have enough strength could account for Pilate's action. Jesus was probably condemned in as confused circumstances as the ones of which the Gospel narratives seem to have conflicting recollections. They meant to write a theologically interpreted history of the events and ended by writing what was taken for literal history, a history all but impossible to reconstruct with precision, however much individual details can be verified or declared probable.

CHAPTER TWO

How Jesus' Death Came to Be Seen as Sacrificial and Redemptive

Luke in his second volume tells the story of the early Jesus community in Jerusalem and of the career of Paul from his first opposing the new movement to his house detention in Rome. Paul was in the capital in the late 50s on appeal of a civil charge of inciting to riot in the Jerusalem temple area. This book of the "Acts of the Apostles"—the latter a title that Luke is unwilling to give to Paul except on the one occasion he seems to find it in his source (Acts 14:4, 14)—serves as the second panel in a diptych to match the story of Jesus. Indeed, Paul's summoning before the temple authorities, then two of Pilate's successors, and finally King Agrippa II of Galilee and Perea closely resembles in the telling the inquests to which Jesus was subjected (Acts 22–26). The report of Jesus' last hours found in the Lukan Gospel is condensed in summaries like the following, with Peter as the speaker but with all the speeches of Luke's composition:

> You men of Israel, hear these words. Jesus the Nazorean was a man commended to you by God with mighty deeds, wonders and signs, which God worked through him in your midst, as you yourselves know. This man, delivered up by the design and foreknowledge of God, you killed, using lawless men [*ánomoi*] to crucify him. But God raised him up, releasing him from the throes of death, because it was impossible for him to be held by it. (Acts 2:22–24)

This direct charge to certain men of power in Jerusalem with the death of Jesus, marked by a total lack of nuance, has been highly influential on Christian thinking over the centuries. It identifies as the actual executioners the "lawless" Romans, a term that could either describe their action against an innocent man or designate their paganism (i.e., their status as outside Mosaic law); but the "delivering up" clearly names some Judaean Jews as the perpetrators, as Luke's Gospel narrative has made clear (22:66–70; 23:1). Not to be missed is the providential explanation of Jesus' death in Acts 2:23. His death came about, Luke maintains, through God's design (*boulē*) and foreknowledge (*prognōsei*). This identifies the death of Jesus as a deed of God before it is a deed of men.

A second speech of Peter in Acts, also addressed to "You men of Israel," summarizes the version of the dispatching of Jesus in Luke's Gospel more thoroughly:

> The God of Abraham, Isaac, and Jacob, the God of our ancestors, has glorified his servant Jesus whom you handed over and denied in Pilate's presence, when he had decided to release him. You denied the holy and just one and asked that a murderer be released to you. The prince [or pathfinder; *archēgòn*] of life you put to death but God raised him from the dead. We are witnesses to this. (Acts 3:12–15)

In still a third passage the Lukan author's uncertainty over who exactly was high priest at the time (he is unnamed in Luke 22:54) continues, but he now provides more data. "Their leaders, elders, and scribes were assembled in Jerusalem" to question Peter and John about the healing of a crippled beggar, and teaching the people, and proclaiming in Jesus the resurrection of the dead (see Acts 3:1–10; 4:2). Joined to them were "Annas the high priest, Caiaphas, John, Alexander, and such as were of the high-priestly class." All these brought the two disciples into their presence and questioned them. They dismissed Peter and John after threats, who then reported it, after which the community prayed: "Indeed, they ['the gentiles, the kings of earth, and the princes' of Ps. 2:1–2] gathered in this city against your holy servant Jesus, whom you anointed, Herod and Pontius Pilate, together with the pagans and the peoples of Israel, to do what your hand and will had long ago planned should take place" (Acts 4:5–7, 21, 25–28). Here again the divine design is paramount, but the multiplication of human players in the drama tends to obscure this fact.

None of the accounts of Jesus' condemnation and death in narrative form was primitive, as has been noted in chapter 1. The written Gospels were composed well after the earliest proclaiming of Jesus as crucified and risen, whatever the first oral forms of the message may have been. When Luke in Acts proposes a basic proclamation of Jesus' death and resurrection (10:34–41), it contains only a fragment of the passion narrative: "They [presumably the people in the region of Judaea and Jerusalem of the same verse] put him to death by hanging him on a tree" (v. 39). The demonstrably earlier proclamations of salvation by faith in Jesus' death and resurrection that occur in Paul's Letters omit all mention of the historical actors. It is to these that we now turn.

The Crucifixion-Resurrection in Paul's Letters

The problem attending 1 Thessalonians 2:14–16 has been noted above (p. 24) and will be reviewed below. For Paul's references to Jesus' death (often, "the cross") or resurrection elsewhere in his correspondence, see 1 Thessalonians 1:10; 4:14; 5:9–10; Galatians 1:4; 2:20–21; 3:13; 6:12–14; Philippians 2:6–11; 1 Corinthians 1:13, 18, 23–24; 2:8; 5:7b; 7:23; 8:11, 32; 10:16; 11:26; 15:1–7, 12–17, 20; 2 Corinthians 1:5; 4:10; 5:14, 15, 21; Romans 1:3–4; 3:25–26; 5:6–8; 6:3–4, 9–10; 8:32, 34. This formidable array of citations, if explored, would show that whenever Paul speaks of Jesus' death or his rising from the dead he has in mind chiefly its effect in the lives of believers ("for us," "for all," "for our sins"). He never refers to either event as a matter of pure history. It is always an occurrence in the contemporary history of the baptized. Paul does not elaborate, moreover, on the circumstances of either death or resurrection except to underscore that in Jesus' dying he suffered.

Paul of Tarsus is often identified by Jews as the Jew they feel most comfortable in despising for his attacks on the law. In fact, the disputed passage from 1 Thessalonians 2 aside ("by the Judaeans [or Jews], who killed the Lord Jesus and the prophets and drove us out, and are so heedless of God's will and such enemies of their fellow men" [vv. 14b–15]), Paul, if he really wrote it, bears no responsibility for the sufferings that the Jews of subsequent ages have endured at the hands of Christians for the way he speaks of Jesus' death. His utterances are always in a theological framework devoid of historical details. To read them in their entirety, together with his sole reflection on the lot of his fellow Jews in God's design (Romans 9–11), is to conclude that the invective of 1 Thessalonians is from a later hand. The all but complete catalog of references above, in the seven letters that are assuredly Paul's, reveals that the union of believers with Christ in his dying and rising is Paul's great concern. First Thessalonians 2:14b–16 stands out as being in a quite different spirit—not to mention the easy transition between vv. 14a and 17 that helps to identify it as an interpolation.

Paul is the earliest witness we have to the effects the early believers thought Jesus' death and resurrection could achieve in them. He says (writing around 50, although some would say the early 40s) that the community members in Thessalonica "await God's Son from heaven, whom God raised from the dead, Jesus, who delivers us from the wrath to come" (1 Thess. 1:10). The "wrath" and "deliverance" from it he speaks of are clearly fragments of Jewish end-time hope. Again, he writes, God did not destine him and believers like him for this wrath (the necessary divine response to unrepented evil) but "for salvation through our Lord, Jesus Christ, who died for us, so that whether we are awake or asleep [i.e., alive or dead] we may live together with him" (1 Thess. 5:9–10).

There are several puzzles here. How could Paul report on the cruel end to Jesus' life in speech so devoid of color and without evident emotion both here and whenever else he refers to it? Has the belief that Jesus rose in glory taken the sharp edge off crucifixion? It cannot simply be the frequency with which Paul proclaimed this death orally that accounts for his dispassion. A person to whom a death means much cannot get so used to its brutal circumstances as never to mention them. It had to be the mythic setting in which Paul had long ago situated this death. The tradition he received and handed on was succinct enough: "that Christ died for our sins in accordance with the scriptures" (1 Cor. 15:3). The center of gravity in the narrative had evidently shifted, some decades before, from the cruel manner of death to the simple fact of death. These events in the life of Jesus did not have their primary importance as regards *him*. They were chiefly important to believers in what God had accomplished through him for *them*. Paul had long ago stopped thinking merely historically, if he ever did so. He was a man of the Bible, and the Bible's only concern with events is what they meant for the lives of the people Israel. So it was with Paul in conjunction with his believing people, whether Jew or Gentile. He saw them as Israel but with an important new, end-time difference, namely, that difference constituted by God's deed in Jesus Christ. He promulgated the fresh reality of the events as a sacred *mýthos*, much as the Bible does with the exodus from Egypt.

The Pre-Pauline Tradition:
A Redemptive Death

Still, a puzzle remains. It goes well behind the figure of Paul. How did the movement that succeeded Jesus interpret his death as expiatory or atoning and, for all we know, do so fairly immediately? There is no evidence that it was interpreted in any other way by believers in Jesus from the beginning than "for our sins." It is true that the experience of Jesus risen from the dead must have radically altered the entire estimate his disciples had of him. Their first thought as they experienced him risen, if they were capable of any thoughts at all in their shaken condition, would have been one of vindication by God of this innocent sufferer. Yet such vindication, as they knew it from the Bible, was a matter of hope and far-off expectation. It must have required some little time for them to take in his resurrection, not only the fact but its sudden following upon his death. It was entirely unlike the divine vindication in the future that the prophets had promised the just. That fact alone would have relativized his death, put it in a new perspective. But to see it as expiatory, as a matter of supreme benefit to those who would survive him in all ages to come? What could have led to this conviction they held relatively swiftly?

The Jewish idea that immediately comes to mind, that a martyr's death is somehow beneficial to others, goes back to the late second-century B.C.E. Maccabean revolt. Even sooner does the daily sacrifice in Jerusalem's temple as expiatory of inadvertent or unconscious sins come to mind. This constant offering "put people right with God." In the case of Jesus, his sacrificial death was thought to be a final buying back of humanity from the grip of sin and death. A third possibility is the rabbinic familiarity with the "binding of Isaac" (*'aqēdat yiṣḥāq*), the paradigm well known in Jewish circles of God's intervention to rescue the innocent one who was let suffer by God's design. Each of these three historically inspired examples has been put forward as best accounting for the primitive view of Jesus' death as expiatory. We must examine them in turn to discover what details they share with the earliest proclamations we have of the saving character of Jesus' death and resurrection.

Even as this is done, it is necessary to recall that no primitive Palestinian proclamation of Jews to Jews about Jesus is extant in the Aramaic tongue. One may harbor the suspicion that the entire New Testament was the work of gentile-oriented Jews beamed at Gentiles on remembered Jewish models, a suspicion that could invalidate its authenticity as a record of Palestinian realities. From the standpoint of critical history, however, it is better to view these writings as containing some authentic recollections of the way Jesus' dying and rising were first presented in Palestine in the 30s. If it were done in any other way, some remembrance should have lingered in the presentation to the hellenized world reflected in the New Testament. No such alternative set of reminiscences exists. Easier still is it to imagine Paul as having devised a theology of human redemption through faith in the cross and resurrection completely on his own. But this picture of Paul as the inventor of Christianity is based more on animus toward him and a grudging respect for Jesus than on solid critical inquiry into the tradition he received.[1]

Why Call a Crucified Man Israel's Anointed King?

Perhaps the best clue we have is that the title of Jesus most closely associated with his given name was Christ—not Son of God, Lord, Savior, or any other but the term in Greek for Messiah, God's Anointed.[2] This both constitutes a problem and offers elements of a solution. Some early evidence indicates that messiahship is not a role that Jesus courted or claimed (see Mark 8:29, then 6:15 and his ambiguous response, much theologized, when challenged to say plainly if he were the Messiah, John 10:24–30). The title had to do with Davidic kingship, the restoration of which in a worthy successor Jews widely entertained. To be literally of David's house and family was less a qualification than to be victorious in David's mold. Whoever claims to see such ambitions in Jesus is seeing more than the Gospels warrant. The first and early second centuries provide a history of failed messiahs. Their successive defeats, ending in that of Bar Kokhba in Hadrian's time (135 C.E.),

1. See E. P. Sanders, *Jesus and Judaism* (Philadelphia: Fortress Press, 1985), 103.
2. For a theory on the early recognition of Jesus as the Christ, see Terrance Callan, *The Origins of Christian Faith* (New York: Paulist Press, 1994), esp. pp. 7–35.

proved that the claims made for each of them were premature. Nothing reported of Jesus, *except for the charge on which he died,* namely, "king of the Jews [or of Judaea]," places him in their company. Whoever may have thought of Jesus in such a role—and fragments in the Gospels indicate that some did—had their hopes dashed when he proved to be no winner but a loser by the royal messianic standard then current: military victory.

There was this difference between the popular acclaim he might have received, culminating in his entry into Jerusalem, and that accorded to the series of self-declared leaders of insurgency. He spoke consistently of a new order of the ages, with himself somehow central to it and his companions having a role. A saying common to Matthew (19:28) and Luke (22:30), hence from the hypothetical early collection known as Q, places "the Twelve" on twelve thrones judging the tribes of Israel, with the Son of man seated on his throne of glory. That sort of end-time envisioning echoes the hope expressed in the *Psalms of Solomon* (17.28–31, 50), the *Testament of Moses* (3.4; 4.9), and the Qumran War Scroll (1QM 2.2, 7; 3.13; 5.1). It is more likely to have originated with Jesus and been remembered than have come to birth as the work of the beleaguered Twelve.

Jesus seems to have used the number "twelve" symbolically for his close companions without a clear recollection remaining in later generations of who exactly constituted the band. (See the variants in Mark 1:16–20; Matt. 4:18–22; Luke 5:1–11; and John's single reference to "the Twelve," 6:67, while providing six of the familiar names randomly and several others that do not occur on any list.) The tradition of the Twelve indicates a concept that is very old and probably goes back to Jesus. Why he called them except "to be with him" to proclaim the gospel, and to drive out demons (Mark 3:14–15), the earliest gospel tradition does not say. But the probable explanation, in light of the use of the number in contemporary Jewish writings, was to symbolize the restoration of Israel. This would include both judgment upon it and rescue of the lost sheep of its house (Matt. 10:6). The Twelve are sent out with a clear purpose in Matthew 10:1, 7–14 (= Luke 9:1–6), namely, to proclaim the gospel with the aid of deeds of power like healing and exorcism, but the accounts are clearly colored by the evangelizing activities of the early church. Best remembered is Jesus' proclamation of the imminence of God's kingship or rule in which they would have a part. After his resurrection the Twelve stayed together continuing this same proclamation, as if they knew he expected them to do so.

The consistent pattern in the Gospels identifies Jesus' project as the restoration of Israel with him under God as restorer. Those among his own people who opposed him, who are described as turning him over to imperial authority, would have been well alerted to his proclamation of a new order. The dream he harbored, whether it was long-term or short-term in fulfillment, had no place in it for them or for the temple. Every report about him that reached their ears would have confirmed this. His words and actions might well have been thought apocalyptic madness by the Sadducees, who were impatient with all post-Torah speculation. He was in any case taken seriously as a political threat to a sufficient number in the ruling body known as the Sanhedrin, whatever its political composition may have been. And its authoritative voice seems to have prevailed.

This relationship between Jesus as an end-time figure in his own mind, though not the Messiah, and the final action taken against him would seem even more compelling in triggering opposition to him than his one symbolic act against the temple reported in all four Gospels. His teaching on law observance was not such as to incline anyone to eliminate him from the scene. Some Christian theologians have affirmed resoundingly reasons why opponents would wish to do so: his "setting his own authority against that of commandments of the Law," "forgiving sins in his own name," "replacing fidelity to commands and precepts with a dispensation of grace and freedom." None of these stands up well to scrutiny. Each reflects a doctrinal commitment in his favor and an ignorance of the rabbinic argumentation in which he engaged, more than close familiarity with sound exegesis. It is clear that Jesus could not have been found blasphemous for any utterance attributed to him before the first-century church theologized his sayings, as a result of belief in him as one in whom the presence of God was bodied forth. It is equally apparent, however, that he was vulnerable in predicting the dissolution of the present condition of Jewish existence as the new and final age came on.

The Earliest Recall of Jesus' Sayings

Important in any hypothesis on why he died is the impact his teaching about God's impending rule would have had on his disciples. The Gospels testify amply to the disciples' incomprehension of his teaching in its depth while he was with them. They would surely have pondered after his resurrection, however, what his proclamation of the final age meant for them. He had not assembled them for no purpose. He had hinted at a role for them in God's mysterious future, however little they understood it. It is not necessary in this reconstruction to call on Jesus' risen-life appearances as a period of teaching, let alone of strategy and tactics. There might have been no extended period resembling the brief christophanies the Gospels describe; the "forty days" of Acts is a theological construct unknown to the other evangelists. But the memory of Jesus' vision for the future would have stayed with them. It would have accounted for their remaining together as a company, thinking of themselves as "the Twelve." It would best explain their self-awareness as a church (Heb. *qāhāl,* or *ekklēsía,* the assembly of the new age), no matter what uneasiness this would cause later New Testament scholars of an antichurch persuasion. In a word, the continuity between Jesus' life and teaching in an eschatological if not an apocalyptic mode, and the origins of a community of believers in a similar mode, is best explained by the compulsion they felt to conduct themselves in a context of God's reign already inaugurated. Without this as the main theme of Jesus' teaching, the post-Easter activity of his companions would be inexplicable.

Paul, the earliest witness we have to the final-age orientation of Jesus, insisted that he handed on only what he had received. To be sure, he developed the message in accommodation to people's needs in the Jewish diaspora. The four evangelists did the same. But all held fast to a core of apostolic tradition that required Jesus' post-Easter disciples to proclaim a reign of God that was to come in its fullness, with Jesus as the anointed human king already in heaven exercising by anticipation the divine rule. Paul's vision of the way it would be consummated at the end of the age spells out the Christ version of this Jewish hope, although for Paul, a Jew, it was clearly a Jewish hope (1 Cor. 15:20–28).

Reports of such a prophetic message delivered by Jesus in his lifetime, although without its Christian elaboration, might have been expected to cause apprehension. Its meeting with popular acceptance could have been his death knell. One thing not explained by the record of his teaching before it was developed theologically is that he did not speak of the restoration of Israel as a matter of this people's victory over all its enemies. He spoke, rather, of his people's living its biblical ideal to the full. There was a place for the Gentiles in most of the apocalyptic dreams then current, but non-Jews would be present at the final days by absorption into Israel. So far as we can reconstruct it, Jesus' end-time teaching had no place for a vindication of Israel against all who had opposed this people of God. The teacher of Nazareth may be presumed as patriotic as the next Jew and as interested in justice for his people against all its oppressors. But, if he featured such conventional expectations, this has not survived. Conspiracy theories have been developed in which his disciples modified his people-centered teaching so as to downplay its stress on Jewish nationalism and thus gain it a hearing outside Jewish circles. One can say little for any theories for which no evidence exists but total silence. Jesus as a protagonist of violent uprising whom his disciples later domesticated must be called a creature of imagination.

The earliest tradition, indeed, goes counter to what one might have expected of a Jewish liberationist movement. Jesus taught the equality of all in the reign of God that was to come. This was not so much if they would repent, as in the movement of John the Baptist (although see Mark 1:15 = Matt. 4:17, where Jesus succeeds John by initially repeating John's message), but an equality that would be theirs if they would emulate "sinners" and submit to God's rule on the terms Jesus set out. These were chiefly submission to that rule now, in readiness for the kingdom to come.

Nothing in the tradition recalls Jesus as an antinomian, a teacher of conduct contrary to the law as the Bible disclosed it. His teaching is a mixture
of familiar Pharisaic positions and some perfectionist refinements of it, but
even more a challenge to reflect on the biblical teaching and *do* it. He had
a normal concern about living an upright Jewish life. He was much more
concerned with the present behavior of those who would let God be king
over them now with a view to the final age. If he had an interest in or even
much contact with non-Jews, we do not know of it (the exceptions would
be fleeting exchanges with pagan and Samaritan recipients of his miraculous
healings; see Mark 5:1–20; 7:26; Luke 17:16; Matt. 8:5). He at times com-
mends these non-Jews in such a way as to indicate that their faith in God is
equal or superior to Israelite faith. If those accounts are authentic they
would be disturbing to normal Jewish piety—but no reason to wish him
dead.

A vision of the future in which no familiar alignments, authorities, or
economic powers would remain could, by contrast, cause total anxiety. Jesus' future-oriented teaching does not closely resemble that of any of the
apocalyptic visionaries of the age immediately before him. One cannot conceive any Jews' wishing to still the voice of the author of *1 Enoch*, or the
Assumption of Moses, or the War Scroll of Qumran. Their visions were redolent of no time and no place. But Jesus' predictions involved the destruction
and reconstruction of the entire social fabric within an identifiable period.

With the memory of Jesus' insistence on the sovereign kingship of God
ringing in their ears ("May your kingdom come," Luke 11:2, a phrase from
the prayer Jesus taught when he was asked to), the disciples did nothing
strange or unpredictable in designating Jesus king-messiah from the start.
He almost certainly never entertained the title as describing himself, because
its meaning as successful liberator of Israel was fixed in the popular mind.
It had no biblical or postbiblical history as a "spiritualized" title, unless its
mythic uses in the apocalypses be so understood. Nothing in the gospel tradition indicates that Jesus wished to refashion its connotations away from
the received political-religious one. The earliest postresurrection disciples
must simply have thought it right as a description of the risen one. He ended
as a crucified Messiah because the reign of God he proclaimed, on its terms,
was resisted by the rich and powerful. The hazards to the apostolic band
were obvious. The title as applied to him would have brought on immediate
ribald laughter. It was totally oxymoronic, a victor whose brush with "the
powers" had ended in ignominious loss. This was a leader with whom no
one had remained loyally except for a band of women and one man: a sorry
end for one more failed messiah.

What, one may ask, made it enter anyone's mind initially to connect the
name of Jesus with a term connoting royalty, if in fact "messiah" connoted
only military victory? His origins as a Bethlehemite by birth and his legal

sonship of Joseph, a descendant of David, would have been known to his close friends (see Matt. 1:16; Luke 3:23; John 1:45). Even if Bethlehem were not his actual birthplace but became such in popular memory *because* he was Davidic, that would only confirm, not place in doubt, his origins as a man of Judah. The remembrance of Jesus' mocking as a king could also have had something to do with the early claims of believers in him that he was the Messiah, although the historicity of this narrative cannot be verified (see Mark 15:18; Matt. 27:29; John 19:3). The *títlos* on the cross denoting obliquely the charge against him may conceivably have been at the root of it: "King of Judaea" (Mark 15:26; Matt. 27:37; Luke 23:38; John 19:19). Mark well, that derisive placard seemed to say, the way all such would-be usurpers end. For believers in Jesus' resurrection who knew how God had vindicated him, the whitewashed board on the stake above his head would have in retrospect said something quite different: "This is the man who pro-claimed a kingship of God"—of "the heavens," in Matthew's later avoidance of the divine name—that began to be realized with his rising from the dead. The taunt of the one who sentenced him to death was prophetic: "Jesus of Nazareth, the king of the Jews [or: of Judaea]" (John 19:3, 14). This most improbable Messiah had begun to reign.

The usage of "messiah" (Gk. *christós*) for Jesus at first blush looks like conscious paradox, a seizing on the least probable designation of him as the one that described him best. This would not only be to grasp the nettle of popular skepticism but to co-opt the most acceptable Jewish term for a pop-ular hero. Still, Jesus' brief life as a public figure and his sorry end so com-pletely contradicted the popular image of messiah that is it doubtful his dis-ciples would have settled on such a rash verbal tour de force. Rather than furthering their cause it would only have invited mockery had they not solid reasons to employ it. They needed a better reason than a paradox intended to pique popular curiosity. Fidelity to their master's proclamation of God's coming kingdom, and their conviction of his centrality in that reign, would have been that reason. It was as the person anointed by God to preach God's reign that he was best remembered (see Luke 4:18, quoting Isa. 61:1–2). But, Jesus, the risen one, was identical with the crucified proclaimer of God's reign. Therefore he was remembered as Jesus Messiah from an early date after his resurrection, giving that title a different meaning than the one it had traditionally had. He was a Jewish king in a quite new sense.

"The Christ" — But a *Crucified* One?

To call Jesus the Christ of God—first in Aramaic then in Greek—was to make a faith statement about his role in the future kingdom. It said nothing about his death on the cross as atoning for sins. In fact, it did quite the opposite. Jewish writings contemporary with Jesus and the decades immediately before and after him knew nothing of the "days of Messiah" being ushered in at the cost of tragic death and loss, least of all of one man's. The concepts "messiah" and "suffering" are nowhere coupled, diligently as Christian theologians have searched for the conjunction. Israel had suffered much at the hands of oppressors. Like the entire people, the just individual in Israel was subjected to ridicule and torment for a show of fidelity (see Wis. 2:12–20). A God of justice would reverse all this. On "the day of YHWH" (sometimes called simply "the day") it would all come right. A conviction of the earlier biblical period had been that all Israel would be elevated in glory on that day and the nations reduced in shame.

After the exile this simplistic view of the divine justice and judgment had yielded to the more nuanced one that the righteous of Israel and even those among the Gentiles would be shown forth for their goodness. The unrighteous, even among Israel, would be disclosed for their wickedness. God would render the judgment in perfect justice on "the day." In some postbiblical visions of the end, God's Messiah would act as judge. Nowhere, however, was this central figure of judgment, by whatever title, seen as suffering let alone dying. By definition he was the person who would lead Israel into the new aeon, leaving all woes behind. Far from dying in the final encounter with evil, he was to be the victor in the name of all the living.

The postbiblical Jewish writings in Greek have no single representation or title for God's vice-regent. They are, however, unanimous in their silence on his having to suffer or die. Obviously, then, Jesus' undergoing an atoning death as the Christ cannot derive from any apocalyptic model. Could the explanation be simpler? He had died in shameful circumstances and there was no getting around the fact. Therefore, the earliest believers might have reasoned, why not make the best of it? A noble or sublime interpretation of the harsh realities of his execution might neutralize the sting of his death. That would do as an explanation if it were not that the earliest presentations of him as someone to be believed in were more than neutral. These sentences of proclamation found positive virtue in his death. An early one was, he "died for our sins in accordance with the scriptures" (1 Cor. 15:3). The death was presented as expiatory from the first we hear of it, which was probably in the pre-Pauline fragment quoted in Romans 3:25–26; but more of that below.

Do We Have Jesus' View of Why He Died?

One way to account for this early belief might be that Jesus himself viewed his impending death as expiatory by God's design. If this could be proved, the search need go no further than his own words on the subject. The difficulty is that we do not have them. The two places in the earliest Gospel, Mark, where Jesus speaks of the meaning of his death cannot be shown to be original with him. Putting them under scrutiny (the texts are Mark 10:45 and 14:24) reveals them to be interpretations put on his death in later, probably Greek-speaking circles. The context of the first is that the true greatness of a disciple consists in service rather than arrogance or dominion, the posture that marks pagans who exercise authority (vv. 42–44). The saying that comes next, v. 45a, seems to have originated in a different context, namely, a polemic against the idea that the eschatological Son of man was to be served when he came. Aside from the probability that the title "Son of man" as attributed to Jesus was the work of the early church, there is the difficulty that giving his life "as a ransom for the many" (v. 45b) may have derived from the early faith conviction that he had indeed fulfilled the prophecy of Isaiah 53: "Through his suffering, my servant shall justify many. . . . He shall take away the sins of many, and win pardon for their offenses" (Isa. 53:11, 12). The one Gospel citation of that fourth Servant Song (Isa. 52:13–53:12), however, relates it to Jesus' cures of the sick, not to his self-perception (see Matt. 8:17). Besides, it is a case of Matthew's view of Jesus, not Jesus' view of himself. In the form in which the Mark quotation appears, "The Son of man . . . [came] to give his life as a ransom for the many" (10:45) is the conviction of the Markan church that Jesus was a vicarious sufferer on humanity's behalf.[3]

The saying of Jesus over the cup at the last meal he ate with his friends labors under the same difficulties: "This is my blood of the covenant which is poured out for many" (Mark 14:24). Matthew retains the entire phrase, adding "for the forgiveness of sins" (26:28), while Luke has "shed for you" (22:20). Paul names as the effect of drinking from this cup in faith a sealing of "the new covenant in my blood," calling it a proclamation of the Lord's death until he come (1 Cor. 11:25b–26). Efforts have been made to show that the cup phrasing could not have originated in Hebraic circumstances, only in Hellenistic, but—disregarding the self-assurance of interpreters about what were religious and cultural impossibilities in those times—the more evident conclusion is that the four versions of Jesus' words over the bread and wine at the supper table were four liturgical formulas that developed in four local churches. We cannot be sure of Jesus' precise words on which they were based. Mark's "which is poured out for many" of 14:24 clearly accords with his theology of Jesus' vicarious death found in 10:45. It may well either underlie (in Matthew) or be common to (in Luke and Paul) the development of thought in other churches. Attributing an expiatory purpose to Jesus' death by his own expressed intent does not, in any case, seem to be grounded in any Gospel text. Broadening this statement, no word of

---

3. "For all" would seem to be the proper translation of *antì pollōn* here, in a parallel with *hypèr pántōn* in 1 Tim. 2:5–6 and Rom. 8:32. See a note on the translation of *pro multis* as "for all" in the Roman Rite in *Third Progress Report on the Revision of the Roman Missal* (Washington, D.C.: International Commission on English in the Liturgy, 1992), 152–54.

Jesus that can be maintained as authentically his indicates what his state of mind was as to the effect of his death.

The Maccabean Martyrs as Paradigm of Jesus' Death

Going backward in history to the book of Daniel and the deuterocanonical or pseudepigraphic writings (i.e., those not accepted into the canon agreed upon toward the beginning of the 2d century c.e., the present Bible of the Jews) and the historian Josephus, we find reference to the deaths of the martyrs of the Maccabean period, 167–75 b.c.e., in the following places: Daniel 11:32–35; 12:1–3; *Testament* (or *Assumption*) *of Moses* 8; 9; 1 Maccabees 1–5; Josephus *Antiquities* 12.241—13.214, which is a paraphrase of 1 Maccabees 1:14—13:42; 2 Maccabees 5:12–14, 24–26; 6; 7. Examining these writings in sequence we will see whether their view of the deaths of the righteous Israelites may have influenced the earliest Christian interpretation of the death of Jesus. We know that these accounts, some of them novelistic, resulted in a cult of the Jewish martyrs and contributed to Pharisaic belief in the resurrection of the dead. That is not the same as saying that any Jews viewed these deaths as profitable to the living, specifically in remitting their sins. This would be required if these martyrdoms were to be taken as the paradigm for Jesus' death as expiatory of sin. The deaths did profit the living, of course, in the sense that they kept the dream of freedom for Israel alive.

Daniel may contain the earliest references to the fate of those Jews who died in the persecution of Antiochus Epiphanes ("the Splendid") around 165. A despicable person "who shall seize the kingdom by stealth and fraud" (Dan. 11:21) will cause some who are disloyal to the covenant to apostatize (v. 32) and punish with the sword, exile, plunder, and flames the nation's wise, who shall instruct the many (v. 33). Few people shall assist the wise as they fall victim (the aggressive Maccabees?) and many shall join them out of insincere motives (v. 34). "Of the wise, some shall fall, so that the rest may be tested, refined, and purified, until the end time which is still appointed to come" (v. 35).

The book of Daniel had previously alluded to the suffering and death of those Jews who held fast to the Law ("the holy ones") and could not be forced into apostasy by the tyrant (see 7:21, 25; 8:24, 25). Nowhere, however, is there mention of the effect of the deaths of the faithful on others, only the good effect of the teaching of the sages until, and concerning, "the end time" (v. 35), on those wise persons who manage to survive. We are left to conclude from what is not said that the death of some of the teachers has purified others by putting them to the test. The time is "unsurpassed in distress" (12:1), but the warriors and others who are slaughtered shall rise from the dust, the innocent to the life of the final age (zōè aiōnios, the phrase adopted by the Gospel of John) but some to everlasting disgrace (v. 2). There is a reward in prospect for the wise and those who lead many to justice. They shall be "resplendent like the firmament . . . be like the stars forever" (12:3). But for those who die in fidelity to the covenant the reward of resurrection is personal. Their deaths will achieve a boon for themselves but nothing for others.

Chapter 8 through part of chapter 10 of the *Testament of Moses* appear to deal with the Antiochian persecution, whereas chapter 6 is more clearly a description of the later Hasmonean kings who usurped the high priesthood. There is a graphic account of the indignities visited on Jews in the Syrian-Greek persecution of the early second century B.C.E., including the crucifixion of those who confess their circumcision, the torture of those who repudiate it, and the attempted surgery on the young sons of Jewish women to "bring forward their foreskins" (chap. 8, where enforced blasphemies against Mosaic law are also described). A tale of Taxo and his seven sons (chap. 9) much resembles the story of the heroic martyrdom of a mother and her seven sons in 2 Maccabees 7. Taxo is determined not to transgress God's commandments and so exhorts his sons to fast for three days and then retreat to a cave in the open country. "For if we do this, and do die, our blood will be avenged before the LORD" (9:7). The "Heavenly One" (10:3), "God Most High . . . the Eternal One alone, in full view, will come to work vengeance on the nations" (v. 7). Some see in Taxo's resistance the triggering of the events of the Maccabean revolt, but this is doubtful. For our purposes, we should note the promise of divine reprisal in the future and the biblical theme that God cannot allow innocent blood to go unavenged. There is no hint, however, of these innocent deaths accomplishing anything for the faithful survivors of the cruel persecution.

First Maccabees, written about 100 concerning the events from 167–65 B.C.E. down to the death of Simon and his succession by John Hyrcanus in 134, is not notably different in theme from the above two books. It is, however, much more a historical chronicle, written in praise of Judah the Maccabee (2:4, 6; 3:8) and his brothers faithful to the covenant. First Maccabees is directed against the Jewish apostates (1:52) more than the Seleucid dynasty of oppressors. Antiochus's defilement of the sanctuary is recorded (1:37–38), likewise his putting to death of the mothers who had their sons circumcised, and Jews who would not eat gentile food (vv. 60–63), and warriors who refused to bear arms on the Sabbath (2:31–38). The last position was not that of Mattathias or his sons and companions (v. 41), who became known corporately as the Maccabees. In this book the reason given for Jewish resistance is the will "not to be defiled by any unclean food, so as not to profane the holy covenant" (1:63). This resulted in violence against "sinners and Law-breakers" by the Hasidean ("pious") supporters of the Mattathias faction, in their testimony to the sanctity of the Law (2:42–44). The author of 1 Maccabees, unlike the anonymous author of Daniel, does not hold out to the just who die for the law the personal reward of being raised up from the grave. Mattathias, about to die, reminds his sons that none who hope in the LORD will fail in strength (2:61). If they are zealous for the law and give their lives for the covenant of the ancestors (2:50) they can expect "great glory and an everlasting name" (v. 51; cf. v. 64).

Josephus in describing the same scene has the patriarch say that the Deity (*tò theîon*), seeing them disposed to die for the laws, will admire their heroism and give them (*autoús*) back to them again. There is, however, no clear indication that the "them" is the laws and, if so, how the restoration will be made (see *Antiquities* 12.281). A preceding passage in the same book (255–56) is more graphic than 1 Maccabees in describing tortures and the details of being crucified alive.

To summarize 1 Maccabees on the point, heroic deaths in testimony to the law will result in an everlasting name for those who die, but we are left to conclude that their sole legacy to the living will be their courageous example.

Second Maccabees is the self-described condensation of five volumes of Jason of Cyrene describing the campaigns against Antiochus and his son Eupator (2:19–23). Not a sequel to the first book, it nonetheless supplements it in some particulars. It attempts to interpret the period theologically by putting edifying discourses in the mouths of the Jewish heroes. The martyrs of the resistance are glorified (6:18—7:42) but they die, as in the previously examined books, saying with the aged Eleazar: "I will leave to the young a noble example of how to die willingly and generously for the revered and holy laws" (6:28). In refusing to eat pork he prefers a glorious death to a remaining few years of defilement (v. 19). There occurs in this book an explanation of the chastisements being visited on Israel for aping the Greeks in its disregard of the laws (4:16–17). The woes are for the nation's correction, not its ruin. It is called a kindness on God's part to punish Jewish sinners promptly, whereas the pagans are allowed to reach the full measure of their sins before they are punished. The divine mercy is never withdrawn from Israel (6:12–17). In "the time of mercy," as the life to come is described, a martyred mother expects to be reunited with her sons (7:29). This treatise sees the Maccabean persecution "in terms of man's sin and God's wrath," without "making the connection between the martyrs' deaths and Israel's deliverance."[4] Those who die will receive, after brief pain, a life that never fails (7:36). The book, in sum, does not suggest

---

4. Sam K. Williams, *Jesus' Death as Saving Event and the Background and Origin of a Concept,* Harvard Dissertations in Religion 2 (Missoula, Mont.: Scholars Press, 1975), 81, 89. This work analyzes the postbiblical writings to see if the cult of the Maccabean martyrs underlay the concept of Jesus' atoning death. It concludes that the pre-Pauline fragment represented by Rom. 3:25–26 derives from the *hilastêrion* ("means of expiation") concept in the apocryphal 4 Maccabees.

any direct cause-effect relation between the deaths of the martyrs and the deliverance of Israel.

In all this one should note that nowhere in the New Testament was Jesus remembered to have died at gentile hands for fidelity to the law or the deliverance of Israel from Gentile oppression. Nonetheless, the question remains, Could the memory of the deaths of the martyrs have influenced the earliest proclamation of him as a messiah who atoned for sins by his death? Some say that the notion of his death as expiatory could not have flourished in the earliest church were it not for the Jewish cult of the martyrs. One cannot, of course, prove that such was *not* the case. The question is whether evidence can be summoned to establish that it *was* the case. The replication of the Seleucid dynasty's cruelty two centuries before was surely etched in the mind of every Jew who believed in Jesus. Still, the search for specific common elements between his death and that of the martyred thousands yields very few. Both he and they died for their loyalty to the God of Israel, but they for ritual purity and covenant fidelity, he (in the interpretation of early believers) for enunciating the terms of a reign of God to come. This was a different cause from those of patriots and purists alike. His first disciples who assembled as a community "called out" from the rest in Israel found in his death the supreme benefit of the rectification of a humanitywide ill. The more important question is, Is there anything like this vicarious sacrifice in the Bible? It can be either one person dying for others or any sacrificial act that is widely believed to profit the many. If such a sacrifice is present, even in a general way, we need only say that the paradigm existed ready-made. No search for specific correspondences as with the Maccabean martyrs, which prove to be inadequate, need be pursued.

The Bible and Expiation by the Deaths of Others

Throughout most of the biblical period death is viewed as God's punishment for sin. Suffering is likewise seen as retributive. From the earliest biblical books down through the writings attributed to the Deuteronomist and the Chronicler, which terminate in the compilation of Ezra and Nehemiah (4th century), some act of wrongdoing is sought to account for every misfortune. The innocent sufferings of someone like Jeremiah alone constitute an exception (see Jer. 12:1–6, which is similar to the questioning on the lips of Job; but see also 2 Sam. 24:17, where David says he understands the reason for his punishment but asks the LORD why the innocent had to die in a plague). The dawning of a new outlook on the causes of suffering came after the exile. With an increased appreciation of the worth and responsibility of individuals came less satisfaction with future reward for the community as an adequate explanation of individual suffering. The author of Job wrestled with the problem mightily but concluded that the mystery was beyond him.

He found his solution in the inexplicable majesty of God. The belief in the resurrection of the righteous that one finds in Daniel and 2 Maccabees yields, in the period around the introduction of the Common Era, to a commitment to immortality in the manner of the Greeks (1 *Enoch* 22:9–13; *Test. Benj.* 10:8; Wis. 3:4; 5:15; 4 Macc. 7:19; 13:17; 16:25; 18:23). The most usual explanation of suffering in this period of Judaism was that God permitted it to test persons in their misfortune. We find this in the first two chapters of Job, where God permits Satan to submit this man of Uz to many trials to see if he will curse God.

This same outlook on the misfortune of the innocent is found in *Psalms of Solomon* 13:10 ("The LORD will . . . wipe away the mistakes of the devout with discipline"); 16:14; Judith 8:27 ("The LORD put them in the crucible to try their hearts"); Wisdom 3:5; 11:9; Sirach 2:1, 3 ("Prepare yourself for trials. . . . Forsake him not; thus your future will be great"). This view of suffering is certainly at odds with the punitive view, although God is seen as the author of the trials in both cases. The notion of testing as in a smelter's refining fire had already appeared in the prophets (Isa. 48:10; Jer. 6:27–30), to be perfected as divine discipline in the later period. It does not stop with the onset of the Common Era but grows in intensity (see 2 *Apoc. Bar.* 13:1–12; 78:3) into the mishnaic and talmudic periods. As to deaths in the Bible and immediately after, they are a personal misfortune in the many cases where they have no retributive character, but no positive value is assigned to them. Warriors die because it is the will of God; they may derive some benefit for Israel out of their victory. They do not give their lives out of patriotic self-sacrifice as in the familiar Greek model. Sometimes individuals in the Bible die to appease YHWH's wrath or to rid the people of transgressors of the covenant, but they never die with the *purpose* of achieving a good.

Do any Hebrew Scriptures claim that one person's suffering or dying achieves expiation for the sins of others? Moses seems to make such an offer to the LORD for the people's sin of casting the molten calf, but it is not clear if his proposal is one of sacrificial mediation. Besides, "strike me out of the book you have written" is in itself an ambiguous phrase (Exod. 32:32). It could mean simply "forget me." The LORD's response settles the question; Moses' offer is not allowed: "Him only who has sinned against me will I strike out of my book" (v. 33). Personal responsibility is at issue here.

In the scapegoat passage that underlies the Day of Atonement, the community's sins are transferred symbolically to a single beast (see Lev. 16:15–22) by "confessing over it all the sinful faults and transgressions of the Israelites" (v. 21). The animal in this rite is accepted by God as a pleasing sacrifice. God then removes the people's sins *if* the symbolic victim conveys their repentant state of heart. It cannot be established that this or any sacrifice of birds or beasts accomplished a transfer such that their deaths were thought accepted by God in place of the deaths of humans who should be dying for their own sins. The transgressions atoned for were normally not deserving of death, and an expiation that did not engage the human will was as abhorrent to the Israelite as it would be later to the Christian. Modern ignorance of ancient religion has made a mechanical transaction of temple cult, as it has the practices of many peoples that our contemporaries categorize as magic. It is not easy—often it is impossible—to know exactly the symbolism intended in worlds we do not inhabit.

Moses says he requires the sacrifice to the LORD of all first-born animals and the redemption of first-born sons as a reminder of the pharaoh's killing every firstborn in the land of Egypt (Exod. 13:11–16). It is clear that the dedication and the slaughter point to what was perceived as righting some ancient wrong or as a preparation for a dedicated life in the promised land. It is not so clear that the sacrifice of animals is meant to be substitutionary, thereby achieving a benefit for the Israelites in the "land of the Canaanites" (v. 11). As to the redemption or repurchase of firstborn males, we do not know whether this was accomplished by the killing of an animal and, if so, what exactly the sacrifice was thought to achieve.

This brings us to the one passage in Israel's Scriptures that is widely supposed by Christian theologians to lie behind the Gospel narratives of the passion even though no evangelist employs it there, namely, Isaiah 52:13—53:12. (Matthew 27:30 is a remote echo of Isa. 50:6, while Luke 22:37, "And he was reckoned among the transgressors," Isa. 53:12c, does little other than declare Jesus' innocence. Luke does quote the passage at Acts 8:32.) It is the prime candidate for what was intended by the phrase "according to the Scriptures" in the summary proclamation provided by 1 Corinthians 15:3. The question is not, Was the suffering servant in the writer's mind the whole people or was it one strong, prophetic voice that brought opprobrium down on the speaker? The question is, What does "he was wounded for our transgressions, crushed for our iniquities" mean (Isa. 53:5a)? Is this a true case of vicarious, expiatory suffering? Or did a faithful servant of God simply have to endure the punishment that was meted out to a wicked people? "Upon him was the punishment that made us whole, and by his bruises we are healed," but in what sense? Is it mere hyperbole?

Everything hinges on what is meant by the "healing" and "making whole" of 53:5b, the "being smitten for the sin of his people" (v. 8). The guilt of us all was laid on him (v. 6). Was he simply made the paradigm of the people's guilt without further effect, a symbol of its wrongdoing in which he had no part? Or did God accept the chastisement he bore to remove the guilt incurred? In the latter case, what the servant suffered is being described as advantageous to many. Israel has sinned and been carried off into exile as a result of its sin. The servant's acceptance of suffering, it seems, has something to do with rectifying the situation by removing what God has against this people. If an individual is not being spoken of and Israel is itself the servant, then Second Isaiah may be describing the people's being brought low in humble acquiescence as the means God intends to bring about a change in its fortunes.

A clue to the passage's meaning may lie in the way it is picked up and interpreted in Jewish writing subsequent to the exile. Wisdom 2:19, already cited, may have Isaiah 53 in mind when it says of the persecutors of "the just one who is obnoxious to us": "With revilement and torture let us put him to the test." More pointedly, "His oppressors who made light of his sufferings . . . will be astounded at his unforeseen deliverance" (5:1–2). Deliverance is thus either being reported or predicted of the just one's efforts. But it is all rather obscure, so much so that the passage cannot be described unequivocally as having followed up on Isaiah 53, assuming for the moment that the latter says the suffering of the servant brings to others deliverance from the guilt of sin. In the Wisdom passage the deliverance promised is of the just one himself from his plight, not of others as in the Isaiah case. Besides, if either biblical text had had any influence on the thinking of Palestinian believers in Jesus, we might expect it to have surfaced somewhere in the four passion narratives. Their sources, after all, were Palestinian in origin. Yet no such use of either passage occurs, despite the fact that Matthew revels in such quotations when they seem apt. John employs biblical allusions rather than direct citations. Yet neither he nor Matthew employs it. The roots of the early doctrine of Jesus' death as saving do not, therefore, seem to lie in the suffering servant of Isaiah or the innocent just one beleaguered by oppressors in the Wisdom of Solomon. Whatever either meant in the first instance, neither Paul nor any evangelist saw fit to find in this passage or passages the paradigm for Jesus' expiatory death.

The Inspiration of Paul's Soteriology

Some passages in the pseudepigraphic 4 Maccabees, dated between 18 and 55 C.E., seem unique to it in the time leading up to or just after Jesus' death. One of these that is claimed to have influenced the way Paul viewed Jesus' death as salvific is as follows:

> [Through the martyrs] the tyrant was punished and our land purified, since they became, as it were, a ransom for the sin of our nation. Through the blood of these righteous ones and through the propitiation of their death the divine providence rescued Israel, which had been shamefully treated. (17:21–22)

The language of ransom, purification, and expiation derives in its entirety from the Jewish Scriptures of the Septuagint canon. The author in speaking of "the sin of our nation" (17:21) means widespread apostasy. Whether the sins be weighty or light, they all equally set the law at nought (see 5:19–21). The main intent of the treatise, however, is to inculcate the "mastery of the

passions by devout reason" (1:1), specifically as exemplified by the endurance of the nine martyrs under torture on whom it concentrates. The vocabulary of this concept occurs throughout. The example the martyrs give to
others of adhering to the law (7:9), thereby living the life of the age of blessing (17:18; cf. 18:23), makes them "responsible for the downfall of the tyranny that beset our nation . . . so that through them their own land was
purified" (1:11). This quite objective result is attributed to the sufferings and
deaths of the resisters. In light of their self-offering the LORD restored to
Israel its land, "as it were a ransom for the sin of our nation" (17:21). God
accepted the offering of their lives as an expiatory sacrifice.

This encomium of the martyrs in florid prose is a much more Hellenistic
product than the pseudepigrapha examined above. The vocabulary frequently has little or no Septuagint occurrence. Platonic and Stoic ideas are
echoed more than biblical (e.g., control of the passions, athletic struggle,
death before dishonor, the exercise of reason as king). In form it resembles
in many places a Cynic-Stoic diatribe. The martyrs die the glorious deaths
of Greek heroes defending their city-state (in their case, the defense is of
religion), approaching death willingly in a most un-Jewish manner.

Jews did not preserve 4 Maccabees; Christians did. It gives clear indication of underlying the second-century *Martyrdom of Polycarp,* even to specific phrases. The fourth-century writers Ambrose, Gregory of Nazianzus
and John Chrysostom made use of it in their eulogies of the martyrs. The
question is, can it be shown to have had currency in Hellenistic Jewish circles
that could have influenced New Testament thinking directly? Ignatius of Antioch seems to have known it in its main lines (see *Eph.* 21.1; *Smyrn.* 9.2;
10.2; but especially in *Poly.* 2.3; 3.1). So does Hebrews (5:8–9; 7:28; 11:35–
38). The one place in Paul's writings that reflects it most faithfully has been
referred to above, Romans 3:25–26.

This Greek text has led some to maintain not only that there is nothing
in the Bible or Jewish thought circulating in Palestine to incline a Palestinian
church to devise a theology of Jesus' death as expiatory, but also that Hellenistic models alone, such as this one, could account for it. This would be the
case even if it originated in a mixed Jewish-gentile congregation.[5]

The thesis is that a primitive formulation preceded Paul's use of it in Romans 3 and had as its purpose to explain how God, out of restraint, has not
punished the sins of the Gentiles up to now but has taken positive action in
Christ to deal with them. Paul writes that "all [i.e., Jews and non-Jews alike]
are justified freely by God's grace through the redemption [*apolytrōseōs*] of
Christ Jesus" (v. 24). This is followed by the verses that are presumed to be
the citation of a pre-Pauline source:

> For God designed him to be the means of expiating sin by his blood [*hilastēr-
> ion*], effective through faith. God meant by this to demonstrate [the divine]

5. Williams, *Jesus' Death,* 55–56, 162–63.

justice, because out of forbearance God had overlooked the sins of the past—to demonstrate this justice now in the present, showing that God is himself just and justifies anyone who has faith in Jesus. (Rom. 3:25–26)

Hilastērion here has to be expiatory because "past sins" is the subject of "passing over" and "forbearance." The passage of 4 Maccabees that is thought to underlie the Pauline source reads: "Through the blood of these pious ones and through the expiation [*hilastērion*] of their death the divine providence rescued Israel" (17:22). There is no closer parallel in all pre-Pauline Jewish literature to the shedding of Christ's blood as expiatory—as achieving a benefit for Jews and Gentiles alike—than the passage just cited. Eleazar had petitioned: "Be merciful to your people and let our punishment be a satisfaction on their behalf. Make my blood their purification and take my life as a ransom for theirs" (6:29). The words that are common to the two texts of 4 Maccabees, "purification," "ransom," and "expiatory" (*kathársion, antípsychon, hilastērios*) are not found in Greek versions of the Bible except for *hilastērios*, which describes the lid of the ark in Exodus 25:17. The roots of the other two words are frequent in the cultic vocabulary of the Septuagint to speak of purification and expiation. Proponents of the thesis regret that they cannot prove that Antioch was the place where 4 Maccabees was written, thinking it would establish that Paul first heard the idea of Christ's death as expiatory developed there.[6] It is at least demonstrable that tales of the Maccabean martyrs were developing in Greek-speaking Judaism in a way that made it impossible for the first believers in Jesus—even among Palestinian Jews—not to be familiar with them.

Tracking Paul's Usage Further

Three other passages in Paul's correspondence have been suggested as containing his inheritance from earlier Christians in this matter. Two of them are remnants of pre-Pauline material, Galatians 4:4–8 (v. 5 parallels 3:13 in verb use) and Romans 8:31–34.[7] A third, Galatians 3:13, is Paul's original development. In the first passage God sends forth the Son (*exapésteilen*) in order to buy freedom (*exagorázein*, v. 5) for the Jews, just as God has sent forth the Spirit of the Son to turn Gentile slaves into children of God (vv. 6–8). As regards the Jews, there is no mention of how the Son redeems them. But Paul's verb *exapostéllō* ("send forth") used in Galatians 4:4 and 6 occurs nowhere else in his letters. In the two biblical cases where one redeems or buys freedom for another, a priest "sends out" a live bird once he has symbolically transferred the impurity of leprosy to it (Lev. 14:7) and "sends out"

---

6. Ibid., 248–53, where Williams tries his best.
7. See the helpful article of Daniel Schwartz of the Hebrew University, Jerusalem, "Two Pauline Allusions to the Redemptive Mechanism of the Crucifixion," *JBL* 102/2 (1983): 259–68.

a goat into the desert once he has made the symbolic transfer to it of the people's sins (Lev. 16:10).

Galatians 3:13 similarly has the language of redemption. Paul says there that Jesus' death "bought us [Jews] freedom from the curse of the law," namely, that incurred by not "doing everything that is written in the book of the law" (v. 10), by "coming under the curse [of crucifixion] for our sake" (3:13). He probably means by this language that Jesus' death accomplished what would set Israel perfectly right in God's eyes, which, as we learn from elsewhere in his letters, he did not think the law could do. If the "sending out" that Paul is most familiar with has a redemptive connotation (and the scapegoat certainly died in achieving its redemptive purpose), an explanation would be ready to hand for how Jesus' death operated on human behalf. His life would have been thought of as accepted by God for the sins of the people as an accursèd one (Deut. 21:23) redeeming others under a curse. Noteworthy is the fact that *Barnabas* (7.6–11), Justin (*Dialogue with Trypho* 40.4), and Tertullian (*Against Marcion* 3.7.7) would all employ the scapegoat figure to illustrate Christ's death.

As regards the third redemptive text, the probability has long been entertained that Paul had in mind the story of the binding (*'aqēdāh*) of Isaac in framing Romans 8:32 (see Gen. 22:12, 16–18).[8] Paul writes: "Will not [God], who did not withhold his own Son but gave him up for all of us, lavish every other gift upon us?" The verb Paul uses for "withhold" or "spare," *pheídomai*, is the Septuagint's verb in the Isaac story. Moreover, Romans 4:13 had spoken of God's promise that Abraham would "inherit the world," an echo of the blessing with which the story of his conduct in the Isaac matter ends: "And by your offspring shall all the nations of the earth gain blessing for themselves, because you have obeyed my voice" (Gen. 22:18). Paul may also have in mind the following blessing on the patriarch in Galatians 3:14, referred to above in connection with the scapegoat: "The purpose of this was that the blessing of Abraham should in Christ Jesus be extended to the Gentiles, so that we might receive the promised Spirit through faith."

Against Paul's having the Isaac story in mind, however, is his failure to develop it in either chapter 4 or 8. There is also the fact that Isaac is not described as having been "given up." More than that, he did not die and Genesis gives no indication that he was to die on anyone's behalf. This means that, while one may discover a general typology of innocent victimhood and sacrifice in Genesis 22, it is not such as to claim that Paul drew on it as his model for Jesus' buying freedom for both Jews and non-Jews by his obedient death.

8. Beginning with Origen, as Nils A. Dahl points out in "The Atonement—An Adequate Reward for the Aqedah? (Ro 8:32)," in *Neotestamentica et Semitica: Studies in Honour of Matthew Black*, ed. E. E. Ellis and M. Wilcox (Edinburgh: T. and T. Clark, 1969), 15–20; cf. Geza Vermes, *Scripture and Tradition in Judaism: Haggadic Studies* (Leiden: E. J. Brill, 1973), 218–21.

Daniel Schwartz spells out the difficulties in the arguments made from all the above texts and follows this with a suggestion of his own. It is the story of the expiation David made to the Gibeonites (2 Sam. 21:1–14). He turned over to them seven men, five of them borne by Merab, Saul's daughter. All were to be impaled on the LORD's mountain at Gibeah (vv. 6, 9). But David spared (LXX *epheísato*) Jonathan's son Mephibosheth "because of the oath of the LORD that was between David and Jonathan son of Saul" (v. 7). He gave them up to the Gibeonites in order to bring the Israelite people's three years of famine to an end. This story has all the elements of the crucifixion as expiatory ("for us") except that David spared another's son, not his own. Schwartz concludes that this might well account for Paul's saying "[God] did not withhold *his own* son" (Rom. 8:32).

Even granting that the 2 Samuel story comes formally closest to the crucifixion narrative, including the essential detail of human lives offered to set right a perceived offense, it does not seem to account for the theory of redemption put forward in Romans 8:32. A believer in the power of Jesus' death who knew the Bible in Hebrew or Greek would undoubtedly be familiar with the tale and would even notice similarities. But it passes belief to maintain that, of itself, it could account for the theology of Jesus' expiatory death. Saul's offspring were undoubtedly innocent, but David's turning them over a millennium before Jesus' judicial execution smacks more of settling a score in a blood feud than Jesus' voluntary death in accord with God's predetermined plan. Most telling of all, the spared son Mephibosheth accomplished nothing by his survival. Only the seven who were not spared achieved a benefit, and of them no favored status is reported. This is quite unlike the theory regarding Jesus' death except in distinct parts. With the Isaac story it is much the same, precisely because the son did not die and because no beneficiary of the father's obedience is named.

As to the influence of the stories of the Maccabean martyrs on a primitive conviction that Jesus' death was expiatory, it is easy to say, if not "with certainty," that at the time of his crucifixion "the notion of vicarious suffering and passive response to persecution were firmly embedded in Judaean consciousness."[9] That generalized fact does not seem sufficient to account for the primitive doctrine that Jesus' death was expiatory for the whole human race. He simply was never considered by those who believed in him to be one Jewish martyr among the many who had died at gentile hands.

On balance, it appears that none of the above images of human sacrifice was responsible for the pre-Pauline conviction of Christians that Jesus had died to expiate sins. Only the Jewish conviction of the efficacy of temple sacrifice in its totality, it seems, could do this. An integral part of this expiatory belief was the conviction that his body was the new temple—glorious now but once offered on the altar of the cross.

---

9. Eugene Weiner and Anita Weiner, *The Martyr's Conviction,* Brown Judaic Studies 203 (Atlanta: Scholars Press, 1990), 47.

How the Cross Came to Be Seen as Redemptive

Paul is the earliest witness we have to belief in Jesus' death on Calvary as expiating human sin and sinfulness. His correspondence from the 50s does not illumine us directly on how this death was viewed in its effects in Jewish Palestine in the 30s and 40s. It does serve, however, as an important cross-reference to the Palestinian traditions on the matter that survived to be included in the Gospels. What is astonishing is that Paul "appears totally uninterested in tracking down and identifying the villains responsible for Jesus' crucifixion, nor does he offer any historical reasons why they did it." [10] The possible exception constituted by 1 Thessalonians 2:14–15 has been noted above. Paul interprets Jesus' death apocalyptically rather than historically in statements such as, "None of the rulers of this age understood this [i.e., the secret wisdom of God decreed before the ages]; for if they had, they would not have crucified the Lord of glory" (1 Cor. 2:8). These rulers, from the context, are not Caiaphas or Pilate but the cosmic forces of the present evil age that are destined to pass away (see v. 6). Paul's overriding interest is not in evil men who have done a wicked thing but in a good God who has done a gracious thing. (On this, see Rom. 5:8, where God is the protagonist behind Jesus' death, and Gal. 1:4, where Jesus takes the initiative but in compliance with God's will.) At all points Paul sees the mystery of Calvary in terms of God's action. In 1 Corinthians 1:18–2:5, for example, the cross is viewed as an expression of the divine wisdom. God is self-revealed as a saving God in the preaching of the cross.

Whether Romans 3:25–26 is a pre-Pauline formula of Christian Jews, or Paul's own synagogue composition on the Day of Atonement, or a post-Pauline interpolation in the middle of a Pauline sentence, it is a clear statement of God's being just in overlooking previously committed sins and the designation of Christ Jesus as "the means of expiating sin [*hilastērion*) by his death." [11] Before it is anything else, Christ's death is proof of God's love for us (Rom. 5:6–8). Nowhere in Paul does one find the notion of a suffering or crucified God, certainly not in the statement that Christ was delivered up for us all (Rom. 8:32). The furthest we can go in the direction of God as fellow sufferer is to cite Romans 8:5: "God shows his own love for us in that Christ died for us while we were still sinners." Loving, yes, but suffering as Jesus did in dying for us, not that.

Many texts in Paul's Letters mention Jesus' death in terms of human sinfulness. That he "gave himself for our sins" is stated in Galatians 1:4, with repetitions or echoes in Romans 5:6, 8; 14:15; 1 Thessalonians 5:10; 2 Corinthians 5:14; Galatians 2:20; 3:13. The question has often been raised whether there was such a widespread consciousness of sin among first-century

---

10. Charles B. Cousar, *A Theology of the Cross: The Death of Jesus in the Pauline Letters,* Overtures to Biblical Theology (Minneapolis: Fortress Press, 1990), 25. See also p. 26.

11. For a discussion of this passage, with ample bibliography, see ibid., 40–41.

Jews that Jesus' followers would immediately have identified his death and resurrection with a divine response to the human predicament of alienation from God. Conformity to God's will was, after all, humanity's true goal for Israel, so failure to meet it should have ranked high as a test of Jewish fidelity.

Anti-Christian polemic has identified the first-century Roman occupation as a time of high anxiety uncharacteristic of biblical Israel, leading Paul, a neurotic diaspora Jew preoccupied with his own guilt, to interpret Judaism in ways quite unlike those of the healthy Jewish psyche. But the whole rhythm of temple sacrifice was geared to restore worshipers who had disturbed a right relation with God by conscious or unconscious sin to a balance of forgiveness. With conformity to the rabbinic interpretation of Torah after 70 C.E. as proper worshipful behavior, the awareness of offending against divine precept, viz., sin, was no less. A careful examination of biblical and postbiblical writing should convince anyone that a consciousness of personal and corporate sin was at the heart of Israel's religion and not a peculiar Pauline hobgoblin. The whole of temple sacrifice was geared to liberating the people from the effects of sin.

For that reason it should not surprise us that when an innocent man was viewed as yielding up his life freely he should have been seen as an offering for sin. That Israel repudiated human sacrifice should not have posed a barrier. The whole Jewish culture was familiar with animal victims symbolic of the repentant human spirit. It was a short step from there to seeing in this sinless human victim Jesus an expiatory sin offering.

Paul reminded the former pagans of Thessalonica that they were waiting for the risen Son of God, now in heaven, to come and begin the process of judgment, this "Jesus who delivers us from the approaching wrath" (1 Thess. 1:9b–10). Gentile proselytes to Judaism were probably familiar with a similar promise about relief from the divine judgment if they would associate themselves with God's people. Paul sees faith in the crucified and risen one as the fulfillment of end-time promise. See 4:13–14 and 5:9–10 for other statements of the same hope. In the latter, his death is "for [*hýper*] us," enlarged in 2 Corinthians 5:14–15 to "he has died for all." The former pagan is "the fellow believer for whom Christ died" (1 Cor. 8:11).

Eating the flesh and drinking the blood of enemies is a repulsive figure in the Bible (see Isa. 49:26; Ezek. 39:17–20), but the early believers in Jesus gave it new mythic significance as they made such eating and drinking an image of solidarity with the victim of the cross (1 Cor. 10:16; see the parallels in the Last Supper wording of Mark 14:22–24; Matt. 26:26–27; Luke 22:17–19; 1 Cor. 11:24–26; cf. John 6:54–56). The blood of temple sacrifice was smeared, then flung on the stones of the altar by the priests who had title to the choicest portions of the animals' flesh (see Lev. 9:8–14; 10:12–15). Ordinary worshipers also ate of the victims offered in proof of solidarity in repentant victimhood, for these beasts represented the contrite hearts of a sinful people.

It is thus no wonder that the blood of the innocent Jesus began to be thought of as resealing the ancient covenant between God and Israel (1 Cor. 11:25; Luke 22:20), this time a new covenant in prophetic fulfillment (see Jer. 31:31) of being final in its effect. When the various early communities partook of this ritual meal they experienced Jesus present in their midst, his body crucified and his blood shed but now in glory, as their spiritual food and drink. They were one with the victim who had been provided them by a gracious God to reconcile them to God and to each other.

The Gospel of John makes Caiaphas remark at 11:50: "It is expedient for you that one man should die for the people." This can be taken as either the callous comment of one who favors sacrificing an individual for the greater good or, in a supreme expression of irony, as unconscious affirmation of Jesus' death as a boon to Israel. That the deaths of the martyrs were on people's minds as "having become as it were, a ransom [*antípsychon*] for our nation's sins" (4 Macc. 17:22) has already been shown as a possibility, but the setting of such an idea "seems to belong to a period of major conflict not evident in the formal expression of 'He died—he rose' and so may be put aside."[12] The traditional formula that speaks of Jesus' death and resurrection "for our sins," 1 Corinthians 15:1–7, was one that Paul said he received and handed on. His insistence in his letter to the Galatians (1:18, 23) that he had spent two weeks with Cephas (*Pétros* in Greek) three years after becoming a believer should provide some assurance that the "good news of faith" he set about proclaiming already had this reconciling death and resurrection at its core.

In identifying temple sacrifice as the paradigm for the earliest conviction that Jesus' death had a beneficent effect on Israel, and with it all humanity, I am not disregarding the passages in the biblical and postbiblical books reviewed above that seem to speak of a vicarious sacrifice by human victims. It is only that they appear to have been resorted to after decades of reflection, whereas the parallel between the shedding of the blood of innocent beasts in expiation of sins and that of the innocent Jesus was staring the first disciples in the face. How could recourse to various places in the sacred books account for something much better accounted for by the great, daily act of Israel's living religion? A people of the Book the learned among the postexilic Jews certainly were, but for the great bulk of them circumcision, the Sabbath, the food laws, and temple sacrifice *were* the religious tradition. The last-named went on quite uninterrupted by Jesus' death and resurrection. Acts could describe the daily temple ritual decades later as something his disciples resumed as a matter of course (2:46). But their reflection on the

12. Kenneth Grayston, *Dying We Live: A New Enquiry into the Death of Christ in the New Testament* (New York: Oxford Univ. Press, 1990), 47. This work is basically an exegetical exploration of all the texts touching on Christ's death or dying and its effects as interpreted in faith by early believers in him.

turning over of the just one to a pagan court by the very guardians of temple worship must have made a profound impression.

The high priest and his associates were a corrupt lot, but that distressing fact was long known to the populace. Could the impenetrable mystery of Jesus' upraising from the dead be best explained as God's revelation of the meaning of his death? They had always called him the Teacher. Might he not also be God's Anointed in a transcendent sense—more than that, the focal point of a pure worship of God in a new age? In that age the temple and its ritual would have no place. A people that had no need of expiation for sin was unthinkable, especially for this latest sin. The step to seeing in Jesus the victim of a perfect sacrifice was a short one. A recurrent memorial rather than a once-yearly meal to make the effects of this sacrifice available would have been an early step. We do not know the steps because they are not recorded, but that it so happened we cannot easily doubt. Within two decades this way of looking at Jesus' death and resurrection and the final meal that preceded it was firmly in place.

The way chosen was the way of myth, just as Israel's deliverance from Egypt and the return from exile and the slaughter by the Seleucids were commemorated mythically. The events were remembered history but they were not remembered *as* history. To be sure, fragments of the actual happenings were retained. Even so, these are mythicized as they appear in the Gospels and Acts. The stress is not on the cross and its horrors but on the death. It was coerced, like all such judicial executions, but in the myth it was seen as voluntary. Jesus' thoughts on his being led to death are not known. It was interpreted as a deed of God, perhaps based on what underlay his statements in the Gospels that by God's will it had to happen so. In any case, the death of Jesus survived in the church's weekly ritual commemoration as the painful preliminary to his exaltation. The two together constituted a human although God-authored atonement for human sin. The apocalyptic view of avoidance of the divine wrath is present—a concept a world away from placating an angry god by a savage letting of blood. No such conception as that appears in the earliest records we have.

There stands apart only a death which, from the first, is given a faith interpretation. Concentration on that death as the sum of its historical details comes much later. It is the product of a demonic mythologizing that popular religion is so good at and true religion so ineffective in exorcising.

CHAPTER THREE

Patristic Attribution of Jesus' Death to the Jews

The twenty-seven books that became the New Testament canon, in a process that extended from their composition (by 125 C.E.?) to the late fourth century (the first complete list being that of Athanasius in 367, followed by others up to 400), were written in Greek in various unknown places in the Jewish diaspora. Only a letter or two of Paul can be traced to its probable place of origin. These are hellenized Jewish writings, some of them fairly remote from Palestinian life. All, however, are concerned to maintain links with Israel, the religion of the writers. Indeed, they think that belief in Jesus Christ and the Spirit common to him and the Father is the true way for Jews and non-Jews alike to profess the religion of Israel.

The writings testify to the existence of numerous communities made up of Jews and non-Jews and Samaritans, who are in tension with the larger body of Jews. This is understandable since the latter envisioned nothing like religious equality of Gentiles with Israel until the final days. Even then, "equality" is not the right term. "A subordinate but harmonious coexistence" would be more accurate. That the Jesus people thought the final days had been inaugurated with Jesus' resurrection evidently made little difference to most of the Jews who heard of it. The progress of the rabbinic movement—Judaism properly so called—after 70 began to lessen end-time expectations among Jews somewhat. But these hopes were the very ones the Jesus people kept alive. Meantime, they were being disqualified as true Jews because of their inattention to halakah. This was the "way" or path of fidelity to written Torah as interpreted by oral Torah, the hermeneutic of the Rabbis. Once this standard was set as a way to determine who were true Jews after the gentile attack on Jerusalem and its temple, believers in Jesus outside Jewish Palestine found themselves unable to meet it. They had a different agenda, one that interpreted all law observance in the light of Jesus whom they called the Christ.

The Palestinian Jews who believed in Jesus may have adhered to the law fully in the way prescribed by the Rabbis of Yavneh (Iamnia, the site of the *gerousía* or academy of elders set up by Yoḥanan ben Zakkai after the fall of Jerusalem). We may assume as much. We do know that outside the situation in the heartland—and on this we have only the scanty information provided by the New Testament and, after 155, by Justin Martyr—there was tension between the two groups. The record is entirely from the side of the Jesus people. No rabbinic references are extant from the first or second century C.E. It is entirely unlikely that the twelfth invocation in the Eighteen Benedictions recited daily, a curse upon the *mînîm* (Jewish deviants from belief in the one God), was devised or even used to entrap the Jesus partisans. Only later were they added to the malediction as *ha-Nôṣrîm* ("the Nazarenes").

As pointed out in chapter 1, the writings of the New Testament had an apologetic cast. Subtle and at times overt appeals were made, not to pagans generally or even to the officials of the empire for favored treatment such as Jews received (these would come much later), but to Greek-speaking Jews. It was they whom believers in Jesus hoped to influence. But, as with the Hebrew Scriptures, the Christian writings contain charges against some Jews in power for infidelity to the covenant as the writers perceived it. This was not a simple diaspora-Judaea struggle but one narrowed down to two groups: the learned among the evangelists' contemporaries (who become "the scribes and Pharisees") and the remembered temple priesthood (called "the chief priests") who were coupled with "the elders" when the Sanhedrin was meant (in John, "the men of Judaea").

Jewish disciples of the risen Christ, like believers in him of later ages, could not comprehend how their fellow religionists could fail to be convinced by their arguments. To these arguments they added charges of resistance to the truth by their forebears. It is as wrong to call this polemic in the New Testament "anti-Semitism" as it would be to speak of anti-Semitism in the books of the prophets or the Dead Sea Scrolls. The New Testament thrusts were one side of the internal polemic of Jews (with some ethnic non-Jews on that side) that provided the raw material for anti-Judaism on the part of a gentile church in the next century. When this contending faction became largely gentile, religious or theological anti-Judaism was the correct name for the phenomenon. The Jewish anti-Christianism of the same period has left only faint traces in the Mishnah and Gemara, but one can assume it was equally vigorous. Such was the religious spirit of the times. There was no other way for religions, including the various paganisms, to go.

Some New Testament Data Reviewed

The Gospels present the crucifixion as part of the preordained purpose of God (Matt. 26:53–56; Luke 24:7, 46–47; John 12:23–24). Luke in Acts 3:17 excuses the guilt of the Jewish leaders through ignorance. A catalog of antipathy to the human agents whom the evangelists and, doubtfully, Paul held blameworthy for Jesus' death was given in chapter 1. Chronologically first in order was 1 Thessalonians 2:14b–16. If as seems to be the case the passage were an interpolation, it was added to Paul's first letter early. No Greek manuscript that contains the whole letter (the parchments we begin to have from the 4th century on) is without it. The relative exculpation of Pilate in the Gospels was overshadowed by Christian Jewish revulsion at the behavior of the highest religious authorities. The opening paragraphs of chapter 2 above examined the speeches of Peter at the beginning of the book of Acts. They are in the same accusatory vein. A prayer attributed to Peter and John divides responsibility for Jesus' death among "Herod and Pontius Pilate, together with the Gentiles and the peoples of Israel" (Acts 4:27). A continued reading of Luke's volume two after Peter's speech in chapter 10 provides ample material for the later antagonism of Christians toward Jews.

Paul is the hero of the second half of the book of Acts. The author uses him to further his plotline of a faithful Israel (Jewish believers in Jesus) versus an unfaithful Israel (Jews who resist the gospel). Paul goes to the synagogue first in every city he visits, starting with Salamis in Cyprus (Acts 13:5). He may well have done so but it is impossible to learn this from his correspondence. In any case, his self-confessed antipathy as a Pharisee to believers in Jesus Christ (see Gal. 1:13; Phil. 3:6) is met with an identical antipathy directed at him in Antioch of Pisidia (Acts 13:45, 50) after an initial warm reception (v. 43). Yet Paul is reported to have made the accusation that the Jerusalemites and their leaders had asked Pilate to have Jesus put to death (vv. 27–29). Paul and Barnabas end by being expelled from that territory by its Jews (v. 50). The same thing happens in Iconium, where Gentiles join the attacking Jews (14:5); Lystra (v. 19, outside agitators but Jews nonetheless); Thessalonica (17:5–9); Beroea (here the commotion was started by Thessalonian Jews (v. 14); Corinth (18:12); Greece (meaning the southern part, Achaia, 20:3); and Jerusalem (21:27–30). All of this may indeed have happened, but such is the narrative technique employed by Luke to establish that Paul's "turn to the Gentiles" was forced on him.

Paul himself reports five scourgings of thirty-nine stripes at Jewish hands by the time he writes 2 Corinthians (see 11:24), so a record of antipathy is no figment. The early Christian hearer of Acts could not come away from it with any impression but that Paul's preaching was resisted violently by Jews in various diaspora cities. Some of this might have been mob action by those enraged at his provocative preaching, but any Jews who heard the Corinthian letter read out would know his scourgings were the biblical punishment that guaranteed clemency by setting a limit (see Deut. 25:2–3), hence legally administered by a Jewish court.

Interestingly Hebrews, the treatise that dwells exclusively on Jesus' sufferings (5:8) and his sacrifice (10:12), says nothing about the human agents who brought it about. A brief document that purports to be written by Paul (1 Timothy at 6:13) speaks of Jesus' "testimony before Pontius Pilate" but is silent about his confession at a Jewish hearing. Revelation, too, while it has much to say of the sacrifice (5:6) of "the lamb who was slain" (v. 12), always does so theologically without citing any human beings as responsible.

Clearly, then, there are three strains in New Testament thought: one exclusively theological in which Jesus' condemnation and the circumstances of his death do not figure, another that has retained bits of reminiscence regarding his last days, and a third—represented by the Gospels and Acts—where Jewish responsibility is featured, if not exclusively. The last of these made the deepest impression on the Christian consciousness.

From the *Didache* to Justin

The effect was not immediate, however. Of the second-century witnesses whose writings we have, only Justin in midcentury and Melito of Sardis toward the end seem to take it for granted that "the Jews" should be identified with Jesus' death. For example, the *Didache* or *Teaching of the Twelve Apostles* (70–125 C.E.?) speaks glancingly at 16.5 of the "curse itself [or himself]" as achieving the salvation of those who persevere. This may be a cryptic reference to Jesus, who died the death of one accursèd (Gal. 3:13; cf. Deut. 21:23). The next verse (16.6) names signs of the end, of which the first is "the sign of the one stretched out in heaven," a preliminary to the Lord's coming on the clouds of the heavens. And that is all; it has no details about Jesus' death.

The *First Letter of Clement,* as it is called (ca. 95 C.E.), refers to "the blood of Christ . . . poured out for our salvation [that] brought the grace of repentance to the whole world" (6.4) and cites Isaiah 53:1–10 and Psalm 22:6–8 (MT 7–9) as prophecies of the Holy Spirit concerning Jesus (16.2–16). The author knows the high-priesthood argument of Hebrews (36, 64). Yet he employs none of the historical data found in the Gospels about Jesus' trial or crucifixion. This may be because he does not know them—as Paul perhaps did not know the primitive narratives that were later incorporated into the Gospels.

It is the same with Ignatius of Antioch, who about 110 sent seven letters from shipboard to communities of believers in the province of Asia and one ahead to Rome. He was being transported to the capital to his death. Judaism and Christianity are already quite separate for him; in two places he distinguishes between *Ioudaismòs* and *Christianismòs* (*Magn.* 10.3; cf. *Phld.* 6.1). He anticipates the Monophysite position (i.e., Christ's having but one nature) by speaking of "God's blood" (*Eph.* 1.1), although he knows that Jesus was "sprung from Mary as well as God" (7.2; cf. *Trall.* 9.1). Elsewhere the phrase is "Christ's blood" (*Philadelphians,* prologue; *Smyrn.* 6.1). When Ignatius speaks of the cross, he seldom gives any details (*Eph.* 9.1; 18.1). He describes it as a "passion," even "the passion of my God" (*Rom.*

6.3), and he once dates it as having happened "when Pontius Pilate was governor" (*Magn.* 11; cf. *Trall.* 9.1 and *Smyrn.* 1.2, "crucified for us in the flesh, under Pontius Pilate and Herod the Tetrarch"). In *Smyrnaeans* Ignatius carries on a polemic against those who think that the crucifixion was a "sham" (*tò dokeîn* = "to seem," 2; 4.2). Despite the frequent mention of faith in Christ's death and resurrection, Jewish complicity in that death is totally absent from Ignatius's epistles.

The anonymous communication attributed to Paul's companion Barnabas dates, like *1 Clement*, to the turn of the second century. It interprets the Bible typologically after the manner of Philo the Jew but is clear in its opposition to Judaism (e.g., God abolished temple sacrifice "in order that the new law of our Lord Jesus Christ . . . might have its oblation not made by man," *Barn.* 2.6). It attributes Christ's endurance of sufferings to "the hand of man" (5.5) and accounts for his "suffering on a tree" by saying that it was "to complete the total of sins" like those of "his apostles . . . lawless beyond the measure of all sin" and the sins of "the persecutors of the prophets" (5.9–14). *Pseudo-Barnabas,* as this treatise is known, sees in the sacrifice of Isaac, in the scapegoat, and in the calf of temple slaughter types of Christ (7–8). It also discerns in some biblical passages foreshadowings of the cross (11.8; 12.1). But, aside from the author's supposition that old rites had been totally supplanted by the one new act of sacrifice, the crucifixion is not given an anti-Jewish interpretation.

The cross does not appear at all in the apologia addressed to *Diognetus* (by Quadratus?) sometime around 125—which does, however, categorize all Jewish ritual observance as "superstition." Hermas's Rome-originated morality the *Shepherd* is made up of visions, commandments, and parables and simply does not mention the crucifixion. The *Epistle of Polycarp* (d. 155/156) *to the Philippians* refers to the cross twice without elaboration (7.1; 12.3). The account of Polycarp's martyrdom speaks only of his joining his pain to Christ's, who "suffered for the salvation of the whole world of those who are saved" (*Mart. Pol.* 17.2).

Justin's first *Apology* (ca. 155) defends the Christian faith for its reasonableness, holding that the pagans accept far more that is incredible in their myths than the Christians do in their mysteries. He writes that Jesus Christ was born for the purpose of teaching us the things that would lead to our living again in incorruption, and immediately goes on to say: "and was crucified under Pontius Pilate who was procurator of Judaea in the time of Tiberius Caesar" (13; cf. 46; 2 *Apology* 6). The Jews had their own ruler and king, Justin observes, up to the time when Jesus Christ came to fulfill the unrecognized prophecies in a book of Moses like the one to Judah, one of Jacob's twelve sons in Genesis 49:10–11 (32). He identifies Herod Antipas as the Jews' king and conspirator with Pilate against Christ (40). Jesus "was crucified in Judaea," Justin writes, "immediately after which the land of the Jews fell to you [Romans] as a spoil of war" (32; cf. 53). He points to no cause and effect here, as later writers will do.

Using the prophecies of Isaiah 11:1 and 51:15, Numbers 24:17 (32) and Isaiah 7:14, he traces Jesus' ancestry from Judah through David ("the root of Jesse") to the virgin who bore him (33). Then, coming to the final days of Jesus Christ, Justin writes: He "stretched out his hands when he was crucified by the Jews, who contradicted him and denied that he was the Christ" (35). Justin's sources for the passion narrative are obscure here. The quotation from Zechariah 9:9 in Matthew 21:5 is attributed to Zephaniah. Jesus' mocking by the soldiers is made out to be a quotation from a prophet but it occurs in a form that is unattested. Justin refers to the *Acts of Pilate,* a document he may assume is available to Antoninus Pius, the emperor to whom the *Apology* is addressed (35). The apocryphal Christian document of that name containing much of this material *may* derive from Justin's mention, but his citation of it in chap. 48, with a quotation from Isaiah 57:1, 2, suggests that such an actual writing may have been his source (48).[1] In any case, Justin has the following charge embedded in an otherwise perceptive paragraph about the various genres of biblical writing: "Not understanding [them], the Jews who are in possession of the books of the prophets did not recognize Christ even when he came, and they hate us who declare that he has come and show that he was crucified by them as had been predicted" (36; cf. 49, where this charge is repeated).

Justin was a pagan native of Shechem in Samaria, modern Nablus (Flavia Neapolis). He couples Samaritans with Jews as possessing the books of prophecy, the Torah, as no Jew would do (53). We do not know the circumstances of his becoming a Christian aside from his expressed admiration for the Christian martyrs.[2] He was put to death for his faith at Rome,[3] but we do not know the circumstances of his journeyings, which ended in what he is quoted as saying (in the letter known as *The Martyrdom of Polycarp*) was his second stay there. Thus we cannot determine where he experienced the mutual hatred between Christians and Jews ("slanders uttered against those who confess Christ," *1 Apology* 49). He gave expression to it from the Christian side in describing the indignities visited on Jesus in his passion, chiefly from passages in Isaiah and the Psalms; but he was also familiar with the mockery of passersby, chief priests, and scribes reported in Mark 15:29–32. Justin concludes this account with: "And that all these things happened to Christ at the hands of the Jews, you can ascertain" (38).

When Justin comes to write his *Dialogue with Trypho*—well after his *1 Apology* (see chap. 80) but as if the exchange occurred shortly after the Bar

---

1. See "Acts of Pilate" in Frederic Huidekoper, *Indirect Testimony of History to the Genuineness of the Gospels* (New York: David G. Francis, 1887), 105–42; also, "The Report of Pilate [to Tiberius]," 142–49.

2. *2 Apology* 12; cf. *1 Apology* 1.1. See G. Rauschen, *S. Justini apologiae duae* (Bonn, 1904) (ET, Thomas B. Falls, New York: Fathers of the Church, 1948; 12, 33).

3. Early in the reign of Marcus Aurelius, according to Eusebius's *Church History* 4.16.7 (SC 31, 44, 55, 73; G. Bardy et al., Paris, 1952–87; 31.192). See "The Martyrdom of the Holy Martyrs, Justin, Chariton [and Others]," trans. M. Dods in A. Roberts and J. Donaldson, eds., ANF 1 (New York, 1908), 305–6.

Kokhba revolt in 135 (chap. 1)—he goes on the assumption that Jews are at fault in not reading biblical "prophecies" as referring to Jesus, as he and other Christians do. For him, "a later covenant voids an older one" (11). This is the earliest expression we have, after Hebrews 8:7, 13, of belief in the supersession or replacement of Judaism by Christianity. (But see Eph. 2:15, which states "[Christ] abolished the law," a verb Paul would not have used. "Law" here seems to mean the ritual precepts no longer required for Gentiles.) Justin thinks that ritual observance in its entirety, including circumcision, keeping the Sabbath, and fasting, has yielded to abstention from perjury, theft, adultery (12), anger, avarice, jealousy, and hatred (14). The whole body of ritual precepts was imposed on the Jews, in fact, because of their sins and hardness of heart (18). Circumcision was given to Israel with God's foreknowledge that it would serve as a sign to the Romans to keep Jews from entering Jerusalem, the capital of their "desolate land with its cities ruined by fire" (16; cf. 19). This judgment on Jews over Hadrian's sack of Jerusalem is unspeakably harsh. Justin thinks it justified because he has evidently heard that "you dishonor and curse in your synagogues all who believe in Christ [although] now you cannot use violence against us Christians because of those who are in power [the later years of the peaceful reign of Antoninus Pius?], but as often as you could, you did employ force against us" (16; cf. 96).

Whatever harassments Justin has in mind, whether reality or rumor, he is able to write that "the other nations have not treated Christ and us, his followers, as unjustly as have you Jews. . . . After you had crucified the only sinless and just man . . . you not only failed to feel remorse for your evil deed but you even dispatched certain picked men from Jerusalem to every land to report the godless heresy of the Christians" (17). This sounds like a reality of some kind within the Jewish community in Rome where Justin resides, which makes Christian proclaiming of the gospel as a legitimate understanding of the Jewish Scriptures hard or impossible. Whatever form Jewish opposition to the Christian movement took in the second century, this antipathy survived in the talmudic writings as a sprinkling of tales about a magician named Yeshu (the son of Pantere or Pandera in several second-century *baraitas*) who was hanged on the eve of Passover.[4] Most Christians could not read mishnaic Hebrew or Aramaic and so these slanders seldom reached their ears, although the pagan Celsus knew of them in the third century.

The Christian opposition to Judaism, according to Justin, took the form of an accusation of responsibility for Jesus' crucifixion. The chief texts are:

4. See *b. Sanh.* 43a; for a discussion of the few possible talmudic references to Jesus of Nazareth, see John P. Meier, *A Marginal Jew: Rethinking the Historical Jesus,* vol. 1 (New York: Doubleday, 1991), 106–7, 246–47, who also discusses the story of Jesus' illegitimacy reported by Origen in Celsus's *True Discourse* (ca. 178) and the slanderous 9th-century(?) *Sepher Toledoth Yeshu.*

"He was pierced by you" (32); "was crucified and died after enduring suffering inflicted on him by your own people" (67); "the Jews planned to crucify Christ himself and to slay him" (72). When Pilate is mentioned he is simply used to date Jesus' death (76) or is someone before whom Jesus appeared (102). The undiluted accusations made by Justin against the Jews were picked up and repeated in the vernacular, Greek (then Latin, Syriac, and Coptic), everywhere there were Christians. Did he get his information from the Gospels and Acts? In a sense it does not matter, but the answer, from his failure to cite any New Testament details touching on Jesus' trial or crucifixion—only the Mosaic books, Isaiah, and the Psalms—seems to be that he possessed the catechetical materials of the sort that went into the composition of the Gospels rather than the Gospels themselves. Whatever the case, the tragic effects for Jews were the same.

Justin's invariable coupling of the harassment of Christians by Jews with mention of Jewish responsibility for Jesus' death makes one wonder how much the former was a factor in interpreting the community reminiscences of the crucifixion that were incorporated in the Gospel accounts. In examining antipathies that go back five generations, as in this case, it is almost impossible to isolate the various factors. The repeated fueling of fires is a constant in such situations. It would seem that the mid-second-century accusations derive from more than recourse to the written New Testament tradition. A memory of subsequent experiences on both sides seems very much part of the story.

Justin's *irenikon* to Trypho is undoubtedly shot from a catapult throughout most of his treatise. He does seem, however, to be making a genuine appeal when he asks Trypho's "brothers" not to "speak harshly against the Crucified . . . insult the Son of God . . . [or] scorn the King of Israel (as the chiefs of your synagogues instruct you to do after prayers)" (41). One can understand, of course, Jewish resistance to such exalted claims made for Jesus.

The origins of the treatise, dedicated as it is to a certain Marcus Pompeius, are puzzling. It seems to be a handbook designed to instruct the learned, whom Justin was arming in Rome against Jewish arguments that stressed the illegitimacy of the Christian movement. The likelihood that it reports actual, sustained Christian-Jewish debate is small. Still, it is impossible to sort out what might have been its original, confrontational core aside from saying that it took its rise from exchanges with a peaceful rabbi.

Irenaeus and Melito

If it is hard to know whether Justin had access to the actual Gospels or only their sources, there is no question that Irenaeus, writing in Lugdunum (Lyon) two decades later, possessed the bulk of the New Testament. This

Greek-speaking Syrian went as a missionary bishop to Gaul after a stay in
Rome, where he may have been Justin's pupil. While residing among the
Celts with their "barbarous language" he did some careful research into the
teachings of the Gnostics, whether recognizably Christian or other. This
he reported in five books directed against them.[5] His chief concern was to
unmask their myths as absurdities and to affirm the corporeal reality of Jesus' birth, career, death, and resurrection against the gnostic denial that anything material can be of God. He does not reach the account of Jesus' career
until book 3, chaps. 9–12. In laying out the preaching of the apostles like
Peter and John reported in early Acts, Irenaeus speaks of their heavy task in
presenting him "whom the Jews had seen as a man, and had fastened to the
cross, . . . as Christ the Son of God, their eternal King. . . . They . . . told
them to their face that they were the slayers of the Lord. . . . They . . . fastened to the cross the Savior superior to them (to whom it behooved them
to ascend)."[6] The setting of this highly convoluted passage is a polemic in
favor of the God who is Father above any Demiurge. For our purposes, the
taking for granted of Jewish responsibility for Jesus' death is the matter of
interest. Most of Irenaeus's quotations in the next section, 7, are from Acts
10, for example: "the Jews [Judaeans?] . . . put him to death by hanging him
on a tree" (v. 39). He returns to the theme in his own words: "To the Jews
[the apostles proclaimed] that the Jesus who was crucified by them was the
Son of God, the judge of the living and the dead" (13). His suffering "under
Pontius Pilate" likewise appears, a phrase we come to expect in these early
writings (8). It is not easy to find the above passages, which by now are
evidently *tópoi* or commonplaces, in the midst of Irenaeus's main argument
against the Gnostics. This argument is that Jesus really suffered for us, not
some Christ incapable of suffering who descended on him (3.18.3; cf. 4.33.2).

One does not find as much animus toward the Jews in this lengthy treatise
as in Justin. When it does surface, it is taken for granted as if it derives from
catechetical formulas already arrived at. Thus, in a discussion of how God's
judgment was visited on ancient Egypt so that the Hebrews could escape
and live, Irenaeus writes: "Unless the Jews had become the slayers of the
Lord (which did, indeed, take eternal life away from them), and, by killing
the apostles and persecuting the church, had fallen into an abyss of wrath,
we could not have been saved" (4.28.3). This is redolent of Paul's argument
about Israel's stumbling as the opportunity for the Gentiles' salvation (see
Rom. 11:11), but with a judgmental twist that is absent from Paul. The passage goes on: "For as they were saved by the blindness of the Egyptians, so
are we, too, by the blindness of the Jews if, indeed, the death of the Lord is

5. Commonly referred to as *Against Heresies* (*Adversus Haereses*) but entitled by Irenaeus
The Refutation and the Overthrow of the Knowledge Falsely So Called, PG 7 and 7 bis (ET,
ANF 1.315–567). An incomplete critical edition of the Latin translation augmented by Greek
and Armenian fragments is Adelin Rousseau and Louis Doutreleau, SC 264, 293, 294 (Paris,
1979–). Critical apparatus is given in vol. 100, 152, 153, 210, 211, 263. Irenaeus's books 3
and 4 meet the Marcionite challenge head on.

6. *Adversus Haereses* 3.12.6.

the condemnation of those who fastened him to the cross and did not believe his coming, but the salvation of those who believe in him." He responds to his own uncertainty by a generalized reflection on believers and unbelievers in Christ without any reference to Jews or non-Jews.

It is not possible, given the few surviving written testimonies between 50 and 175 C.E., to trace the progress of the idea of Jewish responsibility for the death of Jesus, and the persecution of believers in him, as the one thing. There does not seem to be a straight line from the Gospels and Acts to the second-century Apologists, as if the latter simply copied out what they read there and decided to use Pilate as a dating device only rather than the one who condemned Jesus to death. We do not know the impact of the oral tradition or the lost written tradition except in its results, nor can we know the exacerbation caused by a century and a quarter of unrecorded events. What we can confidently say is that the chief priests and elders of Judaea (hoì Ioudaîoi) whom John's Gospel charged with Jesus' death have become, in a gentile church, Jews generally. Further, it begins to be said that Jews generally bear the guilt of the crime because their spiritual descendants of the next century have not repudiated it by coming to faith in Christ. By their continued harassments, they have only confirmed it.

An examination of the earliest extant liturgies[7] shows that this theme occurs in them only in the poetic Easter homily of Melito of Sardis (d. ca. 190). This homily was not the fixed formula of any church but probably exerted its influence on Irenaeus and Tertullian. Early baptismal creeds like that which Hippolytus of Rome gives in his *Apostolic Tradition* (ca. 215), later developed into the Apostles' Creed (first so called at a synod of Milano in 390 and found initially in its present wording in the 7th–8th century Bobbio Missal), confine themselves to the word "suffered" or the phrase "suffered under Pontius Pilate, was crucified, died, and was buried."[8] Melito's sharp departure from the restraint of the creeds and even the Gospels consisted in a succession of fiery images from the Bible establishing that the Jewish *Pesaḥ* (Passover) had been succeeded by the Christian *Pascha*. The author is remembered as a "Quartodeciman," a Christian observant of Easter on the 14th Nisan on whatever day of the week it fell. This Eastern party, which lost out at the turn of the third century, intended to keep Christ's death and resurrection together as the one paschal mystery.

Melito writes of "the new and the old, the eternal and temporal, the incorruptible and corruptible, the immortal and the mortal," in a dizzying array of replacement images. And in one passage:

7. The early third-century church order treatise *Catholic Teaching of the Twelve Apostles and Holy Disciples of Our Savior (Didascalia)* is the work in Greek of a bishop of northern Syria. It contains a doxology after chap. 26 praising "Jesus Christ of Nazareth . . . who was crucified in the days of Pontius Pilate, and slept [died]" (R. H. Connolly, *Didascalia Apostolorum* [Oxford: Clarendon Press, 1929], 258–59).

8. See J. N. D. Kelly, *Early Christian Creeds* (3d ed.; New York: D. McKay Co., 1972), 149–50, where it is identified as a means of rooting the event of Jesus' death in history. The texts are given in Greek and Latin in DS, §§ 10–64.

He was put to death. . . . Where was he put to death? In the midst of Jerusalem. Why?

> Because he had cured their lame,
> because he had cleansed their lepers,
> because he had restored sight to the blind,
> because he had raised their dead.

That is why he suffered. Therefore it is written in the law and the prophets:

> They returned me evil for good,
> and my life has become barren [see Ps. 35:12]. . . .

O Israel, why have you committed this unheard-of crime? You have dishonored him who honored you. . . . you have put to death him who gave you life! Why did you do this, O Israel? Was it not for you that it is written: "You shall not shed innocent blood, lest you die a wretched death"? . . .

> "He had to suffer"
>   but not at your hands. . . .
> He had to be hanged (on the cross)
>   but not by you! . . .

> You were not moved to reverence for him
> by the withered hand of the paralytic. . . .
> You were not moved to fear . . .
> by the dead man he called back from the tomb. . . .

No, you took no account of these, but in order to immolate the Lord as evening came on, you prepared for him

> sharp nails
> and false witnesses
> and ropes and whips
> and vinegar and gall
> and sword and pain
> as for a bandit who had shed blood.[9]

By Melito's time the tradition is in full cry that will understand all the Hebrew Bible's reproaches to Israel—and they are many—to be directed to

9. *Perì Páscha*, found without title on a Chester Beatty Papyrus shared between Dublin and Ann Arbor and published by Campbell Bonner (Studies and Documents; London: Christophers; Philadelphia: University of Pennsylvania Press, 1940). See the critical edition of S. G. Hall (Oxford Early English Texts, 1979) and the rhythmic (but partial) translation of Matthew J. O'Connell in Lucien Deiss, *Springtime of the Liturgy* (Collegeville, Minn.: Liturgical Press, 1979), 106–7, cited here. Eric Werner writes of "Melito of Sardes, the First Poet of Deicide," *Hebrew Union College Annual* 37 (1966): 191–210. In chap. 21, in a chronology of Jesus' last six days

Jesus' tormentors, as the chief priests and temple guard were thought to have been. If the Christian-Jewish tension had not continued uninterrupted, the sins laid to Israel's charge by the prophets might not have been put to this use. We do not have in this rhetoric of reproach anything remotely historical. It is part mythical, part angrily existential.

Tertullian, Clement, Origen

Tertullian's anti-Judaism has been explored in detail by David Efroymson of LaSalle University. It often takes the form of describing Jews, upon simple reference to them, as "that stiff-necked people, devoid of faith in God."[10] As regards the crucifixion, the North African rhetorician (ca. 200) does not content himself with the charge we have already encountered that the Jews put Jesus to death but says that they "not only rejected him as a stranger [*extraneum verum*] but even put him to death as an opponent."[11] This is part of an obscure argument to the effect that the one to come was expected by Jews to be unknown to them (*ignotus et interemptus ab illis*). Tertullian makes it part of prophecy that they would destroy him: "It at once follows that he who was unrecognized by them, he whom they put to death, is the one who who they were marked down beforehand as going to treat in this fashion."[12] He then quotes at length Isaiah 29:14b joined to 6:9b–10 to prove that Christ went unrecognized because God had promised to render this people blind and deaf. He adds a hint of 1 Corinthians 2:8, where Paul says: "If the rulers of this age knew [the plan of God's wisdom] they would not have crucified the Lord of glory."

Tertullian is far from obscure, however, when he finds Jeremiah's proverbial saying about fathers eating sour grapes and children having their teeth set on edge to apply prophetically to the outcry inserted by Matthew into the Markan narrative: "His blood be upon us and on our children."[13] Tertullian wishes to refute Marcion's statement that "the passion of the cross was never

---

not supported by the Gospels, Pilate is exculpated, and it is further written: "Herod commanded that he should be crucified" (p. 191).

10. *Tertullian Adversus Marcionem*, ed. and trans. by Ernest Evans, 2 vols. (Oxford, 1972), 2.18.1; cf. 15.1. Cf. David P. Efroymson, "Tertullian's Anti-Judaism and Its Role in His Theology" (Ph.D. diss., Temple University, 1976).

11. Tertullian *Adversus Marcionem* 3.6.2.

12. Ibid., 6.4.

13. Matt. 27:25. Referring to Jer. 31:29 (again in Ezek. 18:2), Tertullian acknowledges at length that the prophets use this proverb to make the *opposite* point, namely, that inherited guilt is henceforth to yield to personal responsibility, but he makes the legal cavil, "yet without prejudice to that decree which was afterwards to be made." Matthew is recording the fathers' willingness to "call down this judgment upon themselves, *His blood be on our heads and on our children's* [Matt. 27:25]," Tertullian maintains, "if you were to accept the Gospel in its true form [i.e., as a record of truth]" (2.15.2–3). The same text is cited, along with John 19:12 ("If you release him you are no friend of Caesar") in Tertullian's *Adversus Iudaeos* 8.18, CChr, Series Latina 2, *Tertulliani Opera,* Part II, ed. A. Gerlo (Turnhout: Brepols, 1954), 1364.

prophesied concerning the Christ of the Creator" and that it was "quite incredible that the Creator should have exposed his Son to that form of death on which he himself had laid a curse."[14] This he does by identifying Isaac's delivering up by his father in a sacrifice as a case of prophecy "by types and figures" (*figurari*) and Joseph's persecution by his brothers the same.[15] But he cannot refrain from making Simeon and Levi, the violent slayers of Genesis 49:5–7, stand for the scribes and Pharisees who persecuted Christ, "whom after the murder of the prophets they crucified, and with nails wrought savagely against his sinews."[16] Refuting Marcion's claim that it was "the Christ of the other god who was brought to the cross," Tertullian states that the crucifixion was real and that it was the work of the Jews.[17] He makes the same assumption in commenting on 1 Thessalonians 2:14–16, namely, that they "both killed the Lord and their own prophets."[18]

As Efroymson points out, the anti-Marcion debate in which Justin and Irenaeus had also been engaged required Tertullian to prove that the Mosaic law—which Marcion thought base and inferior—was the work of the true God. But if the church had abandoned the law and replaced it by a new law and cult (a point on which Tertullian and Marcion were agreed), what could account for this? As Efroymson explains it, "God's 'old' law and/or cult cannot be due to any inferiority on God's part, [it] must be accounted for by the 'inferiority' of the people with whom God was working at the time. Thus, the God of the Hebrew Bible was 'salvaged' for Christians by means of the anti-Judaic myth."[19]

The importance of this insight cannot be stressed too strongly. The denigration of the Jews and Judaism in Tertullian, pervasive and not found only in *Adversus Marcionem* (*Against Marcion*), seems to be a by-product. It derives from his proof that the God of the Hebrew Scriptures could not have been guilty of all that Marcion charged him with. Since it came from somewhere, the Jews of the Bible must have been the offending parties, the source. Contributing to this mythicizing of the Jews were the four Gospels and Luke's volume two, with their outcries by "the crowd" (Mark 15:8–14; Matt. 27:25) or *toîs Ioudaíois* (John 19:14; the same as "the chief priests and the guards" of v. 6?) that Jesus should be crucified, in response to which Pilate handed him over (Mark 15:15; Luke 23:25; John 19:16, "to them"). Every detail of Christ's passion was foretold in Scripture but God was responsible for none of these. The Jews were.[20]

---

14. *Adversus Marcionem* 3.18.1.
15. Ibid., 2–3; cf. *Adversus Iudaeos* 10.6.
16. *Adversus Iudaeos* 3.18.5.
17. Ibid., 3.23.5–6, 1.
18. Ibid., 5.15.1–2.
19. David P. Efroymson, "The Patristic Connection," in *Antisemitism and the Foundations of Christianity*, ed. Alan Davies (New York: Paulist Press, 1979), 101.
20. See *An Answer to the Jews* 13, for which the translator S. Thelwall provides the heading "Argument from the Destruction of Jerusalem and Desolation of Judea," in ANF 3.168. Most

The first hundred years of Christian writing after the New Testament was completed not only make no critical evaluation of the two testaments of Scripture but also make no distinctions among the varied responses of the Hebrews/Israelites of the Bible to their covenant calling. All the resisters to Moses and the writing prophets and Jesus' learned opponents in the Gospels are lumped together as "the Jews" as if there were no other Jews. The emerging Christians, both outwardly beleaguered and inwardly divided, evidently needed an identifiable opponent to unite them, especially against Marcion's charge that the god of the Bible was an evil god. Their contemporaries the Jews, whom not many of them can have known in an intimate way, served as the occasion. The need for an enemy was the cause.

Clement of Alexandria (d. before 215) was born into the culture of a city and country largely devoid of Jews and Jewish influence since the disastrous revolt against Rome in 115–117. He seems to have known the pagan Alexander Polyhistor's *On the Jews* and the writings of Josephus and Philo. Clement says that he heard the vigorous and animated discourse of a Hebrew in Palestine.[21] On a few occasions he quotes haggadic material, for example, the suggestion attributed to the *Mystai* that Moses slew the Egyptian with a word.[22] Clement's writings provide the earliest sure evidence, fragmentary as it is, of relations between Christians and Jews in Alexandria. In several places he supports his argument with "a Jew told me so."[23] Despite this, he does not seem to have had extensive contacts with Jews, as the paucity of his information about Jewish life in Alexandria indicates. He shares the common assumption of his time (and ever since) that Paul is addressing Jews and Gentiles equally in Galatians—not just Gentiles who were keeping some of the Mosaic precepts—when he says, "We are no longer under a disciplinarian" (*paidagōgós*, 3:25). Clement's comment on the law is that it was "accompanied by fear," whereas now we are "under the Word, the Educator of our free wills."[24] Clement adds to Paul's phrase about being a child and speaking and thinking like a child (1 Cor. 13:11), "that is, of the Law." He continues: "Yet there is a childhood in Christ, which is perfection, in contrast to that of the Law."[25] In a passage in which he disapproves of Christians' garlanding themselves with wreaths of flowers, he reminds them of Jesus' crown of thorns, saying that "no one can approach the Word without

---

authors think that chaps. 9–14, which conclude the treatise, were added by another hand, taken from *Adversus Marcionem* 3.

21. *Stromateis* ("Patchwork," sometimes called *Miscellanies*), 1.1 (*PG* 1.700; also SC 30, 38, 278 [Paris, 1951–81]; ET, ANF 2.301).

22. *Exodus Rabbah* and Rashi on Exod. 2:14.

23. See *Fragmenta* vii (*GCS* 3.225), cited by Robert Wilken, *Judaism and the Early Christian Mind: A Study of Cyril of Alexandria's Exegesis and Theology* (New Haven: Yale Univ. Press, 1971), 41, n. 12.

24. *Paidagōgós* ("Christ the Educator") 1.6.31 (*PL* 8.288; ET, Simon P. Wood, Fathers of the Church 23 [Washington, D.C.: Catholic University of America Press, 1954], 30.

25. Wood, 1.6.34 (ET, 34).

shedding blood."[26] Proceeding to the passion of Christ as a whole by this reminder, he writes:

> [Those who do not believe in the Lord crowned Jesus and raised him aloft] giving clear proof of their lack of understanding. . . . They were people gone astray, who did not know their Lord; they were uncircumcised in mind; not recognizing God, they rejected their Lord and so lost the promise implied in their name Israel [see Gen. 32:29; Clement seems to think it meant "man of God"], for they persecuted God and tried to bring disgrace to the Word. Still, Him whom they crucified as an evil-doer they crowned as a king.[27]

Clement's rambling six books of *Miscellanies* have little reference to Judaism besides the assumption that Christianity has succeeded it, and none to the crucifixion of Jesus. The climax comes in book 6, where Clement describes the Christian intellectual as the true gnostic ("knower"). Anti-Judaism, however, forms no part of his argument against false *gnōsis,* as with Justin and Irenaeus.

Clement tells us little about the relations of Christians with Jews in early third-century Alexandria, and the same is true of Origen (d. 253/254). It was the city where this "first speculative theologian" was born and raised, but we do not know if the knowledge of halakha evidenced in his *On First Principles* was acquired there or on his already extensive travels. We know that Origen had many more contacts with Jews after his move to Caesarea on the seacoast of Palestine. The Samaritans had a colony there in his day. It was the capital of Roman Palestine and had a vigorous pagan culture (to which Origen does not advert); and, while the Palestinian Talmud of a later date helps us to reconstruct life there a century and a half before (i.e., in 250) archaeology has revealed little of Jewish life in Caesarea in the third century. There were certainly Jews, Greek-speaking by and large, who may be presumed to have employed pagan art forms and motifs on their tombs and synagogues, like the Jews elsewhere in the country. Caesarea was resented because the memory of the cruelties of the Bar Kokhba revolt (135 C.E.) was still fresh in the Jewish mind and the opportunities for apostasy and religious syncretism were many.[28]

Origen mentions consulting a Jewish teacher, "the Patriarch Ioullos," whose name Jerome renders as Huillus (Ioudas? Hillel?),[29] but he is not the same as "my Hebrew teacher" to whom Origen frequently refers. This may

---

26. Ibid., 2.8.73 (ET, 156). Cf. 3.12.85 (ET, 263–64): "We have the Cross of our Lord as our boundaryline, and by it we are fenced around and shut off from our former sins. Let us be born again, then, and be nailed to the Cross in truth; let us return to our senses and be sanctified."

27. Ibid., 2.8.73 (ET, 156–57).

28. See N. R. M. de Lange, *Origen and the Jews: Studies in Jewish-Christian Relations in Third-Century Palestine* (Cambridge: Cambridge University Press, 1976), 7–12.

29. Origen, prologue to *Commentary on the Psalms* (PG 12.1056).

be a Christian of Jewish origin or a Jew who has no scruple in helping a Christian understand the Scriptures better. For it is abundantly clear that Origen wants to master Jewish hermeneutical techniques for his own Christian purpose. He repeatedly charges Jews with a literal or "carnal" understanding of the Bible while employing Philo's pattern of metaphoric parallel (or typology, commonly called the "allegorical method") without ever adverting to the paradox. Yet he very much wishes to come abreast of the way the Rabbis play word games and utilize common elements and contrasts in biblical narratives. He hopes to best Jewish teachers in argument, there is no doubt.[30] At the same time, when his learned pagan opponent Celsus points out absurdities in either testament of Scripture, Origen willingly employs refutations derived from Jewish sources.

Important to remember in this is the third-century Palestinian situation. Neither Jews, Christians, nor Samaritans were in the majority. Pagans were. The first three had the Greek language and culture in common, even to their Scriptures (the Samaritans, the Mosaic books only). Jews and Christians were trying to win converts from among the pagans and each other. The two shared a precritical outlook on the probative value of texts but this is not to say they were incapable of sharp insights into textual questions or the meaning of Scripture. From the few extant writings of Origen's voluminous output one can deduce that Jewish converts to Christianity in his milieu were numerous, that Judaism exerted a profound attraction upon Christians, and that "Ebionites" or Jewish believers in Jesus as the Messiah but not the Son of God, and the Christian sect of Elkesaites, were a fact of everyone's experience.[31]

It was to give strength to wavering believers and win new adherents that Origen wrote. He put in the service of this project the best biblical scholarship yet done by a Christian (for there was no tradition of formal exegesis by any but Jews). From his treatise *Against Celsus* one can almost reconstruct the pagan's entire argument against the Christians. One cannot do the same with any books of Jewish authorship in Greek directed against the Christians. The Jews did not keep their writings in Greek of any genre. The Septuagint, the Bible translations of Aquila, Theodotion, and Symmachus, and the works of Philo and Josephus were preserved by Christians only, and for apologetic purposes.

Getting to our main concern: the sign of the cross had been a Jewish symbol well before Jesus' crucifixion, appearing in Jewish underground cemeteries in Rome, on Jewish sarcophagi in Jerusalem from the first century

---

30. See *Epistle to Africanus* 5 (PG 11.60–61); cf. *Against Celsus* 1.45, 49, 55; 6.29 (PG 12.744, 752–53, 761–63, 13.37; ET, Henry Chadwick, *Origen: Contra Celsum* [Cambridge: Cambridge University Press, 1965]). For his familiarity with the Judaism of his time, see the collected texts from his commentaries in Gustave Bardy, "Les traditions juives dans l'oeuvre d'Origène," *Revue biblique* 24 (1925): 217–52.

31. De Lange, *Origen*, 7–12, 15–37, 133–35.

B.C.E. to the third century C.E., and in the third century synagogue at Dura-Europos.[32] Origen says that a Jewish Christian told him that the "sign" of Ezekiel 9:4 was the cruciform Old Hebrew letter *tau*.[33] Like Christian writers before him he compares Isaac to Christ carrying the wood for his own immolation; in this he comes close to a passage in *Genesis Rabbah*.[34] Which influenced which? Or was there no interrelation? The same may be asked of Moses' upraised arms (Exod. 17:11) as a symbol of the cross, already used by Pseudo-Barnabas, Justin, and Irenaeus. Origen borrows from Rabbi Eliezer and Rabbi Akiba the symbolism of Moses' upraised arms to represent human actions and observance of the law but turns it to mean two peoples: the Christians who elevate what Moses wrote by understanding it on a high level and the people who do not see anything deep or subtle in Moses, thus failing to elevate his arms or lift them off the ground.[35] The Jews are, once again, capable of only a literal reading of the text while Christians perceive the mysteries that are but hinted at in the Bible. Thus,

> Both the hardened in heart and the ignorant persons [*idiôtai*] belonging to the circumcision have not believed in our Savior, thinking that they are following the language of the prophecies respecting him. . . . Seeing none of these things [from Zech. 9:10; Isa. 7:15; 11:6, 7] visibly accomplished during the advent of him who is believed by us to be the Christ, they did not accept our Lord Jesus, but they crucified him improperly [*parà tò déon*] because he affirmed that he was the Christ.[36]

Understanding the Scriptures spiritually, that is, in allegorical and typological forms, Origen thinks would have kept them from this unbelief and its consequences: "For although salvation and justification came to the Gentiles through his cross, to the Jews came condemnation and ruin."[37]

Origen represents Celsus as having discovered a Jew who told Jewish converts to Christianity, "Quite recently, when we punished this fellow who deluded you, you abandoned the law of our fathers," and, "as an offender he was punished by the Jews."[38] Origen answers that it was no crime for Jesus to abstain from a literal Sabbath and observances over clean and unclean meats, "rather to turn the mind to the good and true and spiritual law, worthy of God."[39] In this lengthy treatise the charge surfaces that the Jews have suffered and will suffer more than others in the judgment that hangs over the world "on account of their disbelief in Jesus and all their other

32. See Erich Dinkler, *Signum Crucis* (Tübingen, 1967), 1–54.
33. *Selecta on Ezekiel* (PG 13.801A), cited by de Lange, *Origen* 116.
34. *Homily on Genesis* 8.6 (PG 12.206; GCS 6.81.6). See *Genesis Rabbah* 66.3.
35. *Homily on Exodus* 11.4 (PG 12.578); *On John* 28.5.
36. *On First Principles* 4.2.1 (H. Crouzel and M. Simonetti, SC 268 [Paris, 1980], 293–94, 296; ET, G. W. Butterworth, London, 1936; 269, 270).
37. *Homily on Leviticus* 3.1 (PG 12.423).
38. *Against Celsus* 2.4, 5.
39. Ibid., 7.

insults to him. . . . What nation but the Jews alone has been banished from its own capital city and the native place of its ancestral worship?"[40] Origen lays the severity of the punishment of this "most wicked nation" to their sins committed against "our Jesus." Celsus must know the Gospels and some Roman history because he says that no calamity ever overtook the one who condemned Jesus. Origen's reply to this is that "it was not so much Pilate who condemned him, since he knew that 'out of envy the Jews had delivered him up,' as the Jewish people. This nation has been condemned by God and torn in pieces and scattered over the whole earth."[41]

Celsus evidently despises the Jews as a people, saying that they were never of any reputation or account. This Origen hotly denies, pointing out the many centuries during which they enjoyed the divine protection interspersed with their abandonment by God for longer or shorter periods. But God's final and complete desertion of them came in Roman times, when they "committed their greatest sin in killing Jesus. For this, they were entirely abandoned."[42] That theological judgment is tempered with a bit of sober history when, in speaking of the fact that no one sees God with bodily eyes, Origen says that neither those who cried "Crucify him!" nor Pilate, "who received power over Jesus' humanity," could see God the Father directly.[43] The events of the passion were earthly history for Origen, not a fable.

Yet this Alexandrian native at all times also operates theologically in the matter of Jesus' death. His biblical commentaries show him quite capable of critical history, but he never applies these skills to the New Testament accounts of the death of Jesus. These he accepts as sober history without question, taking the reported pressure of Jerusalem Jews (among whom he does not make distinctions) on Pilate to condemn Jesus as equivalent to making them the primary agents of his crucifixion. He derives from this assumption of fact—a fact that horrifies him, given his faith conviction that Jesus is divine as well as human—a providential punishment of later generations of Jews for the sin of their fathers. He was not the first to arrive at this conclusion, but a theory of inherited guilt may have been Origen's chief contribution to the Christian understanding of Jesus' death. This false supposition, in any case, remained firmly in Christian memory.

Origen's outstanding Latin-speaking contemporary in North Africa, Cyprian, martyr bishop of Carthage (d. 258), does not seem to have inherited a

---

40. Ibid., 8; the same relation is established between Jesus' death and the destruction of Jerusalem in 4.22, the latter event being placed forty-two years after the crucifixion. A novel explanation is given of Jesus' prayer in the garden that the cup of suffering pass from him (Luke 22:42): that the Jews might be delivered from the calamities their sins against him would bring on (see *Against Celsus* 2.25).

41. *Against Celsus* 34.

42. Ibid., 4.32. In 7.8 he describes them as "without a prophet since the advent of Jesus. For the Holy Spirit, as people are well aware, has forsaken them because they acted impiously against God and against the one prophesied by the prophets among them."

43. Ibid., 7.43.

full share of Tertullian's anti-Jewish animus. He is only doubtfully the compiler of the biblical texts known as *Ad Quirinum* or *Testimonies against the Jews* attributed to him, and he certainly did not write *Concerning Mounts Sinai and Zion, against the Jews*.[44] But he does write in his treatise on the Our Father that the Jews cannot address God in such an intimate way as this because they "not only faithlessly spurned Christ, but also cruelly slew him."[45] God was their Father but ceased to be such when they abandoned their God. At one point he writes to Cornelius, bishop of Rome, that "we are menaced not only by Gentile and Jew but by heretics as well,"[46] even though there is no special indication of Jewish attacks on third-century Carthaginian Christians. Elsewhere he alludes to a phrase of Paul in Romans (at 2:24, quoting Ezek. 36:20): "The Jews have become alienated from God, for it is due to them that the name of God is blasphemed among the Gentiles."[47]

Eusebius and Fourth-Century Church Fathers

Not long after Cyprian's death under Valerian and Gallienus (253–61), there occurred the persecution of Christians by Diocletian (284–286), then Galerius (305–311). Constantine (305–336) and Licinius (308–324) gave Christians their freedom and confirmed it at a meeting in Milan late in 312 (or early 313). It was some time around 314 that Eusebius, the Greek-speaking bishop of Caesarea in Palestine, completed *Preparation for the Gospel* in fifteen books.[48] All are extant, but of the *Demonstration of the Gospel* (314–18), which the first work was meant to serve as an apologetic introduction, only ten of twenty books remain. Eusebius refers to the "Hebrews" from the time of Abraham to Moses, following which they become "Jews"; but then the prophets and Jesus and his disciples become "Hebrews" again. Despite this erratic terminology, Eusebius has the utmost respect for Moses and his laws. The usage is probably based on the theory of the interim character of the law found in Galatians 3:17–19, but Eusebius cites the vocabulary within the sacred writings as his justification.[49] He speaks early in his first treatise of "adhering to the God who is honored among the Jews in

44. *PL* 4.675–780 and 909–18, respectively. Another spurious work *Against the Jews* accuses them of hating Christ through the stands taken for or against a number of biblical figures; see CSEL 3, Part 3, appendix, 133–44.

45. Cyprian *De Oratione Dominica* 10 (*PL* 4.525; ET, Roy J. Deferrari, *St. Cyprian: Treatises* [New York, 1958], 134, which cites Matt. 8:11, 12 to establish that the Jews are expelled from the kingdom, having once been its sons (Deferrari, *Cyprian*, 138).

46. *Letter* 59 2.3, trans. G. W. Clarke, *The Letters of St. Cyprian of Carthage*, 3, ACW 46 (New York and Mahwah, N.J.: Newman, 1986), 69.

47. *Letter* 13 3.2, ibid., 1, ACW 43 (New York and Ramsey, N.J.: Newman, 1984), 84.

48. Eusebius *Preparation for the Gospel*, ed. E. des Places, SC 206, 228, 262, 266, 215, 369, 292, 307, 338 (Paris, 1948–87; ET, Edwin Hamilton Gifford; 2 vols.; Oxford, 1903).

49. Eusebius *The Proof of the Gospel* 7.6, trans. W. J. Ferrar (London, 1920), 327–28.

their customary rites."[50] Before long, however, he refers to the deeds they wrought against Jesus as resulting in the final siege of Jerusalem and their dispersion and bondage in the territory of their enemies.[51] This kind of language is then absent from the rest of the treatise.

Eusebius quotes Bardesanes the Syrian, Origen, Philo, Josephus, and Porphyry liberally, all in the interest of showing the absurdity of the pagan myths, idol worship, and even philosophy that had bound his ancestors but from which the Gospel has relieved Greeks like him. The plagiarism or at least dependence of writers like Plato and Plutarch on the "Hebrew Oracles" is a constant theme in books 10–15, as it has been with numerous previous Christian apologists. For many who know its title but not its content, the *Preparation for the Gospel* is a classic of supersessionism, but it is scarcely that. It is in fact a long preamble to the *Demonstration,* which in turn hopes to answer all reasonable questions from Jewish or Greek inquirers about Christianity. The major line of approach of this second work is that the Mosaic religion was a decline from the primitive cult of the patriarchs, to which Hebrew original the prophets and Jesus returned.

In this work Eusebius discovers in "the plot against our Savior Jesus Christ," "that through which and after which all the things above-mentioned [the desolation of Jerusalem predicted by Isaiah in chaps. 1–3] overtook them [i.e., the whole people of the Jews that the prophet accused]."[52] It was the "impiety done to our Savior" that resulted in the sieges of Vespasian and Hadrian, following which Jews "were completely debarred from the place, not even being allowed to tread the soil of Jerusalem."[53] This is supported with a series of totally obscure references to Isaiah. When in book 10, the last one extant, Eusebius marshals the biblical passages he identifies as prophetic of Jesus' passion and death, he names the plotters against him as Judas and "the rulers of the Jews."[54] Applying LXX Psalm 108 (MT 109) to Matthew's narrative in chap. 26, he understands the text, "Set a wicked man over him, and let Satan stand at his right hand . . . Let his days be few and let another take his office" (vv. 6, 8), to establish that "a sinful ruler and head was given to the Jewish people, after their presumptuous deeds against the Savior and they were forced to serve strangers and idolators instead of their ancient godly rulers."[55] Having observed Luke's application of this text to the traitor Judas (Acts 1:20), Eusebius proceeds immediately to identify the sinful ruler and head as presumably Rome or its emperor. The presence of "Satan at [the sinner's] right hand," however, is an ominous detail in the use of this psalm in Eusebius's context.

50. *Preparation* 1.2.5c (ET, 1.6).
51. Ibid., 3a (ET, 1.10).
52. Eusebius *Proof* 2.3.37 (ET, 77–79).
53. Ibid., 84.
54. Ibid., 10.1 (ET, 196) and 10.2 (ET, 201).
55. Ibid., 10.3 (ET, 205).

When Gerhart Ladner discusses the homilies of John Chrysostom against the Jews and their religion, preached at Antioch in 386 and 387, he asks: "How could Christianity, a religion of love, produce in one of its most eminent figures such vehemence of anti-Judaism?"[56] He says he does not know of any one reason that will serve as a general explanation, despite all the historical antecedents and socioeconomic, anthropological, and psychological preconditions. He finds the need for a scapegoat too simple an explanation as far as the church fathers are concerned. He does allow, without granting the oedipal explanation, that the assertion of Christian identity "may have some bearing here."

Looking back on these writers, we find in them a primary need to assert Christianity's uniqueness against Judaism and paganism. The apologists and theologians thought their faith much closer religiously to that of Israel than that of the empire. They had to find reasons for God's self-revelation in Christ or they would have had the problem of a divine deed that was needless. Christianity's superiority to Judaism was thus a demand of their logic. The need was heightened by the similarities of Christianity to the old religion and the attraction this Jewish cult exercised on their fellow religionists. Establishing Jewish sin and wrongdoing would accomplish two things: absolve deity from the charge of a change of mind and show the Bible's correctness in its prophetic castigation of Israel's sins. If the Jews had done extreme wrong by working violence on the one whom God had sent them in fulfillment of all prophecy, several things—including accounting for the sufferings of the Jews at Roman hands—would be achieved. That is what made the crucifixion of Jesus by the Jews a kind of theological necessity. His having been done to death by Roman authority, on the contrary, would have been a commonplace of pagan cruelty. There was no place for it in the scheme of prophecy and fulfillment. Providentially speaking, it would not have fit in.

These reflections may help explain without excusing the nodding of three Christian Homers of the fourth and fifth centuries: Ambrose (339–397), John Chrysostom (347–407), and Augustine (354–430). Ambrose had been based in Milano as the *consularis* of Liguria and Aemilia, roughly the position Pilate held, when he was elected as Milano's bishop in 374. Still a catechumen in his thirties, he received in succession baptism and the order of bishop. In resisting the emperor Theodosius's efforts to run a theocratic state, Ambrose opposed the civil rights accorded to Jews, heretics, and pagans that equaled those of Christians, a move of the emperor to show his control over the church. In Julian's brief reign (361–163) churches had been destroyed in Damascus, Beirut, Gaza, and elsewhere without indemnification, Ambrose pointed out.[57] He in turn supported a bishop at the head of a mob that had burned down a synagogue at Callinicum on the Euphrates.

---

56. Ladner, "Aspects of Patristic Anti-Judaism," *Viator: Medieval and Renaissance Studies* 2 (1971): 359.
57. *Epistle* 40.15 (PL 16.1107).

The emperor had commanded that it be rebuilt. Ambrose's words were: "I claim that I would have burned that synagogue . . . so that there may be no place in which Christ be denied."[58] For him it was "a place of unbelief." He asked why Christians should fear Jewish vengeance, saying: "Whom do they have to avenge the Synagogue? Christ whom they have killed, whom they have denied? Or will God the Father avenge them, whom they do not acknowledge as Father since they do not acknowledge the Son."[59] In a public confrontation in his cathedral the bishop made the emperor back down.[60]

There was no understanding of the religious "other" here, only a charge of the Jews' being wrong in religion based on a criminal deed centuries before, from which they had no appeal.

> They insinuate themselves cleverly among people . . . disturb the ears of judges and other public figures, and get on all the better for their impudence. Nor is this a recent matter with them but a longstanding evil going back to their origins. In time past they even persecuted the Lord and Savior within the praetorium, condemning him before the judgment of the one who presided (Matt. 27:2ff.). In that place innocence was oppressed by the Jews, religion condemned, what was hidden betrayed. For with the killing of Christ all truth and justice was condemned; he is innocence itself and thus the religion of holiness, too, and mystery.[61]

Almost contemporaneous with Ambrose was the Greek-speaking Antiochian John Chrysostom. His rhetorical excesses in the eight sermons he preached against the Jews immediately after his ordination as a presbyter of Antioch (aged thirty-seven) are well known. Fearful of the influence of the Arians upon Catholics, he launched a series against them but shortly interrupted it in the fall of 386 with two sermons against the Jews as their holy days came on. He identified as "a disease flourishing within the body of the church" the attendance of "many who belong to us and say they believe in our teaching, attend their festivals, and even share in their celebrations and join in their fasts."[62] He was convinced that such participation amounted to apostasy, although an explanatory detail may be the evidence that there was a late survival of early judaizing tendencies in Christian Antioch.[63]

58. Ibid., 8 (PL 16.1104).
59. Ibid., 26 (PL 16.1110).
60. Theodosius's protection of the Jews and their meetings is defended at law against "the excesses of those who under the name of the Christian religion are committing illegal actions, or attempting to destroy or ruin synagogues" (Codex Theodosianus, ed. T. Mommsen and P. Meyer [Berlin, 1905], 16.8.9).
61. Ambrose Sermon 7 (PL 17.618).
62. John (Chrysostom) of Antioch, Against the Jews, Homily 1.1 (PG 48.844). Robert Wilken has translated homilies 1 and 8 in Wayne A. Meeks and Robert L. Wilken, Jews and Christians in Antioch in the First Four Centuries of the Common Era, SBL Sources for Biblical Study 13 (Missoula, Mont.: Scholars Press, 1978), 86.
63. See Marcel Simon, Verus Israel: A Study of the Relations of Christians and Jews in the Roman Empire, 135–425 (New York: Oxford Univ. Press, 1968), 379–80.

Chrysostom was brutally harsh in his descriptions of the Jews as ungrateful to God, given to drunkenness and overeating, licentiousness, and dancing with naked feet in the marketplace. He could not let stand the opinion of many that the Jews are holy and that oaths taken in synagogues are especially sacred; that opinion must be uprooted. As part of his polemic he spoke of one who worships Christ dragging a person off "to the haunts of the Jews who crucified [Jesus]."[64] "Not only the synagogue but also the souls of Jews are the dwelling places of demons."[65] "Do anything to rescue [your brother] from the devil's snare and deliver him from the fellowship of the Christ-killers [Christoktónōn]."[66] Chrysostom identified those Jews who are now fasting with the people who shouted "Crucify him! Crucify him!" (Luke 23:21) and "His blood be on us and on our children" (Matt. 27:23, 25). "Is it not folly for those who worship the crucified to celebrate festivals with those who crucified him?"[67] "They killed the son of your Lord, and yet you dare to gather with them in the same place? When the one who was killed by them honors you by making you a brother and fellow heir, you dishonor him by revering his murderers, those who crucified him, and by attending their festival assemblies."[68]

John Chrysostom was not always as violent as this in his condemnation of the Jews, as Ladner observes. His best argument in favor of Christianity is already foreshadowed in Homily 7. The eclipse of the Jewish law's validity is "not because of the sins of the Jews but because of its own inherent imperfection which required the new dispensation of Christ."[69] A new order of sacrifice was instituted, Chrysostom gets around to saying, as a transformation of the old: the order of Abraham's contemporary Melchizedek, which Hebrews 5:6 identifies as the order of Christ.[70] This explanation cannot be expected to have given much comfort to the Jews of Antioch who were hearing of the slanders against them from the dual-attendance Christians against whom the fiery new preacher's remarks were directed. But it is the latter that live in Jewish memory. Christians, meanwhile, tend not to have heard of Chrysostom's anti-Judaism, though the poisonous remarks he authored became part of their anonymous heritage.

The immensely influential Augustine entertained no thought that the Jews could lose the stigma of having disbelieved in Jesus. "You have killed Christ in your ancestors," he wrote. Clearly he thought of it as a collective guilt.[71] It is certainly easy for us to put down the Jews' lack of faith to the root cause

64. *Against the Jews,* Homily 1.3 (*PG* 48.847. ET, Wilken, *Jews and Christians,* 91).
65. Ibid., 4 (*PG* 48.849; ET, 92). Cf. 6 (*PG* 48.862; ET, 98).
66. Ibid., 4 (*PG* 48.849; ET, 93).
67. Ibid., 5 (*PG* 48.850; ET, 94).
68. Ibid., 7 (*PG* 48.854; ET, 100).
69. Ladner, "Aspects," 360.
70. *Oratio* (Homily) 12.45 (*PG* 48.921ff.). Hebrews at that place is citing Ps. 110 (LXX 109): 4.
71. *A Sermon against the Jews* 8.11 (*PL* 42.60).

of free choice, he wrote, "for many . . . willed to believe neither him nor those he raised from the dead."[72] Despite the severity of his judgment, Augustine was convinced it was the right one. His theory of grace forced him to believe that the Jewish people over four centuries had had the possibility of believing held out to them by a God who forces no one's will, and they had freely rejected the option. What we would call "social factors," or the possibility of God's grace given them to persevere in covenanted peoplehood, do not figure in Augustine's reckoning. In the world of his day, no religion showed itself capable of making such allowances. The wrong were simply wrongheaded.

What Augustine could and did say, in a sermon delivered in the last five years of his long life, was that "what the Jews read [in Scripture] they do not understand." By "understanding" he meant interpreting the Bible spiritually as Christians did. He was not so foolish as to think Jews could be invited just to read their sacred writings and thereby come to faith. On his own principle he required that they first believe so as to understand.[73] What we must do, Augustine says, is preach to them in love, whether they hear us willingly or not, "not with the presumption of insult [insultando] but with an awesome rejoicing [exsultando]." But the preaching in love he counseled was never purged of insult, largely because Christians were incapable of recognizing the wounds they caused by the grounds for argument they chose.

Pope Gregory the Great

Aside from Ambrose's literally fiery opinion on the Callinicum synagogue expressed to Theodosius, little in the writings of the church fathers tells of their relations with actual Jews. Gregory, bishop of Rome (590–604), provides an exception. It is a welcome one, because in the thirty or so of his eight hundred letters that deal with the Jews he shows himself solicitous for justice in their regard and the preservation of their rights under Roman law.[74] He favors their becoming Christian, as one might expect, but is set against anything smacking of duress, knowing that such "conversions" cannot be expected to be meaningful. From Gregory's correspondence much can be learned about Jewish life toward the end of the sixth century: the deep

72. On the Gift of Perseverance 9.23 (PL 45.1005–6). I owe this citation and the preceding one to Ladner (who does not give an English version), with an assist from Robert Wilken.

73. Enunciated clearly in his Sermon 43.3, 4 (PL 38.255): "A person says to me, 'Let me understand that I may believe,' to which I reply: 'Believe, that you may understand.'"

74. James Parkes, no friend to fellow Christians in these matters, devotes several pages to a breakdown of fully half of Gregory's letters in The Conflict of the Church and the Synagogue: A Study in the Origins of Antisemitism (London: Soncino, 1934), 210–21. See now Shlomo Simonsohn, The Apostolic See and the Jews: Documents: 492–1404, Studies and Texts 94 (Toronto, 1988). This eight-volume work gives documents from the Vatican Archives dating from Gelasius I (d. 496) to Julius III (d. 1555).

involvement of Jews in the slave trade, their living in amity with Christians in some regions and being dealt with sharply, even cruelly, by them in others, and the Jewish-Christian tensions that arose from close living, like churches and synagogues troubling each other by the volume of their song.

When Pope Gregory acts as a theologian rather than an administrator, his voluminous writings betray no sympathy whatever for Jews or a wish to receive them into the church. In referring to them he uses such terms as superstition, vomit, perdition, and *perfidia,* and describes them as the enemies of Christ.[75] "[Gregory's] practical treatment of problems connected with the presence of Jews in Christian society," the Tel Aviv historian Simonsohn says correctly, "laid the foundations of papal Jewry policy in the Middle Ages."[76] In his allegorical reading of the Bible wild asses, unicorns, basilisks, and serpents turn out to stand for Jews. This wise and practical renderer of judgments that protect Jews is the captive of a theological position which, carried to its logical extremes, resulted in harassment of them and even bodily harm. The bishop of Rome does not see that. There is right in religion and there is wrong. The Jews, regrettably, are wrong; and an inerrant Scripture, every verse of which contains a secret meaning, is employed to lay this bare.

Conclusion

What can be said to summarize the attribution of responsibility for Jesus' death to the Jews by the church fathers of the years 100–600? First, that they thought it clearly taught in the New Testament. For this they relied on the Acts of the Apostles as much as on the Gospels. That Pilate sentenced Jesus—whatever the measure of temple priestly encouragement—was thought to be a nonfact except in the creedal statement that served to date Jesus' sufferings. It came to be assumed very early in the patristic age that every member of subsequent generations of Jews concurred in this wicked deed. There was, of course, no evidence for this assumption, but it was thought that their failure to become Christians proved it. The latter argument was based on empirical observation, coupled with some harassment at the hands of Jews, even though the conclusion drawn was false. The main argument was a deduction from biblical data. The prophets had foretold Jesus' sufferings at the hands of his own people, it was supposed, because of all the texts that spoke of the abuse heaped on an innocent one by fellow Jews. It had all come to pass in the case of the singularly just Jesus. His rejection at the hands of others was freely willed by them in the fulfillment of prophecy. The failure of later generations of Jews to believe in the cross

75. Simonsohn, *Apostolic See,* Documents 5, 12, 13, 23, 24, 25, 26.
76. Idem, *The Apostolic See and the Jews: History,* Studies and Texts 109 (Toronto, 1991), 10.

and resurrection as saving events confirmed the hardness of heart of their first-century forebears.

The whole construct was a totally false elaboration of a partially valid myth. But this fact gave the Jewish people of the patristic era, particularly from Constantine's day onward, no consolation whatever. They began a centuries-long history of being stigmatized as the killers of Christ on the cross, when in fact they would have repudiated to a person the small number of Jews in power who had a part in the deed.

CHAPTER FOUR

Theories of Expiation and Satisfaction: From Tertullian to Anselm and Beyond

Death by crucifixion was so horrible a fate that the marvel is that the earliest Christians dealt with Jesus' death as blandly as they did. They made no effort to suppress the mode of his death. Such an intention cannot have been at work in the deemphasis on the manner of his execution. The public fact of his shameful death was acknowledged in Galatians 3:1 as part of the original proclamation of the gospel (cf. 1 Cor. 1:13). It was turned to good account by the open declaration in Acts 5:30 and 10:39 that he died "upon a tree [or stake]." Paul and the pre-Pauline tradition on which Romans 3:24–26 depends are at ease in describing Jesus' death as a "means of expiation" (*hilastērion*, v. 25). It was a "sacrifice of redemption" (v. 24), the passage says, achieved "by faith, through his blood" (v. 25). Blood here clearly means death.

The Gospel narratives of his last hours do not hesitate to report a flogging of Jesus at Pilate's order (Mark 15:15b; Luke 23:16, 22), his mocking by soldiers and crowning with thorns as a claimant to kingship (Mark 15:17–20a par. Matt. 27:28–31a; John 19:1–3), and the spitting in his face and blows he was subjected to (Mark 14:65 par. Matt. 26:67; Luke 22:63; Mark 15:19 par. Matt. 17:30). Yet all of this is described very matter-of-factly, with as little color as the summary of it that Mark's Gospel presents as a prophecy of Jesus (10:33–34). Jesus' words from the cross, notably the psalm verse expressing abandonment by God (Ps. 22:1; cf. Mark 15:34), may well have been the evangelist's contribution; likewise his death "with a loud cry" (Mark 15:37). The marvel, I repeat, is that the awful fact of a criminal's death was recorded so dispassionately. Hebrews tries to enter into his anguish, but that only briefly (5:7–8). First Peter is almost alone in proposing Jesus' sufferings as a model for those of believers (2:21–24); but see Philippians 3:10; Colossians 1:24. First Timothy, uniquely among non-Gospel writings, refers to a detail of Jesus' final hours (6:13), his appearance before Pilate.

A number of factors may account for this relative silence. From an early date, it is evident that the death was viewed as primarily a deed of God rather than of human beings. Its character as expiatory was likewise to the fore, not the manner of the death. A narrative mode was adopted in the gospel tradition that described tortures and mockeries in the same flat tone as that employed for Jesus' major miracles or the incarnation of God's word in a human being. While the passion accounts were framed to elicit sympathy for the innocent Jesus, the technique adopted was not one of playing blatantly on the hearers' sympathies. A low-key description of the events was used, perhaps to underscore their horror. Even when, in the third century, the accusations of Jewish responsibility for Jesus' death began to proliferate, there was no special emphasis on the gruesome details.

The explanation cannot have been that the ancient world was inured to cruelty and torture. There was as much—and as little—sensitivity to brutality then as now. It was more that the Christian option was to center on God's authorship of the deed even though an immense miscarriage of human justice accompanied it, and not on the physical pain or the mental anguish Jesus underwent.

The Blood of the Cross as Transcendent Symbol

Christ's sufferings and death were early transposed into the theological key of *mýthos*. "Paul thought of Jesus' death as a sacrifice and in specifically Day of Atonement terms," as the phrase "an expiation . . . by his blood" (Rom. 3:25; cf. 4:25) establishes.[1] The first layer of gospel tradition does not describe his death as particularly bloody, although the scourging, crowning with thorns, nails, and spear thrust would have accounted for considerable loss of blood. The substitution of "blood" for "cross" as the word to describe Jesus' death was meant to convey its ritual character, which was established early. The association of his death with the blood of sacrifice in Jewish ritual, particularly the Day of Atonement sin offering (Leviticus 16), was central in the pre-Pauline fragment that underlay Romans 3:24–26. In Leviticus the blood of a goat is sprinkled on the cover of the ark (Lev. 16:2; LXX *hilastērion*) and before it. This practice is reflected in the reference to "covenant blood" in Mark 14:24 par. (see also Exod. 24:8); in the superiority of Christ's blood in what it achieved to that of goats and bulls (Heb. 9:11–14); and in the phrase delivered as an axiom in 1 Peter 1:19: "You were ransomed . . . with the precious blood of Christ as of a spotless unblemished lamb." Hebrews later says that he "consecrates the people by his own blood" (13:12).

The word "cross," to be sure, had a history in Paul's Letters, standing for the total mystery of redemption (see Phil. 2:8). It had a "content" (1 Cor.

1. James D. G. Dunn, *Romans 1–8*, Word Biblical Commentary 38 (Dallas: Word, 1988), 171.

1:17) and a "message" (v. 18), namely, that believers in it are redeemed. The cross is, in Paul's view, a "stumbling block" or "scandal" (Gal. 5:11). Whoever puts faith in it risks persecution (6:12). Those who profess belief in the cross are capable of behavior inimical to what it stands for (Phil. 3:18). "Our old self was crucified with him, so that our sinful body might be done away with" (Rom. 6:6). In a hymn similar to that of Philippians 2:6–11, Jesus reconciles all things in the heavens and on earth, "makes peace by the blood of his cross" (Col. 1:20). By it he brings an end to the enmity between Israel and the pagans (Eph. 2:16). In a complex metaphor, "the invoice with its claims at law against us" is said to have been nailed to the cross, presumably declared paid by being affixed to the wood (Col. 2:14). Hebrews speaks of Christ's death (2:9, 15) and crucifixion (6:6) and many times of the shedding of his blood in sacrifice by this great high priest (7:15–16, 26; 8:1; 9:11–14; 10:12, 21). "He put up with the cross, despising its shame . . . [and] enduring opposition from sinners" (12:3). The tone is generally, however, ritualist rather than naturalist. Jesus acts as priest and victim in a way that recalls temple sacrifice rather than the brutal events of Calvary.

Two things emerge from the body of New Testament texts just cited: they do not linger on the circumstances of Jesus' death, the only point featured being that he shed his blood in a ritual sacrifice; and his sacrifice was effective in achieving the purpose God had for it, the redemption from sin of the whole human race.

Does the New Testament Have a Theory of Reconciliation?

One needs to ask at this point whether the New Testament writers provide anything like a full-blown theory of human atonement or reconciliation by the shedding of Christ's blood. The answer seems to be no. There is only the tradition, already in place when Paul becomes a believer in the risen Lord, "that Christ died for our sins" (1 Cor. 15:3). This tradition he both received and passed on in all the churches he founded (ibid.). One other form in which he received it has already been alluded to: "All who believe are justified [i.e., acquitted] freely by God's grace through the redemption in Christ Jesus, whom God set forth as a means of expiation in his blood, through faith, to demonstrate God's righteousness, because in the divine forbearance God had let the sins committed in the past go unpunished to demonstrate his righteousness in the present, that God might be righteous and justify anyone who believes in Jesus" (Rom. 3:24–26).

These verses begin with a participle in Greek, "the justified," which may indicate that they are an inserted quotation commenting on all who will be justified (v. 22) and some who will not (v. 20), the first group by faith, the second by observing the law. Paul may have added to an earlier traditional formulation the phrases, "freely by [God's] grace" (v. 24); "by faith" (v. 25); "justification/acquittal" (v. 20); and "righteousness," all found previously in his letter (1:17; 3:5, 20, 22). The terms for "redemption" (*apolýtrōsis,* v. 24), "in his blood" (v. 25), and "expiation" (*hilastérion,* v. 25) are part of the primitive tradition that saw Jesus' death, if it were rightly believed in, as accomplishing all that temple sacrifice did and more. Another expression of the tradition Paul received occurs in Romans 5:8–9: "It is in this that God proves his love for us: that while we were still sinners Christ died for us. Now that we have been justified by his blood, it is all the more certain that we shall be saved through him from the wrath" (cf. 1 Thess. 1:10). This expresses the primitive belief—the justification figure apart, which is Paul's—that humanity is to be rescued ("saved") from the fitting divine recompense for sins at the end of the age. "Indeed, if while we were enemies we were reconciled to God through the death of [God's] son, how much more, once reconciled, will we be saved by his life" (Rom. 5:10). This teaching on redemption through Christ's blood for the remission of sins is repeated in a letter and a treatise in the Pauline tradition, respectively Colossians at 1:14, 20 and Ephesians at 1:7; 2:13.

The tradition that Paul received at an early date and passed along was that Christ eliminated the guilt of past sins by his sacrificial death. His blood was expiatory, even as that of bulls and sheep and goats had been. Sinners were redeemed by it just as were captives taken in war when the ransom price was paid. Paul never denied this primitive theory of expiation. He accepted it and transmitted it, but he did more. This earliest tradition is often presented as if it were Paul's great contribution. But he built on it in a way that was distinctively his own. He developed the idea that Christ gave himself for human sins to deliver the entire race from "the present evil age" as he conceived it. In this he went beyond viewing Jesus' death as expiatory for past sins, teaching that Jesus identified believers with himself as Lord of the new age over which he now presides.

For Paul there is purpose in Jesus' death that transcends the expiating of *past* transgressions. When he speaks of Christ's dying "for all" in 2 Corinthians 5:14–15, he has in mind a death that notably affects their *future:* "The love of Christ controls us, because we have come to the conclusion that one has died for all and therefore all have died" (v. 14). Solidarity with the saving and reconciling Christ is thus an important effect of his death. "He indeed died for all, so that those who live might no longer live for themselves but for him who for their sake died and was raised" (v. 15). This describes a death to the *power* of sin and not just one that atones for past trespasses. E. P. Sanders suggests that Galatians 1:4 should probably be read in the same way: Christ "gave himself for our sins that he might rescue us from the present evil age in accord with the will of our God and Father."[2] This goes be-

---

2. E. P. Sanders, *Paul and Palestinian Judaism* (Philadelphia: Fortress Press, 1977), 465.

yond the traditional faith that Jesus expiated past sins. It describes believers as being in a quite new condition, placed in a new aeon over which Christ presides, as a result of their faith in "Jesus Christ and God the Father who raised him from the dead" (v. 2).

A third text in Paul puts the matter beyond all doubt: "For if we live, we live for the Lord, and if we die, we die for the Lord; so then, whether we live or die, we are the Lord's. For *this is why* Christ died and came to life, that he might be Lord of both the dead and the living" (Rom. 14:8–9, emphasis added). Unequivocally, Paul holds that the purpose of Jesus' death on the cross and his resurrection goes beyond atoning for past transgressions. It is to establish Jesus' lordship over those who by faith are one with him. This new lordship replaces that of death, sin, and Satan (see 16:20). Its correlative is the mystical union of believers in Christ. They have died to sin with him and risen from that death to a life for him in the new epoch (see Rom. 7:4: "so that you might belong to another, to the one who was raised from the dead in order that we might bear fruit for God").

It is important to observe that Paul never stresses the physical details of Jesus' time on the cross. It is always his "death," the "cross," or his "blood," without further elaboration. The piety centered on Jesus' passion that was to dominate later centuries has little warrant in Paul's exposition of the redemptive mystery or, indeed, in the whole New Testament. Interesting, too, is Paul's relatively greater stress on Jesus' rising from the dead than on the sufferings that preceded it. Death and resurrection are at times coupled (e.g., in Rom. 4:25; 6:5, 9; 8:34; 1 Cor. 15:3–4; 2 Cor. 5:15; Phil. 3:10), but much more often Jesus' rising from the dead is mentioned alone (e.g., Rom. 4:24; 6:4; 7:4; 8:11; 10:9; 1 Cor. 6:14; 15:12, 20; 2 Cor. 4:14; Gal. 1:1; 1 Thess. 1:10).

The convention of the last few centuries in evangelical preaching of "proclaiming Christ and him crucified" (1 Cor. 1:23) in isolation from his resurrection has little New Testament support. It is puzzling that some theological circles should repudiate Luke in his book of Acts for identifying the crucifixion as a necessary precondition of the resurrection (see 2:32–33; 3:26; 4:33; 5:31; 7:56; 10:39–40) and not the whole mystery, when Paul the champion of Reformation faith is consistently guilty of the same emphasis. An exploration is required and will later be attempted of how Jesus' death on the cross, its painful aspects especially, became the all but exclusive symbol of God's redemptive deed.

The Cross and Resurrection as Redemptive in the Second Century

A search in the second-century literature for the crucifixion as the sole means by which the human race was redeemed will lead to disappointment. *The*

Letter of the Church of Rome to the Church of Corinth, commonly called *1 Clement,* puts the words of Christ on a par with his sufferings as the "provisions" or "rations" he has issued to the members of the Roman community (2.1). It quotes Isaiah 53:1–12 in full and Psalm 22:6–8 to illustrate Christ's humility but without any overt reference to his passion. Imitating his example and being obedient to his teachings are proposed throughout as a means of salvation. The closest the treatise comes to speaking of redemption by the cross is 7.4: "Let us fix our eyes on the blood of Christ and let us realize how precious it is to his Father, since it was poured out for our salvation and brought the grace of repentance to the whole world." This is echoed in 12.7: "by the blood of the Lord redemption was to come to all who believe and hope in God." Jesus' giving "his blood for us, his flesh for our flesh, and his life for ours" is the way God accepted us (49.6), *1 Clement* says. We found our salvation through a "sacrifice of praise," to which Psalm 50:23 alluded, offered by "Jesus Christ, the high priest of our offerings" (*1 Clem.* 36.1).

Ignatius of Antioch (ca. 110) speaks of the crucifixion as having been undergone by Jesus Christ for "God's fidelity" (*pístin theoû; Eph.* 16.2) and in one place says, against gnostic thought, that he was "really crucified" (*Trall.* 9.1). He writes of the cross under the figure of a crane that hoists us up to God (*Eph.* 9). Quite unlike the Christology of the New Testament, Ignatius celebrates the "blood of God" (*Eph.* 1.1); more traditionally, "of Christ" (*Phil.,* Introduction; *Smyrn.* 6.1). Jesus endured death and other sufferings (*Trall.* 2.1; 11.1; *Eph.* 7.2) in what Ignatius calls, as above, "the passion of my God" (*Rom.* 6.3; cf. *Phil.* 3.3; *Smyrn.* 1:2; 12.26). Passion and resurrection are coupled four times (*Eph.* 20.1; *Phil.,* Introduction; 9.2; *Smyrn.* 6.2), lest it be thought that this author is the first to depart from the twofold redemptive mystery.

The *Didachē* describes the eucharistic meal on the Lord's day, for which it provides a formula of thanksgiving, as "your sacrifice," along with a reference to the pure sacrifice demanded by the Lord in Malachi 1:11. The anonymous *Letter to Diognetus* of the same period (ca. 125) says that God, out of mercy, "took up the burden of our sins. [God] gave up his own Son as a ransom for us—the holy for the unjust, the righteous for the unrighteous, the incorruptible for the corruptible, the immortal for the mortal" (9.2). The letter has God showing the Savior's power to save even the powerless (v. 6) by the righteousness of one who justifies the many who are sinners (v. 5). The phrasing is redolent of Romans 5–8. The cross is only obliquely referred to.

Justin mentions it directly in his *1 Apology* (ca. 155), providing the first extant reference after the Gospels to details of Jesus' crucifixion. He applies the text of Isaiah 9:6, "and the government will be upon his shoulder" (meaning the broad band that supports a heavy wooden key), to "the power of the cross . . . which he took upon his shoulders" (*1 Apology* 35). He further refers to the pierced hands and feet of Psalm 22 (LXX 21): 16, 18 and the mockery reported in Mark 15:18 (see *1 Apology* 38 for other prophecies employed by Mark). Since Justin's purpose is to prove to pagans and Jews that prophecy was fulfilled in Jesus, we should not expect a theory of the cross as redemptive and he does not provide one. He is interested to maintain such things as that Plato's letter *Chi* (X) in the universe (*Timaeus* 36BC) imitated Moses' form of a cross on which the bronze serpent was placed (Num. 21:6–9; cf. John 3:14).

From New Testament times to the third quarter of the second century the prevailing Christian conviction was that humanity was bought back or ransomed from the guilt of sin by Jesus' sacrifice (his "blood"), much as God accepted the blood of beasts and birds as vicarious of human life. There was no theorizing on whether Christ's blood was an actual purchase price and, if so, paid to whom. Faith in the offering of his life was sufficient to bring total release from sin on the last day, but an upright life was the condition of this faith, "when he will come to redeem (ransom) us, each according to deeds performed, and [unbelievers] . . . will be surprised to see the sovereignty of the world given to Jesus."[3] His death had acquired the status of a rite, universal and cosmic in its effects. The culpability of those who had brought it about was not a feature of this simple redemptive theory. Justin might make much of Jewish guilt in his *Dialogue with Trypho* (see chap. 3 above) but it does not figure in his theory of atonement for sins by faith in Jesus' blood.

The same is true of Irenaeus, who has been called the most distinguished witness to Catholic tradition of the second century. Christ as redeemer is the center of Christian faith for him, but Irenaeus situates the redemption he accomplished in the incarnation rather than the cross. God's choice of being united with humanity in Jesus Christ was essentially, in his view, what accomplished human salvation. "The Word of God, Jesus Christ our Lord, because of his great love for us, became what we are in order to enable us to be what he is."[4]

The Greek-speaking bishop of Lyon was in a mortal encounter with the Christian Gnostics who denied the reality of the incarnation. His whole effort in his five books against false *gnôsis* was to demonstrate this reality. God's having become a human being was alone enough to redeem us, making Christ's death on the cross the corollary of that initial divine choice. "The word of God was made man," Irenaeus wrote, "God recapitulating in himself the ancient formation of man in order to kill sin, annihilate death,

---

3. *2 Clement* (a Christian homily of ca. 150 C.E.), 17.4–5; see C. C. Richardson, trans., *Early Christian Fathers* (New York: Macmillan, 1970), 200–201. The translation of second-century writings in this collection, with notes and commentary, contains the works of Clement, Ignatius, the *Didachē, Letter to Diognetus,* and Justin's *1 Apology* cited above.

4. *Adversus Haereses* (*Against Heresies*), preface to book 5 (*PL* 7 bis.1120; ET, ANF, A. Roberts, W. H. Rambaut, and J. Donaldson; 2.55). See the treatment of Irenaeus in Louis Richard, *The Mystery of the Redemption,* trans. J. Horn (Baltimore: Helicon, 1965), 133–41.

and give life to humanity." [5] This exchange was at the heart of all his thought: life to give life to humanity, death to achieve the death of sin. God's Word restored us, making us his own disciples.

> [He] gave his soul for our souls and his flesh for our bodies, and poured out the Spirit of the Father to bring about the union and communion of God and the human race—to bring God down to humans by [the working of] the Spirit and raise humanity up to God by his incarnation—and by his coming firmly and truly to give us incorruption, all the teachings of the [Gnostic] heretics are destroyed by our communion with God. [6]

Incorruptibility, of course, was the very thing the Gnostics sought through their schemes of redemption. Irenaeus made use of Paul's figure of the two Adams, expressing it this way:

> When [the Son of God] became incarnate, and was made man, he recapitulated in himself the long line of human beings. He obtained salvation for us in miniature so that what we lost in Adam, namely our being in the image and likeness of God, might be recovered in Jesus Christ. [7]

Yet this first formal theologian, as he is sometimes called, was not ignorant of the tradition he had inherited on how human redemption was ultimately achieved:

> He is the mighty Word and true human. Redeeming us by his blood in a spiritual way, he was given as a ransom for those who had been led into captivity. . . . The Word of God, powerful in all things . . . and unfailing in his justice, was just even when he confronted the apostasy itself [Satan, the primordial sinner] and redeemed from him his own property [humanity]; for he did not do it by violent means—as the apostasy had obtained dominion over us in the beginning by insatiably snatching what was not his—but by persuasion. Thus it was fitting for God to be persuasive and not violent in obtaining what he wished to recover. [8]

It has been much argued whether Irenaeus in this passage granted any rights to the devil, who is portrayed as having humanity captive to him. Did Christ pay the devil a just ransom by handing himself over? This cannot be the case, since elsewhere Irenaeus calls the devil a rebel and a usurper, denying that he has any rights over sinful human beings. The "justice" of the ransom he alludes to is in the order of divine wisdom. [9] It does not mean that

5. *Adversus Haereses* 3.18.7 (ET, 1.344).
6. Ibid. 5.1.1 (ET, E. R. Hardy in C. C. Richardson, *Early Christian Fathers*, 2.56).
7. Ibid., 3.18.1 (ET, Roberts and Donaldson, 1.338).
8. Ibid., 5.1.1.
9. Ibid., 3.23.2.

the devil has acquired any rights over the human beings he has violently taken captive. "We were debtors to no one except to him whose commandment we had disobeyed in the beginning. . . . thus becoming [God's] enemies."[10]

The ransom figure has the biblical meaning of liberation, not of paying another what is his or her due. Christ does not free us by handing himself over to the devil but offers his blood in sacrifice. Its acceptance by God is liberating in its effect. The lifelong struggle of Jesus with the devil began in the desert and ended with the passion, where the devil instigated the death sentence. Jesus seemed to be defeated in handing himself over freely for us. But he was the victor, not only over the devil but also (and chiefly) over sin and its concomitant, death. Irenaeus knew that Christ accomplished the work of a high priest by undergoing death, "so that exiled humanity might go forth from its condemnation and recover its inheritance without fear."[11] The drama was a divinely ordered one, at the heart of which was always the cross:

> So by the obedience whereby He obeyed unto death, hanging on the tree, He undid the old disobedience wrought in the tree. And because He is Himself the Word of God Almighty. . . [through whom] everything is disposed and administered . . . . the Son of God was crucified [in the length and breadth and height and depth of the whole world], imprinted in the form of a cross on the universe.[12]

The emphasis in the mystery of the crucifixion here is on Jesus' obedient self-offering as victim, while he is at the same time active offerer as priest. Irenaeus, like Paul, sees human redemption as a cosmic happening as well as a historical one, in which God acts on human behalf. Calvary and the resurrection, the manifestation of Christ's victory, while centered on a human being are never presented as a merely human drama. The gospel account of the condemnation of Jesus as a criminal has yielded to a theological construct in which the divine-human Jesus Christ achieves the salvation of all humanity. The innovative thought of Paul, in which the chief effect of the cross and resurrection is mystical union with Christ in the new age, has survived in Irenaeus in the form of an interiorly divinized humanity. A weakened human race has been replaced by another that has as its strength the gift of the Spirit.

10. Ibid., 5.16.17
11. Ibid., 4.8.2.
12. Irenaeus *Proof of the Apostolic Preaching* 34 (*PG* 22.), trans. Joseph P. Smith (from the Armenian, the earliest translation extant; Westminster, Md.: Newman, 1952).

The Third Century: Sacrifice as Satisfaction, Redemption as Divinization

An important term was added to the Christian vocabulary of redemption when, fifty years later, the legally oriented layman Tertullian used the term "satisfaction" to characterize the reparation required of sins committed after baptism by fasting, almsgiving, and the like. In Roman law "satisfaction" meant personal repayment for injury or public punishment. Tertullian did not develop this concept as a description of Christ's death in sacrifice. He confined himself to speaking of God as "one to whom you may make satisfaction."[13] A person who repented was "making satisfaction" "to the Lord"; one who lapsed after repentance was "making satisfaction to the devil by repenting his repentance."[14]

Another writer toward the end of the fourth century, Hilary of Poitiers, "the first doctor of the Latin West," would pioneer in applying the term "satisfaction" to the death of Christ. This is an important move in the theology of redemption. Hilary equated the cross with sacrifice and saw in it the reparation made to God on behalf of sinners. This concept would acquire great significance in the Middle Ages in the Western church. He wrote:

> [Our Lord Jesus Christ] delivered us from a curse, as the Apostle says . . . [Gal. 3:15; cf. Deut. 21:23]. He therefore offered himself up to the death of the accursèd that he might remove the curse of the Law by offering himself to God the Father voluntarily. . . . to God who refused the sacrifices of the law by offering the pleasing victim of a body assumed. [Hebrews 7:27 recalls this]; the complete salvation of the human race will be accomplished by the offering of this holy and perfect victim.[15]

Stress was placed above on the importance the incarnation acquired in Irenaeus especially as the root principle of human salvation. In all the christological disputes of the third through the fifth century and beyond, the church fathers of East and West assumed that the redemption was already accomplished through the incarnation of the Son of God. The cross and resurrection made it manifest. Humanity was redeemed by virtue of its close union with the human being who was joined to the Word. The Greek fathers expressed the effect of this union by the term *theopoiēsis,* "divinization."

Pseudo-Dionysius, the early sixth-century Syrian monk, was alone in using the better-known Hellenistic word *theōsis.* Among the witnesses to the conviction that humanity was divinized by the incarnation are Athanasius

---

13. Tertullian *On Repentance* 7 (PL 1.1242; ET, W. P. Le Saint, *Tertullian on Penitence,* ACW, 28 [Westminster, Md.: Newman, 1959], 29).
14. Ibid., 5 (PL 1.1235–36; ET, 23).
15. Hilary of Poitiers *Exposition of the Psalms* 3.12–13 (PL 9.345).

("If indeed he became man, it was in order to deify us in himself"), Gregory of Nyssa ("The Word who revealed himself became mingled with perishable nature so that humanity might be deified with him by this participation in the divinity"), and Cyril of Alexandria ("The Son came to enable people to become in some way what he is by nature and to share what is his own").[16]

There was great concern that the incorruption of human flesh be brought about by faith in the incorruptible flesh of the risen Christ. At the same time, the power of the cross to redeem was not disregarded. It simply followed from the mystery of divine union with human nature. Thus, John of Damascus could say in his catechetical summary, so influential on later generations: "that is why, through his birth or incarnation, through his baptism, passion, and resurrection, he delivered the human race from the sin of its first parent, from death and corruption."[17]

The Western fathers mentioned the doctrine of the divine life in humanity frequently, even if they were not committed to it as universally as their brothers from the East. Thus, Ambrose and Hilary refer to humans' becoming gods as a result of God's becoming human.[18] The theology of deification does not seem to have been a secondary aspect of the doctrine of redemption but its basic principle, "much more intrinsic, than if we considered only the meritorious value of one or other of his various *actions,* such as his passion and death."[19]

Yet complementing this are the repeated affirmations of the same fathers that the Son of God, having become like us in everything but sin, underwent death to deliver us from sin and ultimately from death itself. "For the one who alone died [to be] raised up," we hear Athanasius saying, "accomplished [our salvation] on the cross."[20] And Cyril of Alexandria: "Had he not died we would never have been saved, and the cruel [*krátos*] empire of death would not have been broken."[21]

To Whom Was a Ransom Price Paid?

To say that Christ bought the human race back from the slavery of sin by the price of his blood is one thing. Is it the same thing to say, as Basil did, that, "If the Lord had not come in the flesh the Redeemer would not have turned over *to death* a ransom for us"?[22] Since the fathers used the terms

16. Athanasius *Letter to Adelphios* 4 (PG 26.1077A); Gregory of Nyssa *Great Catechesis* 37 (PG 45.97B); Cyril of Alexandria *Book 1 on John* (1:12) (PG 73.153A; and see B).
17. John Damascene *On Orthodox Faith* 4.13 (PG 94.1137C).
18. Ambrose *On the Incarnation of the Lord* 4.23 (PL 16.825); Hilary of Poitiers *On the Trinity* 2.24 (PL 10.66).
19. Pierre Rousselot, quoted in Richard, *Mystery,* 149.
20. Athanasius *On the Incarnation of the Word* 26 (PG 25.140C).
21. Cyril of Alexandria *Commentary on Exodus* 2 (PG 69.437B).
22. Basil of Caesarea *Letter* 261.2 (PG 32.969).

"death," "hell," and "the devil" interchangeably, has Basil in his metaphor said that a ransom was paid to Satan? Even if it were maintained that God had turned the Son over to Satan as the price of redemption, and the resurrection proved how badly the devil miscalculated, is there a sense in which men like Basil saw in the redemption a bargain between God and Satan? Did they, in other words, press the ransom figure too far?

It seems that Origen was the first to speak of Christ's having been turned over by God to demonic powers. Earliest Christian thought supposed that demons were the primary cause of evil in the universe and the devil the master of death. Origen speculated that God delivered Jesus over to the devil who, in turn, transmitted him to those in his earthly setting who were opposed to him. This outlook put the human race in the devil's possession until the ransom of the soul of Jesus was paid to him.[23] Referring to Paul's statement that we were "bought at a price" (1 Cor. 6:20; 7:23) Origen wrote:

> Obviously we were purchased from someone whose slaves we were, who claimed the price he wanted in exchange for the release of those he held captive. Now it was the devil who held us, since we had sold ourselves to him by our sins. He therefore claimed the blood of Christ as the ransom.[24]

Basil was not the only one to pick this up, as indicated above, but Ambrose and Jerome as well. Gregory of Nyssa is the person best remembered for his use of the figure because of the strange twist he put on it. From him the West derived the following image: Since humanity had fallen into this calamity voluntarily, God, who was to give us our freedom, had to take the way of justice and not of violence, the way by which the devil snatched us. This was one means of paying to the one who had achieved dominance over us the ransom he wanted.[25]

Gregory goes on to say that the devil would yield up his captives only if he had in prospect a greater ransom price, namely, Jesus, the powerful worker of miracles:

> God therefore hid himself under the veil of our nature so that the devil, throwing himself like a ravenous fish on the bait of mankind, might be caught on the hook of Deity. . . . He thought he would hold it in death like a man, but Christ acted according to his nature. As the Light, he dispelled darkness; as the Life, he destroyed death.[26]

23. See Origen On Matthew 16.8 (PG 13.1397B).
24. Origen On Romans 2.13 (PG 14.911C); cf. 4.11 (PG 14.1000C).
25. A paraphrase of Gregory of Nyssa Great Catechesis 22.6 (PG 45.59). See J. H. Srawley, ed. The Cathechetical Oration of Gregory of Nyssa (Cambridge, 1956), 84–85.
26. Great Catechesis 24 (PG 45.65A, B). See Srawley, Oration, 92–93. Rufinus of Aquileia, writing in Latin early in the next century, has it this way: "When he who had the power of death seized the body of Jesus, he failed to notice the hook of Deity enclosed within it; so, when he swallowed it, he was immediately caught and, bursting the bars of the underworld, was dragged out from the abyss to become a bait for others" (Commentary on the Apostles' Creed 16; PL 21.354–55; ET, J. N. D. Kelly, ACW 20 [Westminster, Md.: Newman, 1955], 51).

This crude metaphor shocked Gregory's contemporary, Gregory of Nazianzus. He was repelled by the notion that Christ was the object of an exchange between God and Satan:

> If it was to the devil, what an insult! How are we to suppose that he received not only a ransom from God, but God himself as a ransom, under the pretext of offering him such a great payment for his tyranny that he would in justice have to spare us? And if it was to the Father, I ask how this was done. It was not [God] who held us captive.[27]

The Nazianzen (who was archbishop of Constantinople) goes on to point out that, while God received the ransom price, it was because it was necessary that the human race be sanctified by the humanity of God. God had to free us and bring us back into the power of deity through the Son as mediator, thus triumphing over "the tyrant." By this move Gregory of Nazianzus preserved the New Testament figure of human redemption by Christ's blood—with its patristic elaboration of victory over the devil—while adhering to what had become a theological commonplace, namely, that it was the incarnation that deified and saved.

If the contemporaries of Gregory of Nyssa found his literal reading of the metaphor bizarre, one should remember that he was, in other passages, as committed to the saving power of the incarnation as they. He wrote that

> [the Lord] conjoined himself with our nature in order that by its conjunction with the godhead it might become divine, being exempted from death and rescued from the tyranny set against us. For his triumphal return from death inaugurated the triumphal return of the human race to life immortal.[28]

This was mainstream theological thought, not the unfortunate sortie into payment of a price to Satan out of justice. That extravagance captured the Christian imagination, though, and long survived in the West through the influence of Rufinus.[29] Popular religion was intrigued by the thought of the much-feared devil's being deceived and caught on the fishhook of Christ's divinity. The metaphor was slow in dying.

Augustine tried to modify it by removing the inconsistencies of a bargain between God and the devil in which Jesus was the object of exchange. He did this by introducing the idea that Satan had come to have some power over the human race, not in strict justice but by God's just permission. The devil abused this power "by killing Christ without having found anything in him that deserved death. It was therefore just that the debtors he held [i.e., human sinners] should be set free, those who believed in him who was not a debtor and whom he [the devil] had killed [as the cause of death]."[30]

27. Gregory of Nazianzus *Oration* 45.22 (PG 36.653A).
28. Gregory of Nyssa *Great Catechesis* 25 (PG 45.65, 68).
29. Rufinus *Commentary on the Apostles' Creed* 16.
30. Augustine *On the Trinity* 13.18 (PL 42.1028). See 12–13 (PL 42.1026–27).

This interpretation, namely, of the devil's abuse of the power he had by "a certain justice," survived well into the medieval period.[31] It was even the theme of the eighteenth-century Oberammergau passion play written by Ferdinand Rosner, which reached full production before the season of 1980 but at the last minute was not staged. The village council probably decided that modern audiences were not prepared for such activity on the devil's part, and that the charge that the text was anti-Jewish (which they did not believe) would not be met by the substitution.[32]

In defense of the church fathers it should be said that the New Testament pits Christ against the devil from the temptation in the desert to the passion (see Mark 1:12–13 par., especially Luke 4:13: "And when the devil had ended every temptation he departed from him until an opportune time"; and John 13:27: "After [Judas] took the morsel, Satan entered him. So Jesus said to him, 'What you are going to do, do quickly'"). An important text in this theorizing process was Hebrews 2:14–15:

> Now since the children [spoken of in Isa. 8:18, just quoted] share in blood and flesh, he likewise shared in them, that through death he might destroy the one who has the power of death, that is, the devil, and free those who through fear of death had been subject to slavery all their life.

First John 4:4 was influential, too, with its promise that believers of the Johannine community have conquered every spirit that does not acknowledge Jesus Christ come in the flesh, "for the one who is in you is greater than the one who is in the world" (cf. "the prince of this world," John 12:31).

Even as the church fathers discuss the incarnation as itself redemptive, they have in mind the deed done by God out of love for sinful humanity that expresses the love. For them, the redemption proceeds from earth to heaven as praise to God, not only from heaven to earth as reconciliation. The value of Jesus' death on the cross is that it is a universal expiation of human sins and sinfulness by Christ, the new Adam. "Atonement" is the English word for the Latin-derived "expiation." God and humanity are "at one," reconciled by the divine acceptance of the life thus offered. The fathers do not think of God as having tolerated a cruelty by countenancing the death of the Son. That is because their concentration is not so much on the human drama of Calvary as on Christ's blood as symbolic of his self-giving. A scouring of patristic sources yields the repetition of the biblical phrases that describe his voluntary self-offering: "[Christ] himself has borne our sins in his body on the tree of the cross" (1 Peter 2:24). "He is the lamb who takes away the sin of the world" (John 1:29). "Him who did not know sin, God

---

31. J. Rivière, in *Le Dogme de la Redemption au debut du moyen-âge* (Paris: J. Vrin, 1934), 53–59, gives a lengthy catalog of pseudo-Augustinian sermons that kept the idea alive.

32. See Saul S. Friedman, *The Oberammergau Passion Play: A Lance against Civilization* (Carbondale, Ill.: Southern Illinois University Press, 1984), 164.

has made to be sin for us" (2 Cor. 5:21). "God, by sending his own son in the likeness of our sinful nature and to deal with sin, has passed judgment against sin within that very nature" (Rom. 8:3). There is no hint of propitiating the divine wrath in these texts because the temple sacrifice on which Christ's death is patterned does not know the idea. The blood purifies the offerers, reconciles them to God, prepares them against the day of just judgment. It does not placate God.

The Popular Liturgies on Redemption by the Cross

The patristic texts marshaled above tell us how the learned were thinking about the mystery of redemption. But how were ordinary people praying it? The hymn of Melito, bishop of Sardis, in his long homily *On the Pasch* is one indication of the quality of sung prayer in the province of Asia around 175. It says in part, with Christ as the speaker:

"For I am your forgiveness,
    I am the Pascha of salvation,
    I am the lamb slain for you;
    I am your ransom,
    I am your *life*,
    I am your *resurrection*,
    I am your *light*,
    I am your salvation,
I am your king.
I will raise you up by my right hand;
I am leading you up to the heights of heaven;
    there I will show you the Father from ages past. . . ."

It is he . . . .
who was hung upon a tree,
who was buried in the earth,
who was raised from the dead
    and went up to the heights of heaven.
who sits at the Father's right hand,
who has the power to save all,
through whom the Father did everything from the beginning to all
    ages.[33]

The beautiful poetry of this homily is marred by the claim that the law was marvelous before it was made void by the gospel and, worse still, by a

---

33. *Melito of Sardis on Pascha*, Greek text ed. and trans. Stuart George Hall (Oxford, 1979), 60–61; cf. the translation of Lucien Deiss, *Springtime of the Liturgy: Liturgical Texts of the First Four Centuries*, trans. M. J. O'Connell (Collegeville, Minn.: Liturgical Press, 1979), 109.

sustained attack on "Israel" for killing the Lord that had done nothing but good to it.[34] This kind of invective was probably more influential with the masses than any theological developments of the mystery of redemption. The eucharistic prayer of Hippolytus of Rome (ca. 215) is neutral in language when describing the stark events of Calvary:

> He it is who accomplishes your will and who, in order to obtain a holy people for you, spread out his hands while he suffered in order to deliver from sufferings those who believe in you. When he handed himself over to suffering in order to destroy death and break the chains of the devil, to trample hell underfoot, enlighten the just, establish the covenant, and show forth his resurrection, he took bread, gave thanks, and said. . . .[35]

The roots of the Syriac anaphora of Addai and Mari go back to the third century. This eucharistic prayer speaks of "this great mystery of the passion, death, and resurrection of our Lord Jesus Christ." The church is described as "redeemed by the precious blood of your Christ, offering up [praise, honor, thanksgiving and adoration]."[36] In the Maronite liturgy called "The Third Anaphora of the Apostle Peter," which has affinities with the previous one, a memorial is made of the Lord's passion, beginning: "In the night in which you were betrayed to the Jews. . . ." Christ is called a spiritual Lamb who descended from heaven, "to be an expiatory sacrifice for all."[37] The gift of life is asked for through his "life-giving death," with which is coupled "and resurrection." In general, the early liturgies in all the languages speak of Jesus' "sufferings" as a sacrifice without specifying them and refer in a single phrase to his resurrection from the dead, return to heaven, and glorious coming. Some will speak of the offering at the meal as a "spiritual and unbloody sacrifice." Mention of Christ's body broken and his blood shed is frequent, deriving from the New Testament liturgies, but without further elaboration.

The earliest complete liturgy to have survived, that found in book 8 of the *Apostolic Constitutions* (ca. 375), is Antiochene in origin. Uncharacteristically, it has these details from the Gospels and Acts:

> And when he had achieved all these things [in his public ministry], he was seized by the hands of lawless so-called priests and high-priests and a lawless people, by betrayal through one who was diseased with wickedness. He suffered many things at their hands, endured all kinds of indignity by Your permission, and was handed over to Pilate the governor. The Judge was judged

34. *Melito of Sardis on Pascha*, 21, 41–57.
35. *The Treatise on the Apostolic Tradition of St. Hippolytus of Rome* 4.7–8 (trans. B. S. Easton, New York, 1934). Cf. the later edition of Gregory Dix, ed., (London: SPCK, 1968).
36. R. C. D. Jasper and G. J. Cuming, *Prayers of the Eucharist: Early and Reformed* (New York: Oxford University Press, 1980), 28.
37. Ibid., 30–31.

and the Savior was condemned; he who cannot suffer was nailed to the cross; he who was immortal by nature died, and the giver of life was buried.[38]

The liturgy of John Chrysostom may well have gone back to his lifetime (d. 407). It is the principal rite for most of the Eastern churches, Orthodox and Catholic. Both it and the Roman canon of circa 400 have no details about Christ's sufferings and death.[39] They speak of his death, resurrection, and return in glory in a single phrase, and feature the everlasting life that Jesus Christ won for us by these holy mysteries.

The hymn over the paschal candle in the Easter Vigil that sings praise to Christ the Light, the *Exultet,* tells of Jesus Christ, our Lord,

> who has paid the debt of the eternal Father for us and, with his sacred blood, has erased the debt of the ancient crime.
>
> For this is the paschal feast in which the true Lamb is immolated, whose blood sanctifies the doorposts of the faithful. . . . This is the night in which Christ broke the chains of death and arose from the netherworld as conqueror. There would have been no advantage for us in being born unless we had been redeemed. . . .
>
> O unspeakable tenderness of your love: to ransom the slave, you have handed over the Son!
>
> O, yes!—the necessary sin of Adam, since the death of Christ has destroyed it!
>
> O happy fault, since it obtained such and so great a Redeemer![40]

In What Sense Did Jesus "Suffer for Our Sins"?

It was the conviction of all the early church writers—bishops and nonbishops alike—that by the shedding of his blood on the cross Christ had achieved the expiation of universal human sin. The human race had been sanctified, at least at root, when the divine Word became a member of it in the person of Jesus Christ. What had been achieved radically for all became a reality in the lives of believers by their appropriating his incarnation, death, and resurrection. They expressed their faith by accepting baptism and living the eucharistic life of the church. How others might receive the benefits of this redemption the early writers did not know, but they were convinced

38. Ibid., 76.
39. Ibid., 88–92, 118–24.
40. *Missale Romanum, Benedictio Cerei* ("Easter Proclamation"), Easter Vigil. The similarities of phrasing between this hymn and the writings of Ambrose are so many and so close that Dom Bernard Capelle could designate it, "L'Exultet' pascal, oeuvre de saint Ambrose," *Miscellanea G. Mercati,* 1 (Rome, 1946), 228. From ca. 1000 onward, some expressions were removed from it in certain manuscripts as too optimistic about the conquest of sin, especially the pontifical of Mainz and those used in places influenced by the Cluniac reform. L. Richard, *Mystery,* 173, n. 96, gives the citations in Ambrose's writings that make Capelle's case.

that the whole human race was somehow the recipient of this benefit.[41] They believed without exception that Adam's sin had brought death to our race and that Christ, the second Adam, had made reparation for this sin and its effects. This he did in the first place by freely giving his own life. Thus far they were agreed.

When they spoke of Christ's death as a penalty or curse, they based themselves on Paul's rhetorical declaration that Christ "became a curse for us" (see Deut. 21:23) to "ransom us from the curse of the law" (see 27:26). This occurs in his letter to unspecified Galatian churches at 3:13 of that epistle. Paul's citation from the Torah in the first instance is talking about the condition of those who willfully disobey Mosaic law. By omitting any part of it they bring a curse upon themselves, says Deuteronomy. In the second instance Deuteronomy describes the condition of one who dies by crucifixion; more accurately, it is the punishment itself that the law declares "accursèd." The church fathers used the quotation from Galatians in Paul's double sense, slippery as such a colorful figure is in the service of a cosmic theology: Christ bore the sins of humanity by accepting the curse of death leveled at it for its sins (implicit in Gen. 3:19c), but not the curse that will be delivered to sinners on the last day. Acutely aware of Paul's statement that "God made him to be sin who knew no sin" (2 Cor. 5:21), they nonetheless confined "sin" in this sinless one to the penalty for sin, death.

Some statements about Christ's sufferings and death in lieu of ours are important and should be quoted here. They represent a turn away from the penalty for sin, death, in the direction of the sufferings themselves that Jesus underwent. Eusebius of Caesarea, best known as a church historian and Constantine's theologian at the Council of Nicaea, wrote:

> Not only did the Lamb of God endure sufferings and punishments for us. . . . but he suffered torments and tortures he did not deserve. It is we who deserved them because of our sins. He became for us the cause of our sins' being forgiven, for he accepted in our place the death, the blows and the disgrace we deserved. He transferred them to himself and took upon himself the curse that was rightly ours, thus becoming a curse for us. What was he, except the substitute for our life?[42]

41. Augustine of Hippo is the notable exception. He thought that a consequence of the fact that no human will could determine the divine will was that the will of God predetermined all free human choices. This led him into his theory of double predestination. Pressed to answer how a gracious God could predestine anyone to hell, he said that it was necessary in order to manifest the divine wrath and to demonstrate the divine power (*A Literal Commentary on Genesis* 11.8; *PL* 34.434). So sure was Augustine of his position that he consistently took 1 Tim. 2:4, "God wills all to be saved and come to a knowledge of the truth," to mean "wills all to be saved who will be saved." He was followed in this opinion by few contemporaries. The Council of Orange (529) adopted his teaching on grace almost in its entirety but passed over this part in respectful silence. Trent (1547) took special pains not to teach the predestination of anyone to hell (DS, 1567).

42. Eusebius *Proof of the Gospel* 11.1 (*PG* 22.724D).

Cyril of Alexandria says that the Son of God accepted death, the penalty for our sins, but he also calls him "the just equivalent of our life."[43] For Gregory of Nazianzus Jesus offered himself "in the place of humanity."[44] This claim of equation or substitution of Christ for us would cause considerable confusion in subsequent ages. Augustine was clear on the point in a regrettably titled treatise: "He had no sins of his own but he bore ours," which could mean death, the penalty of our sins, but could as well mean the sufferings that should have been ours.[45]

The solidarity of the whole redeemed race, potentially the body of the incarnate Word, is central to the conception of Christ's union with us in his death. It is easy to see how later generations unfamiliar with the biblical and patristic idea of a humanity in solidarity with Christ could interpret him crassly as "the substitute for our life." His expiation is ours, the fathers taught, if we consciously and willingly become members of his body. It is not accomplished by accepting the assurance that "he died in our place" with the understanding that the torments he endured should have been ours for our sins, hence no punishment can be exacted for our forgiven sins. Christ endured death, the penalty of sin, for us. He did not take upon himself the guilt of our sins or absorb all the punishment that that guilt might deserve.

From Repetition to Exploration of the Mystery

In adopting the reparation achieved by temple sacrifice as the paradigm for Jesus' death, Christians of the early centuries praised both the gracious deed of God that wrought the incarnation—God's Word become human—and the deed of Jesus, a member of our race, that redeemed us. In recognizing that the debt humanity owes to God was paid by Christ's willing self-sacrifice, they did not probe deeply into the way it operated. It was enough for them to repeat, out of the biblical sources, that he was led as a lamb to the slaughter and obtained thereby remission for the sins of the world. Sacrifice was a way of expiation in the Israelite and pagan worlds. God had both initiated and accepted this supreme sacrifice. There were problems, of course. In seeing prefigurings of Jesus' sacrificial death in the paschal lamb, the scapegoat, the sacrifice of Isaac, and the Maccabean martyrs, the Christian fathers placed this sacrifice in a unique category. "He offered himself

43. Cyril of Alexandria *On Adoration and Worship in Spirit and Truth* 3 (PG 68.293D–296A); *That Christ Is One* (PG 75.1341C).

44. Gregory of Nazianzus *On the Coming of the Lord* (PG 36.1165B), probably the work of Basil of Seleucia.

45. Augustine *Against the Jews* 5.6 (PL 42.54). He says much the same writing *Against Faustus the Manichean* 14.4 (PL 42.297): "Christ took [on himself] our punishment but without guilt, that he might remove our guilt and even bring to an end our punishment."

according to our nature," Ambrose wrote, "in order to accomplish a work beyond our nature."[46] Augustine put it in his familiar epigrammatic way: "He remained one with God to whom he offered [this sacrifice of peace]; he united in himself those for whom he offered it; he himself was the one offering; and he was what was offered."[47]

Sometimes these writers saw Christ's sacrifice as so transcending that of the temple or Mosaic law generally that they felt they had to make a point of the latter's crassness. They described temple sacrifice as mere toleration on God's part lest Israel fall into idolatry. The former was an offering of birds and beasts but this one was the sacrifice of a human life. The contrast, of course, led them into new difficulties as they tried to explain how God, who could not abide human sacrifice in Israel, could approve this one. The commonest way out of dealing literally with the symbol of blood—their initial difficulty—was to stigmatize all former sacrifice as "carnal" (surely a redundancy) but to hymn Jesus' death as a death in the Spirit. What went before was shadow; this was substance. Gregory the Great wades in directly, without blinking. He says that only a human would do to be offered for human beings. A sinless man, at the same time, could best serve as victim to purify the race from its sins.[48]

Not all patristic explanation of Christ's sacrifice was embarrassed by its Israelite antecedents. Some writers could see that there had to be a relation between what went before and what was happening now, that Christ's death as sacrifice would be meaningless for the church unless it had its setting in the sacrifices of the temple and before. The temple was no more and its priesthood was no longer active. The Jewish people now saw the fulfillment of "what was hidden under the veil of signs" (to use the phrase of Pope Leo I)[49] in the study of Torah and fidelity to its precepts. The Christians looked to the sacrifice of the true Lamb as taking the place of all previous victims. The church's present eucharistic sacrifice was seen as making manifest in symbol what had once been accomplished in history.

So far as we can tell, the West continued to teach through the sermons of Augustine for a full six centuries after his death in 430. Preachers repeatedly presented the even more popular teaching of Pope Gregory I (d. 604). The bishop of Seville, Isidore (d. 636), put much of the doctrine of Augustine in the jejune form of lists and in that dress it survived into the Carolingian period and well beyond. Bede and Alcuin, England's great teachers, and the "apostles of the nations" like Boniface, Denis, Willibrord, Augustinus, and

46. Ambrose On the Sacrament of the Lord's Incarnation 6.54 (PL 16.832).
47. Augustine On the Trinity 4.14, 19 (PL 42.901).
48. See Gregory's Moral Lessons on Job 17.30, 46 (PL 76.32–33).
49. See Leo's Sermon 50.7 (PL 54.341); he writes: "That which remained hidden under the veil of signs in the one Jewish Temple is now celebrated everywhere, manifestly and openly, in a sacrament, by the piety of all peoples."

Ansgar simply brought with them the Western theology sketched above. The East, for its part, conveyed the concept of redemption as divinization basically unchanged.

It was the task of Anselm, archbishop of Canterbury (d. 1109), an Italian monk of the French abbey of Bec, to hammer out a redemptive theory that was both new and would prove lasting in the West. Anselm lived a thoroughgoing life of faith, was one of the "new men" in his dependence on intellect, and was Augustinian in method if slightly more sanguine than Augustine about the possibilities of a "darkened intellect." He wrote his *Cur Deus Homo?* ("Why the God-Man?") in dialogue form, in part to prove to Jews and Muslims that the doctrine of a crucified Son of God was not an absurdity.[50] For this purpose he adopted principles he thought they could accept: the justice and mercy of God, the reconciliation of an alienated world to God, and suffering and death as realities foreign to God but evidently necessary to restore humanity to the divine friendship. Anselm started from a vantage point of faith but sought understanding of what he termed the "necessary reasons" for the incarnation. He accepted as axiomatic, as a person of the eleventh century could, that something was known of the nature of God, that the human plight was widely realized (he called the human race "altogether ruined"), and that God had overcome sin and death on humanity's behalf.

The ingenious argument Anselm mounted goes as follows. The primordial human sin and its consequence, the sins of humanity, have derogated from the divine *honor* (by which he means the essence of godhead). For this, reparation must be made to God's glory, which is simply God's infinite greatness or deity. The latter cannot be detracted from, least of all "injured" after the manner of human lèse-majesté. Anselm would have thought such a notion absurd. But since humans owe to God an acknowledgment of the divine greatness, the cosmic imbalance caused by sin must be restored. God, in an exercise of the divine mercy, could obviously have achieved a reconciliation with humanity by a sheer act of will, declaring all human sin forgiven. But the infinite justice of God had also to be taken into account. "Anselm's problem was to provide 'necessary reasons' why, given the nature of God and the straits in which humanity found itself, the dilemma could not be solved in any other way [than by the incarnation]."[51] Knowing well the biblical tradition of Christ's death as sacrifice and his blood as ransom from sin, and also the theology of deification, he nonetheless went in a fresh direction.

Satisfaction was due to God. In light of the infinity of godhead, only God could provide it. By "satisfaction" Anselm did not mean payment or repayment but the correction of an omission. In his *Proslogion* Anselm had pre-

50. *PL* 158.359–432. An excellent translation, "Why God Became Man," accompanied by an expository introduction occurs in *A Scholastic Miscellany: Anselm to Ockham,* ed. Eugene R. Fairweather (New York: Macmillan, 1970), 100–83.

51. Gerard S. Sloyan, *Jesus: Redeemer and Divine Word* (Wilmington, Del.: Glazier, 1989).

viously described God as "one than whom nothing greater can be thought." A sin against God is an offense than which no greater can be thought because of the magnitude of the one offended. Hence only infinite satisfaction will serve as restoration of the balance. At the same time, since the one who derogated from the divine glory was the human race in solidarity with Adam, this creature had to make creaturely satisfaction. A finite humanity had brought about an infinite offense but was not capable of infinite satisfaction.

When humanity praises God or is repentant for sin, this is but the acknowledgment of God's infinity proper to finitude. The cosmic balance is merely observed in this repentance; the previous imbalance is not restored. Human sin denies to God the glory owing to deity from creaturehood.

> Something is lacking, so to say, on God's side. Hence only the action of God infinite can restore the balance. At the same time there must be a human reconciler because there was a human offender. This leaves the necessity of human salvation initiated and carried through at all points by God, yet at the same time a thoroughly human work.[52]

The medieval monk and bishop solved a problem he thought to be fairly self-evident by positing the necessity of a *Deus-homo,* a God who is human without any compromise of deity or humanity. The only way out of the dilemma posed by the rebellion of the free human creature was by the incarnation of the Son of God, who would freely make recompense to God by offering his human life. In that way, the divine justice would be satisfied and human responsibility preserved. Anselm called the satisfaction made to God by the incarnation "necessary" only if it is understood that God acts under no compulsion.

> Now this necessity is nothing but [God's] changeless *honor,* which [God] has [*a se*] and not from another, and on that account it is improper to call it necessity. Nevertheless, let us say that it is necessary—on account of [God's] own changelessness, for God's goodness to complete what was undertaken for humanity, even though the whole good that [God] does is of grace. . . .

> Is it not right for humanity [*homo*] which, by its sin, stole itself from God as completely as possible, to make satisfaction by giving itself to God as fully as it can?. . . But nothing that a human being can suffer for God's honor, freely and not as an obligation, is more bitter or harder than death. Nor can anyone give himself more fully to God than when there is self-surrender to death for God's honor.[53]

52. Ibid., 101.
53. Anselm *Cur Deus Homo?* 2.6 (ET, Fairweather, *Scholastic Miscellany,* 150, adapted); 2.11 (ET, 161).

There is nothing of feudalism in Anselm's theorizing, as has often been charged. For him, sin against God is nothing like wounding the honor of a knight or noble. It is in a unique order since there is no one like God. Neither is his theory to be likened to a commercial transaction, since no sum is paid or received. A life is offered by a divine-human person. God sees the fittingness of the offer and accepts it. The one major flaw of the theory is that it bases everything on the demand of divine justice, whereas Scripture presents human salvation as a matter of the divine mercy or gratuity. Anselm's response would probably be that the biblical authors did not probe the divine nature sufficiently, for if they had they would have come to a conclusion quite like his.

Abelard (d. 1142) was not satisfied with the retention of a place for the devil in a theology of the redemption, even though Anselm had set aside the Augustinian theory of the devil's abuse of power. He taught that Jesus joined us to himself by love and by his painful passion revealed his love for us, soliciting ours in return.

> A person also becomes more just after the passion of Christ than before, that is to say, loving the Lord more, because the benefit accomplished arouses still more to love than the mere hope of that benefit.[54]

Abelard retained the traditional notion of Christ's merit as valid before God, foreseen and prepared beforehand for our benefit. But he was accused, even in his own time, of so stressing the example Christ's passion set for virtue and the incentive it provided for love that he overlooked the "objective" character of the traditional doctrine of redemptive incarnation and the sacrifice of the cross.

Thomas Aquinas (d. 1274) created a powerful synthesis of the Western theology that had preceded him. He did not treat the redemption separately but made it part of his consideration of the incarnation—which was basically the way God "rescues us from our wretched condition." Thomas found the incarnation eminently "appropriate" (*conveniens*)—not necessary, in the sense that the restoration of human nature could not have been accomplished without it, but in the sense that it was required for the better and more expeditious attainment of God's purpose.[55] He taught that mortal sin has "a kind of infinity" (*quandam infinitatem*), not that it was an infinite offense.[56] Duns Scotus went further, saying that to call the human merits of

---

54. *On Romans* 3.2 (*PL* 178.836B). Cols. 105–6 (bottom) report his submission to theological condemnation, professing the traditional teaching that "the Son of God became incarnate to free us from the slavery of sin and the yoke of the devil, and to open the way to eternal life by his death."

55. *Summa theologiae* 3.9.1, a.2, *responsio;* cf. 3, q. 46, a.3 ("Was There a Better Way to Free Humanity Than the Passion of Christ?"), where five reasons are given why we were more fittingly (*convenientius*) delivered by this means.

56. Ibid., a.2 *ad* 2.

Christ infinite was exaggeration, for despite the union of the eternal Word with Jesus' humanity, they were still the merits of human acts.[57] Thomas, for his part, situated the merits of salvation that Christ won for us by his passion in the "grace of headship" that God gave to Christ when his humanity was joined to the Word. They were so great that they were sufficient for every human purpose.

When Thomas speaks of the death of Christ he sometimes calls it "a certain sacrifice" and sometimes "a true sacrifice" without explaining the difference. Perhaps the indefinite adjective "certain" describes his death understood as a rite. The "principal sacrifice" of Christ for Thomas was interior self-offering in his passion made voluntarily. This was eminently pleasing to God because it originated in the greatest love. "It is therefore clear that Christ's passion was a true sacrifice."[58] The Thomistic explanation of how the redemptive sacrifice of the cross "worked" retained all the traditional elements of ransom and freedom from slavery to sin and the devil, but it exorcised completely the themes of a payment of ransom to the devil and that of his abuse of power. The perfection of Thomas's argumentation came with his identification of the obedient human spirit of Christ in going to his death as that which, above all, pleased his heavenly Father. Sinful men were the authors of his death: the leaders of the Jewish people, not the uneducated (to whom Thomas attributed only a small measure of guilt for compliance), the Roman governor, and the soldiery. But behind these agents stood the whole of sinful humanity and also Satan. As for Jesus himself, he gave up his life in obedience to God (John 10:18) and in complete freedom by not preventing something that could have been prevented.[59]

Thomas devoted three questions of the Third Part of his *Summa theologiae* to the resurrection of Christ and one each to his ascension, his sitting at the Father's right hand, and his power as judge. He viewed the resurrection as a necessary "complement to our salvation," already achieved by the cross, and as "the cause of our own resurrection through the power of [Jesus'] union with the Word."[60]

An important question that must be left for another chapter is how the popular piety of the Middle Ages removed the center of attention from the fact of Jesus' voluntary and obedient death and placed it on the circumstances that attended it, the human agents, and chiefly the human anguish Jesus experienced in his tortured state.[61] This move left Western theology—largely Anselmian—unchanged. The same was true of liturgical forms. Both

57. *Book 3 Commenting on Peter Lombard's "Opinions,"* d. 19, 9.unica, n.4.
58. *Summa theologiae* 3.9.48, a.3, *responsio;* cf. 9.46, a.10, *responsio.*
59. Ibid., 9.47 ("On the Cause of Christ's Passion"), aa.1–6.
60. Ibid., 3.53.1, *responsio ad* 5; 56.1, *responsio ad* 1.
61. See 3.9.46, aa.5 and 6, where Jesus' physical sufferings are cataloged, without elaboration, and his mental anguish is declared greater still because he suffered "for all sins at once" (9.46.6, *responsio ad* 4).

were "cool" media, in Marshall McLuhan's terms. Popular piety centered on the passion was "hot."

Martin Luther's thought is indicative of this influence. He conceived human redemption as the outcome of a conflict between the curse of God—the divine wrath—and the divine blessing. He made the opposition sharper than anything found in previous Western theory. There a satisfaction was achieved that won remission of punishment in response to a demand for punishment. This was all too neat and rational for Luther's taste. In his sharply dualistic outlook, God wins a decisive victory over the curse and the wrath. The love of God breaks through the wrath. Humanity has nothing to do with the victory but accept it as God's victory. Luther feared that the idea of the sanctification of humanity by the incarnation was the opening of the door to redemption as a human work, as something that could be laid hold of by human power. But the human race was absolutely powerless in this matter. All its works were sin. The only thing it could do was gratefully accept the outpouring of divine love made manifest in the cross.[62]

62. The core of Luther's teaching on God's gracious action in redeeming humankind is probably to be found in his *Commentary on St. Paul's Epistle to the Galatians*. See the translation of P. S. Watson (London: J. Clarke, 1953).

Plate 1: Face of Christ at Center of Cross. Ravenna: S. Apollinaire in Classe (6th c.).

Plate 2: The Crucifixion (detail). Duccio, Italian, 14th c.

Plate 3: Crucifixion. Lucas Cranach the Elder, German, 16th c.

Plate 4: Christ Expiring on the Cross. Theodor Boyermanns, Flemish, 17th
c. Metropolitan Museum of Art, New York. Religious News Service Photo.

Plate 5: Crucifixion Icon. School of Novgorad. Russian Museum,
Leningrad.

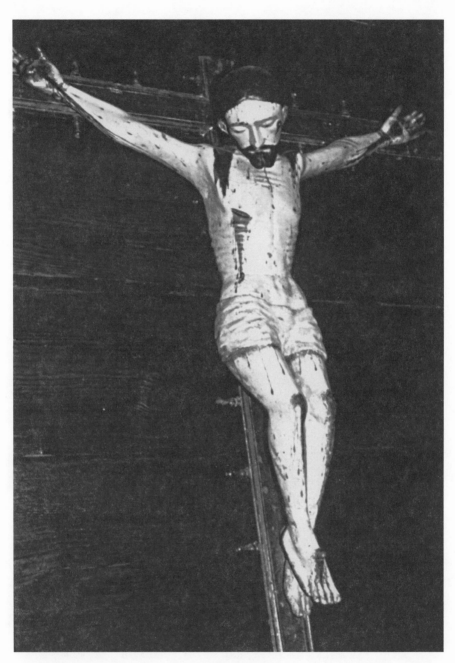

Plate 6: Crucifix, c. 1650. Michodean, Mexico. Denver Art Museum.

Plate 7: Crucifixion. Sadao Watanabe, Japanese, 20th c.

Plate 8: Le Crucifix (1943). Marc Chagall. Vatican Museum.

Plate 9. Headpiece to "Apparition": Christ on the Cross (1939). Georges Rouault.

Plate 10: 7 Last Words. Sandra Bowden. Mixed media.

CHAPTER FIVE

The Popular Passion Piety
of the Catholic West

The first ten centuries of Christianity went largely unmarked by devotion to Jesus' flagellation and crowning with thorns, his progress toward the hill of Calvary (Latin, "skull place"; Aramaic *gûlgaltā'*; akin to Hebrew *golgōlet*, "skull"), and his sufferings on the cross. Paul had written that baptism unites believers to the death of Christ (Rom. 6:3–6), and several places in the New Testament propose his sufferings as an example (1 Peter 1:21; Col. 1:24; 1 Cor. 2:2; 4:16; 11:1). In the late first and early second century, the writings of Clement of Rome and Ignatius of Antioch, which were long considered to be Sacred Scripture, asked Christians to keep Christ's passion before their eyes, to be united with him, and to be nailed to the cross.[1] The same Ignatius counseled the necessity of imitating Christ in his passion.[2] The various Acts of the Martyrs from the second century through the fourth present these witnesses to the faith as patterning their acceptance of torment on the sufferings of Christ. Beginning in 333 with the chronicle of the anonymous pilgrim of Bordeaux, accounts of pilgrimage to the so-called holy places testify to a route in Jerusalem the pilgrims followed from one Constantinian edifice to the other.[3] This does not have the character of a *via crucis* or a *via dolorosa*, however, tracing the steps of Jesus from Pilate's judgment seat to the knob of earth where he died.

Melito of Sardis (fl. ca. 170) in his Easter homily is the first Christian writer extant to engage in graphic detail, deploring the cruel event in these words:

> Listen while you tremble before him on whose account the earth trembles:
>> He that suspended the earth was himself suspended.
>> He that fixed the heavens was fixed [with nails].

1. *1 Clem.* 2.1; Ign. *Phil.* 3.3; *Smyrn.* 1.1; 4.2; 5.3.
2. *Eph.* 9.1; 10.3; *Magn.* 5.2; *Rom.* 4.9; 6.3.
3. P. Geyer, ed., *Itinera hierosolymitana, saec. IV–VIII*, CSEL 39 (Vienna, 1898), 22–23, 71–77.

He that supported the earth was supported on a tree.
The Master was exposed to shame,
God put to death![4]

It has been theorized that the reason there were no pictorial representations of the cross or the crucified Jesus in the early centuries was that his manner of death would be repulsive to candidates for baptism. There is no solid proof for this deduction. The Basilidean Gnostics, it is known, denied his death and some think this denial was influential.[5] The verbal descriptions of the way he died, however, would seem to tell against the theory that second-century catechesis suppressed it.

The Cross in Early Inscriptions, Carvings, Sketches

Earlier than Melito's hymn a Christian inscription in Aramaic found at Palmyra in central Syria contains two crosses: "To him whose name is blessed forever! Made by Salmon, son of Nesa . . . for his salvation and those of his children. In the month of Nisan of the Year X447X [134 C.E.]."[6] There is no known punctuation mark in the shape of an X. The probability of its representing the cross of Christ is heightened by the fact that the same X-shaped cross is found in other Syrian monuments (X is also the Greek letter *chi,* the first letter in *Christós*).

A red jasper amulet carved on two sides, found at Gaza in Syria in 1867, shows a naked man with arms outstretched, a halo around his head, flanked by a man and a woman, their arms folded in prayer.[7] The inscription on the reverse has not been deciphered. Two other gems of carnelian, one from the second and the other from the third century, depict a naked Christ with arms extended. The earlier one was found at Costanza on the Black Sea in Rumania and is in the British Museum. The figure of Jesus has a crossbar in the shape of a pole behind his shoulders; six small figures whom he dwarfs stand on a pediment on either side of him; the acrostic *IXTHVC,* in reverse for signet purposes, flanks his head (the initial letters of "Jesus Christ, Son of God, Savior," in Greek spelling "fish"). The other carnelian stamp or die is of the third century and depicts a haloed Jesus, arms rigidly outstretched, standing on a small platform on a stake half his height. Again, twelve evenly divided figures stand well below him on a thin bar supported by a lamb and by the last two letters of a reversed inscription that has begun under his arms: *EHCOXPICTOC,* "Ieso Christos."

These small carved gems were clearly owned by wealthy Christians who multiplied their message of faith in the cross in wax. Of another sort is the

4. O. Perler, trans., *Sur la Pâque* (Paris, 1966), 116.
5. See Irenaeus *Against the Heresies* 1.15.
6. H. Leclercq, O.S.B., "Croix et Crucifix," *DACL* 3/2 (Paris, 1914), 3048.
7. Ibid., 3049–50.

much better known graffito found on a wall of the imperial palace on the Palatine Hill in Rome in 1856, one among many scratched there in what may have been, according to another graffito, a *paedagogium* or hall of the pages.[8] In this crude line drawing a *T*-cross is sketched on a horizontal line depicting the earth with another bar against the buttocks of a standing human figure, reversed, arms outstretched, whose head is that of an ass. A smaller human figure stands below the cross to the left, one hand upraised in a gesture that may be veneration. The head of the ass looks over its human shoulder at the devotee, identified by name in the taunting phrase: "Alexamenos worships [his] God." Elsewhere in the same house there was discovered in 1870, this time in Latin rather than Greek, the possible response of the person jeered at: "*Alexamenos fidelis*," that is, "Alexamenos, a [Christian] believer." Paleographers are inclined to date these graffiti to the first half of the third century, a period when pagans are known to have employed the taunt involving a god with an ass's head against Christians, used also against Jews. An animal's head on a human torso in pre-Christian times was a common depiction of the absurdity of another's worship. The technical term *fidelis* and the human body on the *tau* (T-shaped) cross specify the graffito as directed against a Christian.

Crosses in the catacombs are relatively rare, some twenty or so having been found in these underground cemeteries in the form + or T, usually accompanying a name such as Rufina, Victoria (both in Greek spelling), or Gaudentia.[9] Tertullian in Latin and Origen in Greek twenty-five years later, both in the third century, spoke of the custom Christians had of tracing a T on their foreheads in self-dedication to the crucified Christ before beginning any prayer or work.[10] The crosses in the catacombs are sometimes disguised by the twin hooks beneath as anchors, a symbol that would not be read as signifying salvation by the cross if there were not fish displayed nearby. Memorial shafts found in Asia Minor show a cross with arms of equal length or a shorter shaft above the crossbar inscribed within a circle or concentric circles. These artifacts and inscriptions—and surely there were many more—convey that both the cross and the corpus of Christ were a commonplace before the Constantinian settlement, even though outnumbered by representations of fish, shepherds, and doves. Religious people "who traced the forehead with a cross . . . at every entry and departure . . . before washing, at table . . . upon retiring" was a desciption Tertullian had for his fellow believers, while Clement of Alexandria spoke of the cross as "typical of the symbol of the Lord."[11]

The commonest types of Christian crosses were the following: (1) *decussata* in the form of an *X* or number ten, *decussis* from the Greek *deka*, later

8. Ibid., 3051.
9. Ibid., 3056–59.
10. Tertullian *On the Soldier's Crown*, chap. 3 (PL 2.80); cf. Origen *Selections on Ezekiel* chap. 9 (PG 13.801).
11. *Apology* 16 (PL 1.365–66); Clement of Alexandria *Miscellanies* 6 (PG 9.305).

known as the cross of St. Andrew; (2) *commissa* ("placed there") or *patibulata* from *patibulum*, "crossbar," in a T-form; (3) *immissa* or *capitata* ("capped"), the familiar Latin cross with a short shaft above the point of juncture; (4) *quadrata*, or Greek cross with arms of equal length; (5) *gammata* in the form of the capital letter Γ (*gamma*), *g*; four of these going clockwise, their foot upon a central point, form a swastika (from Sanskrit, meaning "be well"); (6) *ansata*, the Egyptian hieroglyph *ankh*, ☥, standing for the future life; (7) *florida*, a cross scarcely disguised by ornamentation such as flowers.[12] Some of these had ancient histories in design far removed from the instrument of torture used by the Romans. All the above forms of crosses served as conventional representations of the way Jesus died.

Devotion to the Cross in the Age of Constantine

The Constantinian decree of freedom of religion of 313 and the discovery of the "true cross" in Jerusalem by the emperor's mother Helena in 326 resulted in some important iconographic changes. Constantine reportedly introduced the labarum or tracing of the cross in chrism on shields for battle and depictions of himself holding a cross in hand. A notable innovation was the striking of coins throughout the empire bearing the monogram ℞ (for *Iēsoũs Christós*) and *XP* (*chi rho*, the first two letters of Greek *Christós*), as well as ☩ and T, all of them later circled or garlanded. The encircled T survived on imperial coins into the Byzantine period.[13] Eusebius of Caesarea tells of the emperor's erecting the sign of the Lord's passion "decorated with gold and precious stones" in an eminent place in the palace.[14]

Two church historians of the time, Aurelius Victor and Sozomenos, report that Constantine abolished the punishment of crucifixion, although another, Firmicus Maternus, writing in 334 and again in 357, describes it as still in force.[15] Constantine's abolition of the practice of breaking prisoners' legs seems well attested, and this may be code language for his bringing crucifixion to an end, at least in effect. By the beginning of the fifth century, according to the testimony of Augustine, it had ceased being administered.[16] It was not officially outlawed, however, until the Code of Theodosius (438). Whatever the case, the encircled cross and *chi-rho* began to multiply after 350, especially on sarcophagi, through the emperor's open employment of the cross symbol.

Cyril, bishop of Jerusalem, in his instructions to catechumens of 348 or 349, speaks of pieces of wood of the true cross as having been distributed

---

12. Leclercq, *DACL*, 3/2.3061–62.
13. Ibid., 3062–64.
14. Eusebius *Life of Constantine* 3.49 (PG 20.1109).
15. Leclercq, *DACL*, 3/2.3064.
16. Augustine *On the Psalms XXXVI* 2.4 (PL 36.366).

throughout the world. By the end of that century, Ambrose, Rufinus, and other bishops had heard of this *inventio* or "finding" by the queen mother, Helena. The first we hear of pilgrimages to Jerusalem is the itinerary of the anonymous pilgrim of Bordeaux in 333, largely a list of stopping places and changes of mode of transport. That writer describes going in Jerusalem from the *Anastasis,* Constantine's rotunda over the presumed site of the resurrection, to the *Martyrium,* his recently erected basilica at the place of the crucifixion.[17] According to later pilgrims, this route was extended to other sites of the passion. When the Constantinian buildings were destroyed, the pilgrims normally went in procession with lighted candles to the traditional sites of Calvary and the Holy Sepulchre. Petronius, bishop of Bologna in the fifth century, returned to Italy from his pilgrimage to the holy places to replicate some of the buildings he found in Jerusalem in the monastery of San Stefano, where since medieval times there has been a cluster of seven churches around that of the Holy Sepulchre.[18] Beginning in the ninth century, many cities in what are now Italy, Austria, and France had reproductions of that central church, doubtless impelled by the piety of returning pilgrims.

The Cross in the Lives of Monks and Martyrs

As early as the fourth century the hours of the divine office in the Greek-speaking East were being placed in relation to the scenes of Christ's passion. According to the late fourth-century *Apostolic Constitutions,* prayer was set at the third hour (9 A.M.) because it was at that time that Pilate sentenced Jesus,[19] at the sixth hour because it was then he was crucified, and at the ninth hour because at that point he yielded up his spirit. "We participate in the sufferings of Christ patiently," the prologue to St. Benedict's sixth-century rule concludes, "so that we may deserve to have a share in his kingdom. Amen."[20] In the Egyptian desert, according to the *Life of Pachomius* (d. 346), the solitaries "placed before their eyes constantly the examples set by Christ crucified so as to imitate them."[21] Not many Christians of the early centuries could go into the desert as cenobites or anchorites, but those who did presented a model of self-abnegation and of suffering with the crucified Christ to the rest who lived more ordinary lives. These desert dwellers were a paradigm of virtue for the laity.

---

17. Geyer, *Itinera,* 23.

18. M.-J. Picard, "Croix (Chemin de)," *Dictionnaire de Spiritualité,* 2 (Paris, 1953), 2578.

19. *Apostolic Constitutions* 8.33.

20. Rule of St. Benedict, prologue. See Timothy Fry, O.S.B., et al., eds., *The Rule of St. Benedict: In Latin and English with Notes* (Collegeville, Minn.: Liturgical Press, 1981), 166.

21. E. Bertaud and André Rayez, "Devotion à la Passion," *Dictionnaire de Spiritualité,* 3.767; see Armand Veilleux, trans. and intro., *Pachomian Koinonia,* vol. 1, *The Life of Saint Pachomius and His Disciples* (Kalamazoo: Cistercian, 1980), 38, 41, 135, 302, 304, 365.

If the monks and nuns of Egypt and Palestine served as exemplars for the Christians there, the Christians of Gaul, Rome, and North Africa were exposed to a still more potent example of enduring pain in union with the Crucified, in the martyrdoms that prevailed between 175 and 300. Torture and death in testimony to Christ has been called the greatest influence on Christian spirituality after the New Testament itself. Tertullian was the first, after Ignatius and *The Martyrdom of Polycarp,* to express this solidarity with Christ. It occurs early in his brief treatise *A Book [Addressed] to the Martyrs.* Their struggle begins in prison, which he calls a kind of retreat for future martyrs on the eve of battle: "For the Christian, what the desert was for the prophets."[22] There the imitation of Christ, even to the point of his passion, began. The martyrs to be, whom Origen exhorts by name as Ambrose, Protoctetus, and others, now

> go in procession bearing the cross of Jesus and following him who brings you before governors and kings. . . . to suffer martyrdom . . . and complete what is lacking in Christ's afflictions [Col. 1:24]. . . . Those who share in sufferings will share also in comfort in proportion to the suffering they share with Christ [2 Cor. 1:7]. . . . For the martyrs in Christ disarm the principalities and powers with him and share his triumphs as participants of his sufferings, becoming in this way also participants in the courageous deeds wrought in his sufferings [see Col. 2:15]. . . . We learn, moreover, that the person who drinks that cup which Jesus drank will sit with Him and rule and judge with the King of kings.[23]

Clement of Alexandria speaks of faithful Christian life culminating in death as a kind of martyrdom:

> If martyrdom consists of confessing God, all who conduct themselves with purity in the knowledge of God, who obey the commandments, are martyrs in their lives and in their words; in whatever way their souls are separated from their bodies, they will pour out their faith, in the manner of blood, all during their lives and at the moment of their departure.[24]

---

22. Tertullian *Ad Martyres* (PL 1.623).

23. Origen *Exhortation to Martyrdom* 36; 42; 28 (PG 11.609, 612; 617, 620; 596–97; ET, Rowan A. Greer [New York: Paulist Press, 1979], 67, 73, 60).

24. Clement of Alexandria *Miscellanies* 5.4.30 (PG 8.1228). This view of utter fidelity to Christ as quasi martyrdom is found in Maximus of Turin (d. ca. 470), who points out that the Latin word for "martyr," *testis,* like the Greek, means witness, "and, every time that we accomplish by our own acts the commandments of Christ we render him testimony of our faith; and it is thus that we build the Saviour's cross, not truly the cross of wood which was constructed for his Passion, but the one of which we make up the parts by submitting the whole course of our life to every kind of discipline" (*Homily* 82; PL 57.429–30). Cited by Louis Gougaud, O.S.B., "The Desire for Martyrdom," in *Devotional and Ascetic Practices in the Middle Ages,* trans. G. C. Bateman (London: Burns & Oates, 1927), 205–6.

We do not have a record of the Christian lives of ordinary lay people in the fifth and sixth centuries, only the preaching of their largely bishop teachers and the liturgical forms in which they took part in baptism and the Eucharist in their own spoken languages. These rites proclaimed Jesus' death on the cross and his rising from the dead in terms of total rhetorical restraint. The prose they employed featured a gracious deed of God to achieve human salvation. The preaching and teaching of the patristic period, unlike the liturgical formulas, indulged in patterns of speech about Jesus' passion and death that included some detail but was marked by two features in particular: an invitation to emulate his innocent suffering by accepting the trials of life as a witness to him, and an emphasis on the fact that the divine Man who was the framer of the universe had freely subjected himself to the indignities of his human tormentors. There was stress neither on the physical pain he endured nor on seeking out suffering quite like his as reparatory, in the spirit of Colossians 1:24: "I rejoice in my sufferings for your sake, and in my flesh I am filling up what is lacking in the afflictions of Christ on behalf of his body, which is the church."

The Cross at the Onset of the Middle Ages

Gregory the Great, the first Roman bishop of that name (590–604), is sometimes called the last of the Latin fathers but one, Isidore of Seville (d. 636) having come after him. But it is wise to see the Middle Ages as having already begun when Gregory came on the scene. He had spent sixteen years in Constantinople without learning Greek, living a monastic life there as he had in his native Rome after being its prefect, the same imperial post Ambrose had held in Milan and Pilate in Judea. His was a practical and contemplative approach to Christian life, not a speculative one. Best known for his letters, *Morals on Job* and *Pastoral Rule,* his writings made him even more than Augustine the spiritual father of the Latin Middle Ages. There are some, he writes in his *Homilies on Ezekiel,* who are the *parvuli* ("little ones"). They "cling above all to [Christ's] humanity; others, the *perfecti,* reflect more on his divinity." [25] But this is a difference of emphasis only. All must contemplate the two inseparable realities.

Whenever Gregory counsels the recollection of Christ's passion he presents it as a stimulant of the love we owe to God, a love that has as its proof the imitation of Jesus Christ and as its fruit, contemplation. He speaks of Jesus' sufferings of mind and body in a context of what to say to the sick, but even there he does not attempt to arouse compassion for Christ, who is

25. Dom Jean Leclercq, Dom François Vandenbroucke, and Louis Bouyer, *The Spirituality of the Middle Ages* (London: Burns & Oates, 1968), 16. Cf. *Homily 9, Book 1.31 on Ezekiel* (PL 76.884).

now in glory.[26] Gregory's concern is much rather with the objective adoration of the *opprobria* of the passion, in which God's love is manifested and by which our salvation is achieved. He considers not so much the human feelings of Christ as the dignity of the person who experienced them.

He shows no tendency to humanize the figure of the Lord, who is always divinely transcendent. "Christ now suffers in his Church, as he formerly suffered in Job."[27] The grounds of human hope for Gregory are, above all, Christ's resurrection and ascension. He is in heaven, concealed from us, yet dwelling among us in a more spiritual way. Meditating on Jesus' sacred humanity, Christians conceive a longing to contemplate it in the light of the divinity. There is no lingering here on the sufferings of Jesus in themselves. They are but a stage on the road to his present glory. Referring especially to early writers like Bede of Jarrow (d. 736), Ambrose Autpert, an Italian monk (d. 784), and Odo of Cluny (d. 942), J. Hourlier, a modern Benedictine, says that the common lesson they teach is that one "begins with the humanity of Christ's flesh to reach the glorified body of the Risen One in the depths of the Trinity."[28]

It is different in the writings of the Irish missionary Columbanus (d. 615), who founded the monasteries at Luxeuil in Gaul and Bobbio in Lombardy. Although he had a great respect for Gregory the Great, he was in all matters more rigorously ascetic than his Roman contemporary, little though his *Rule for Monks* differs from Gregory's. Christ, "a true father [this usage is also characteristic of Gregory], the charioteer of Israel . . . over the swelling flood, reached even to us."[29] Now that he is in glory we must follow him there. "This is the truth of the gospel, that the true disciples of the crucified Christ should follow him with the cross . . . in it are hidden all the longed-for refreshments, the mysteries of salvation."[30] The severe penitential exercises engaged in by Columbanus and the Irish monks generally do not, however, seem to be patterned on the sufferings of Christ. They were done to achieve conversion of heart and in reparation for sins with a view to divine absolution. Added to the Eastern genuflections and prostrations were long prayers while the monk was immersed in cold water or held his arms outstretched in the form of a cross. Pilgrimages were engaged in "for the love of Christ" or "for the healing of the soul." Self-imposed exile was the greatest renunciation these Irish men and women could make, so attached were they to their own people and family. This accounts for their journeyings, even those of

26. *Pastoral Rule* 3.12 (PL 77.69). On devotion to Christ in the patristic period more generally, see Irénée Noye, S. S., et al., *Jesus in Christian Devotion and Contemplation* (St. Meinrad, Ind.: Abbey Press, 1974), a translation of "Humanité du Christ (Dévotion et contemplation)," *Dictionnaire de Spiritualité* 7.1033–1108.

27. Leclercq, *Spirituality*, 17.

28. J. Hourlier, O.S.B., in Noye, *Jesus*, 37.

29. Epistle 5.11. See *S. Columbani Opera*, ed. G. S. M. Walker, Scriptores latini hiberniae, 2 (Dublin, 1957), 48. Quoted in Leclercq, *Spirituality*, 37.

30. Epistle 4.6 (Leclercq, *Spirituality*, 30, 32).

the monks vowed to stability of place. Everywhere they went they erected "high crosses" before their monasteries (the familiar Celtic design with arms slightly splayed and linked by a circle), like the ones they had carved at home in Clonmacnoise, Clonard, and Glendalough.[31]

Some have said that there was no devotion to the humanity of Christ or his sufferings on the cross until the eleventh century in the West with the writings of Bernard. This is hardly true, as the spread of Gregory's piety and that of the Irish and British monks and nuns to the barbarian peoples of northern Europe attests. While those under vow were reciting the Divine Office daily, chiefly made up of the Psalter in Latin, they compiled in the Irish language, and later the Anglo-Saxon and Latin, collections of private prayers (*preces peculiares*) inspired by the liturgy. Some of these, especially the poetic ones, ended up in the breviary. Their subject matter was the praise of Mary and various saints, but especially the cross of Christ. Two nonvernacular hymns of the late sixth century that came to enjoy great currency were Venantius Fortunatus's *Pange, Lingua, gloriosi lauream certaminis* ("Sing, my tongue, the Savior's glory," from which come the well-remembered verses in translation: "Faithful Cross above all other, / One and only noble tree, / None in foliage none in blossom, / None in yield thy peer may be; / Sweet are the nails and sweet the tree / But sweeter the fruit that hangs on thee. / Bend thy boughs, O tree of glory! / All thy rigid branches, bend! / For a while the ancient temper / That thy birth bestowed, suspend; / And the King of earth and heaven / Gently on thy bosom tend") and *Vexilla Regis prodeunt* ("The Royal Banners Forward Go"). It continues: *Fulget Crucis mysterium, Qua vita mortem pertulit, Et morte vitam pretulit,* in a fine Augustinian wordplay that speaks of the "mystery of the resplendent cross, on which life bore death and brought forth life from death." Venantius, an Italian, who died as bishop of Poitiers, is hailed as the first of the medieval poets.

In the later Carolingian era (843) a noblewoman named Dhuoda wrote a handbook of devotion for her son, who was at the court of Charles the Bald. It was one of many such ninth-century treatises provided for the educated laity, even as the monks were proposing to them patterns of piety based on the monastic.[32] Dhuoda suggests for her son's devotions extracts from the psalms and invocations to the cross. Rabanus Maurus (d. 856), the abbot of Fulda and archbishop of Mainz, likewise wrote a lengthy treatise in praise of the holy cross, seeing in it the symbol of Christ's victory and the scepter of his triumph.[33]

31. Gougaud, *Christianity in Celtic Lands,* trans. Maud Joynt (London: Sheed & Ward, 1932), 93–95.

32. *Liber Manualis* 10–11 (PL 106.113–14). See the *Commentary on Matthew* of Christian Druthmar, monk of Corbie, in the same volume: "Miserable wretches! You should have kissed his feet and instead you bound his hands!" (col. 1480).

33. Rabanus Maurus *De Laudibus Sanctae Crucis* (PL 107.133–294).

The Cross in Second-Millennium Monasticism

The roots of mediation on the life of Jesus and especially the events of his last days and hours are to be traced to the monastic *lectio divina,* a reading of the Bible slowly and meditatively in private.[34] This practice led to an identification with him and a desire to emulate his virtues, even a wish to suffer with him in his passion. There are eleventh-century figures especially associated with this type of meditation, Peter Damiani (d. 1072), John of Fécamp (d. 1078), and Anselm of Canterbury (d. 1109), all three Italians by birth. Peter Damiani wrote very specifically: "He [Jesus] is stripped of his clothing; he is beaten, bound, and spat upon; his flesh is pierced by a fivefold wound, so that we may be healed from the entry of vices which reach us through the five senses."[35] John addresses Jesus as *Carissime,* begging that by his passion and cross his heart be filled with an inextinguishable love and unbroken remembrance, that by the holy effusion of his precious blood he be given a contrite heart and a flood of tears. In another place he calls Jesus "the very medicine for our wounds who hung on the cross." Vernet says that his *Symbol of Faith,* "by its detailed enumeration of the circumstances of Our Saviour's life," contains the whole cult of Christ's humanity in its embryonic stage.

One of Anselm's prayers reads:

> Kindlest, gentlest, most serene Lord,
> will you not make it up to me for not seeing
> the blessed incorruption of your flesh,
> for not having kissed the place of the wounds
>   where the nails pierced,
> for not having sprinkled with tears of joy
> the scars that prove the truth of your body?

And another:

> As much as I can, though not as much as I ought, I am mindful of your passion,
> your buffeting, your scourging, your cross, your wounds, how you were slain
> for me, how prepared for burial and buried; and also I remember your glorious
> Resurrection and wonderful Ascension.[36]

34. See Jean Leclercq, *The Love of Learning and the Desire for God: A Study in Monastic Culture,* 2d rev. ed. (New York: Fordham University Press, 1974).

35. Peter Damiani *Opusculum* 43 chap. 5 (*PL* 145.683); John of Fécamp, *Confessio theologica,* in J. Leclercq and J. P. Bonnes, *Un maître de la vie spirituelle au XIᵉ siècle* (Paris, 1946), 172–73; cf. Félix Vernet, *Mediaeval Spirituality* (St. Louis, 1930), 91; Anselm, "Prayer to Christ," in *The Prayers and Meditations of St. Anselm,* trans. Sister Benedicta Ward, S.L.G. (New York: Penguin Books, 1979), 93. There is also a "Prayer to the Holy Cross," 102–4.

36. Anselm, "Prayer to Christ," cited by Ewert Cousins from Ward, *Prayer,* 95, in "The Humanity and the Passion of Christ," in *Christian Spirituality: High Middle Ages and Reformation,* ed. Jill Raitt (New York: Crossroad, 1987), 387–88.

"Why, O my soul," Anselm asks, "were you not there to be pierced by a sword of bitter sorrow when you could not bear the piercing of the side of your Saviour with a lance? Why could you not bear to see the nails violate the hands and feet of your Creator?" And to Mary: "What can I say about the fountains that flowed from your most pure eyes when you saw your only Son before you, bound, beaten and hurt?" This summoning of the Crucified in imagination through prayers addressed to him should help dispel the notion, perhaps created by the *Cur Deus Homo?*, that Anselm conceived Jesus' redemptive death as some kind of bloodless exchange made necessary by the awesomeness of the divine glory and the awfulness of Adam's sin. He was trying to speak to Jews in that treatise and to Muslims, whose Holy Qur'an was not open to Jesus' painful sufferings.

John Gualbertus (d. 1073) is one among many reported in this century and the next as having the image of the Crucified bow toward him. This occurred in a monastery chapel near Florence, in acknowledgment of his having forgiven an enemy. Similar appearances are reported of Alfonso Narvaez, self-proclaimed king of Portugal, Bernard, and Thomas Aquinas.[37]

Ailred of Rievaulx in England (d. 1167) wrote a treatise for his sister, a recluse, in which in true Cistercian fashion he counseled her against images or pictures in her cell.[38] The two were children of a Saxon priest of Hexham. He said that a single image would do, that of the Savior hanging on the cross, flanked if she liked by images of his mother and the beloved disciple, a twofold emblem of charity. The outstretched arms of the suffering God should be all she needed to invite her to loving embraces. Ailred's contemporary William of St. Thierry (d. 1148) recommended to novices contemplation of Christ in his earthly life and in his passion as a means of access to God; they could later rise to thoughts of him in glory, clothed with human flesh in heaven, from where his blood always flows for the redemption of believers.[39]

Jesus' humanity had begun to be depicted historically if not yet realistically as early as the Constantinian era, for example in catacomb art. The adoption of Christianity by the empire shortly began to show the influence of the imperial court: Christ portrayed as a royal, even a superhuman, figure. By 400, continuing through the Theodosian age and well beyond, he is shown reigning from a throne or on a mountain, at times surrounded by the twenty-four elders or four living creatures of Revelation 4. The great apsidal

37. Gougaud gives these claims as much documentation as can be summoned in their favor in *Devotional and Ascetic Practices,* 78–80, as well as of the stigmata reportedly granted to Francis of Assisi in September 1224. The latter occurs in a most enlightening discussion of devotion to "The Five Wounds," 80–91.

38. *Regula inclusarum* 27 (PL 32.1460). See A. LeBail, "Ailred of Rievaulx," *Dictionnaire de Spiritualité,* 1.225–34.

39. Hourlier in Noye, *Jesus,* 40. Citations from William's writings include *The Golden Epistle to the Carthusians of Mont Dieu; On the Song of Songs* 16 and 18; *Meditations* 10; *On Contemplating God* 10.

Christs, as of Ravenna near Venice and Monreale in Sicily, are examples of this depiction. He will at times be crowned and hold a scepter or the globe of the earth in his hand. Homage to him as Christ the victorious king is thus solicited. If the cross is shown it is either jeweled or of burnished gold. This Christ is the Word of God, the Light of the world, the Pantocrator "who rules all things and contains all things."[40] Some Gospel manuscripts of the sixth century, however (e.g., of Sinope on the Black Sea, Rossano, Zagba in Mesopotamia, and one housed at Cambridge), express the personal, physical aspects of the participants in the gospel drama.

Bernard and His Forerunners

Irénée Noye's article on the "Cross" in the book to which he is the first contributor, along with those on "The Instruments of the Passion" and the "Passion" in the same source, shed light on early devotion to Christ's wounds, to the spear that pierced his side, his holy face, and the true cross itself.[41] Kept alive by groups of nuns and women called canonesses through the Carolingian era and the bitter late ninth and tenth centuries, devotion to the crucified Jesus gained new devotees in the eleventh and twelfth. Among these were the women in monasteries founded by the itinerant preachers Norbert of Xanten (d. 1134) and Blessed Robert of Arbrissel (d. 1117).[42] The former, a native of the Cologne area, founded the male Order of Prémontré; and Robert founded numerous communities of nuns of which the first was at Fontévrault. The religious renaissance of the twelfth century was everywhere marked by a tender devotion to the humanity of Christ, both in monastic settings and among the laity.

With all these predecessors it is surprising that Bernard of Clairvaux (d. 1153) is singled out as the initiator of devotion to the humanity of Christ in the West. The reason probably is that he wrote so extensively and in such a good Latin style. His writings stand as a peak, in part because of the mists that cover the lowlands of the previous five centuries. But there is more to it than that. Bernard is more overtly affective in his prose, more disposed than those who preceded him, to disclose his sentiments in a world that was just beginning to express its feelings openly without shame or embarrassment. He recognizes "the lawfulness of the part played by the affections," Leclercq writes, "in any consideration of the life of Jesus, he enumerates for our loving compassion the sufferings of our Lord, adding that the safeguard of this love is the imitation of Christ, that is the practice of

40. Noye, *Jesus*, 12–13.
41. *Dictionnaire de Spiritualité*, 2.2617–18; 7.1820–31; 3.26–33. See n. 6 above.
42. Leclercq, *Spirituality*, 142, 145–50.

mortification in our daily duties, and the renouncing of every form of self-feeling."[43] Bernard writes in one of his sermons:

> Two things console the Church in her exile: the memory of the Passion of Christ in the past and in the future the contemplation of what she both thinks and believes will be her welcome among the saints. . . . [The Church's] contemplation is complete because it knows not only what it is to expect, but the source from which it is to come. It is a joyous expectation with no hesitation in it, because it rests on the death of Christ.[44]

"What can be so effective a cure for the wound of conscience and so purifying to keenness of mind," he asks in that sermon, "as steady meditation on the wounds of Christ?"[45] Bernard wrestles at length with the statement in Hebrews, "He learned obedience from the things he suffered" (5:8). At first the idea does not trouble him:

> We have an example in our Savior. He wanted to suffer so that he would know how to suffer with us (Heb 2:17), to become wretched so that he could learn mercy. . . . He learned mercy in the same way [that he learned obedience]. It is not that he did not know how to be merciful before. His mercy is from everlasting to everlasting (Ps 102:17). But what he knew by nature from eternity he learned from experience in time. . . .

Thus, "he learned" can be taken to refer not to our Head in his own Person, but to his body, which is the Church (Col 1:24), and then this is the sense: "And he learned obedience from the things he suffered" means that he learned from his body from what he suffered in his Head. For that death, that Cross, the opprobrium, the scorn, the beatings which Christ endured, what else were they but outstanding examples of obedience for his body, that is, ourselves?[46]

This shows a way of thinking that modernity is almost incapable of. It is not so much that Bernard cannot think of Jesus' passion as separate from his future (and for us present) glorification. He cannot, rather, think of Christ as separate from us. There is only a corporate Christ, head and members. There is no isolated Redeemer out of the past whose sufferings we look back upon with gratitude for the benefits they represent to us. The suffering Christ of *then* is identical with the suffering Christ of *now*. His pain is ours and our pain is his, all obediently borne. Christ exercises a psychological role on us from the fact that he knew human misery. "He gives humanity the experi-

43. Ibid., 198.
44. "Sermon 62," *Bernard of Clairvaux: Selected Works,* trans. Gillian R. Evans (New York: Paulist Press, 1987), 247.
45. Ibid., 4.7, (pp. 250–51).
46. Ibid., "On Humanity and Pride," 107.

ence of being one with Him, and therefore of imitating Him and of conforming itself to Him."[47]

Franciscan and Dominican Devotion to the Passion

Coming to Francis of Assisi, we find the facts of his life obscured by the literary legacy he generated: the two *Lives* written by his companion Thomas of Celano, the two *Legendae* of Bonaventura, who lived a generation after him, and the *Fioretti* penned by the repudiated "Spiritual Franciscans" a century after his death. He seems to have drawn up a *Testament* in April 1226, shortly before his death, recording that he had received the wounds of Christ on September 17, 1224, in the hermitage on Mt. Alverno that Count Orlando of Chiusi had given him eleven years before. There is no record of a precedent to this miracle. It was a sign that he had thoroughly identified himself with the Redeemer by penance, by prayer, and by love.

There can be no doubt that all of Europe and the lands beyond it to which the friars—Franciscan, Dominican, Carmelite, and Crosier—traveled, were brought closer to the humanity of Christ by their preaching. The theory of suffering as the sole way to glory may have peaked with Bernard a century before, but no one made the infant Jesus or the Jesus who healed or suffered torment more real in people's lives than the sons and daughter of the Poverello. Among the Franciscan mystics of the passion are Bonaventura (d. 1274), Blessed Angela of Foligno (1309), Jacopone da Todi (d. 1306), author of the *Stabat Mater,* Ramón Lúll of Palma (1316), and the anonymous author of *Meditationes vitae Christi.*

Great theologians, mystics, and saints came to birth and flourished in the thirteenth century, but a number of tragedies were on the horizon that would change the shape of all European life and with it Christian piety and prayer. The Crusades (1095–1396) were the first of these, then the Hundred Years' War (1337–1453) in the midst of which came the Black Plague of 1348–49, and finally the Great Western Schism of 1378–1429. Probably as a result of these multiplied dislocations, people became fearful, apprehensive, and superstitious. The faith Catholic and the theology based on it were breached from mystical experience in a way that had never previously been the case. Apocalyptists and charlatans blackened the roads of Europe proclaiming that the millennium was near. A strange kind of voluntarism not to be confused with affectivity replaced the intellectual approach to theology, leaving the people confused as to the difference between the two. The mid-thirteenth century had witnessed the writings of a woman of Antwerp, Hadewijch, who was perhaps a Beguine and who left *Visions, Letters and Poems* that had love as their central theme. This was an ecstatic love that borrowed the

47. Hourlier in Noye, *Jesus,* 41.

language of the courtly love of the previous century. The following poem is from a later collection attributed to Hadewijch, possibly influenced by Meister Eckhart:

> In love's pure abandon
> No created good can subsist:
> For love strips of all form
> Those whom it receives in its simplicity.
>
> Freed from every modality,
> Alien to every image
> Is the life here below
> Of the poor in spirit.[48]

Eckhart (John by baptism or in religious life), a native of Hochheim in Thuringia who was a Dominican friar and frequently held administrative posts in his order, died sometime before 1329 while proceedings against him for heresy were in progress. In that year Pope John XXII reviewed the adverse sentence of the archbishop of Cologne and condemned twenty-eight of Eckhart's propositions as heretical or dangerous. The case was handled badly and there is every likelihood that the charge of heresy was unfounded. In any case, he left behind him numerous commentaries on Scripture and theological treatises in Latin and sermons in German (taken down by listeners, often imperfectly), although much was destroyed as a result of his trial.

Eckhart's thought was not "passion-centered" in comparison with that of his later, fellow German Dominicans John Tauler and Henry Suso. There is "no lingering at all on the physical details of Christ's suffering and death. Nevertheless, the theme of the imitation of Christ, especially in adherence to the law of the cross, does appear in enough places to show that the Meister did not in any way minimize the importance of the Passion."[49] This judgment of Bernard McGinn is followed by the observation that his Latin sermon 45 contains "the most extended meditation on the significance of the cross as the model for the life of the Christian," a theme present in a number of places, especially the vernacular works. Eckhart is insistent that God suffers with human beings, quoting Psalms 34:19 ("The Lord is close to the broken-hearted") and 91:15 ("When he calls to me, I shall answer; I shall be with him in time of distress") to this effect:

God suffers with man, he truly does; he suffers in his own fashion, sooner and far more than the man suffers who suffers for love of him. Now I say, if God

48. J. B. P[orion], *Hadewijch d'Anvers,* "Poem XXVI," cited by Vandenbroucke in Leclercq, *Spirituality,* 362–63. The English translation is by the Benedictines of Holme Eden Abbey, Carlisle.

49. Bernard McGinn, "Theological Summary," in *Meister Eckhart: The Essential Sermons, Commentaries, Treatises and Defense,* trans. Edmund Colledge, O.S.A., and Bernard McGinn (New York: Paulist Press, 1981), 46.

himself is willing to suffer, then I ought fittingly to suffer, for if I think rightly, I want what God wants. . . . I say with certainty that since God suffers so willingly with us and for our sake, if we suffer only for love of him, he suffers without suffering. Suffering is for him so joyful that it is not suffering. And therefore, if we thought rightly, suffering would not be suffering for us; it would be our joy and consolation.[50]

Late Medieval Concentration on Jesus' Passion

The fifteenth century saw the introduction of the cyclic dramas of the passion, which provided

> "close-ups" of favorite scenes from the life and especially the Passion of Christ, of His person, His behavior, His actions, and His body; "film-strips," to which the actors of the liturgical plays and the *Mysteries* of the preachers added the sound effects. . . . In its own way, this piety recognized in Christ, whether child or suffering, the God-man who was born and suffered for the salvation of the world.[51]

The piety of the faithful at the end of the Middle Ages was particularly attracted by Christ's sufferings and death, by the instruments of the passion and the cross. "From Bonaventure, Thomas Aquinas, and Hugh of Strasbourg up to Henry Suso, Thomas à Kempis, Gerson and Bernardine of Siena, the Passion of Christ is considered to be in all respects more painful than the sufferings ever endured by anyone."[52] There was thought to be no greater ignominy than these sufferings in the circumstances that accompanied them, "among the wicked" (Isa. 53:9). Jesus, it was supposed, had the most sensitive and most perfect constitution, hence his was the keenest and the most total suffering. "From the sole of the foot to the head there is no sound spot: / Wound and welt and gaping gash, not drained, or bandaged, or eased with salve" (1:6) was a favorite Isaian verse attributed to Jesus' passion. This theme was developed by the authors of meditations, by preachers and artists using texts from both Testaments of the Bible indiscriminately and embellishing as their imagination or devotion dictated. There developed, as a result, devotions to the way of the cross, to Christ tied to the pillar, to the holy face, to the wounds, and to the side of Christ. There even came to be the practice of self-flagellation in imitation of the Crucified.

The cross was the center of it all: the Savior dying on it, his words spoken from it, his deposition from it and entombment. The cross as the sacred emblem of the redemption was found everywhere: on buildings sacred and

---

50. Ibid., 232–33.

51. See G. Cohen, *Mystères et Moralité: Manuscrit 617 de Chantilly* (Paris, 1920), cxliv, cited by A. Rayez in Noye, *Jesus*, 50, 52.

52. Rayez, in Noye, *Jesus*, 107, n. 26.

profane, in wayside shrines, in private homes, on one's person. Bruges had its "procession of the precious blood" toward the end of the fourteenth century. Mystics recounted from their visions the number of blows Jesus had received. People recited in vernacular tongues offices *Of the Passion* and *Of the Compassion,* often saying the psalms from memory. Toward the end of the fourteenth century "Passion Clocks" were devised to keep track of the hours of the office by the hours of the day. It was as if the Christian populace of Europe was smitten by the new license it was allowing itself and was terrified by the shortness and brutality of life; hence it was determined to make reparation by joining itself to the sufferings of the Savior.

More restrained than most mystics of the period in her concentration on the passion was the anonymous recluse whose cell was attached to the Augustinian church of St. Julian in Conisford near Norwich. Known simply as Julian (d. after 1413), this female solitary—highborn enough to have a maidservant—recorded thirteen of the visions she experienced in her thirty-first year, described by her as *Shewings* ("revelations"). This she did shortly after they occurred in 1373 in twenty-five brief chapters. Later in life she elaborated on them in the so-called Long Text of eighty-six chapters. Julian writes that early in life she had had great feeling for the passion of Christ but asked for more: for the Savior's bodily pains in the form of an illness. It was granted to her. Indeed, she had a near-death experience. She recovered "by God's secret doing" and was shown by "our Lord a spiritual sight of his familiar love."[53]

Her chief "showing" is of Jesus on his suffering:

> Suddenly I saw the red blood trickling down from under the crown, all hot, flowing freely. . . . I saw the body bleeding copiously. . . . a living stream. . . . And I saw this in the furrows made by the scourging, and I saw this blood run so plentifully that . . . if it had been happening there. . . . the bed and everything around it would have been soaked in blood.[54]

She knows that the cause, not the pain, is of supreme moment here. The blessed blood has flowed to wash us of our sins. Her descriptions of the suffering Jesus are extremely graphic but free of the usual clichés. The Long Text says at one point: "He was hanging up in the air as people hang up a cloth to dry."[55] This comes after a description of the crown that made the sweet skin and the flesh break all in pieces and the hair be pulled from the bone: "The skin and the flesh of the face and the body which showed were covered with fine wrinkles and of a tawny color, like a dry board which has aged, and the face was more brown than the body."

53. Julian of Norwich, "Showings," trans. Edmund Colledge, O.S.A., and James Walsh, S. J. (New York: Paulist Press, 1978), chap. 4, the Short Text, 128, 130.
54. Ibid., 129, 137.
55. Ibid., 208.

Remarkable about her description of Jesus' state in his passion is that he seems to confide in her how he devised and carried out the work of human salvation. "It was done as honourably as Christ could do it, and in this I saw complete joy in Christ; but his joy would not have been complete if the deed could have been done any better than it was."[56] "Are you well satisfied that I suffered for you?" he asks, and when she says yes, "It is a joy, a bliss, an endless delight that ever I suffered my Passion for you; and if I could suffer more, I should suffer more."[57] She writes that, despite "the common teaching of Holy Church" (from which she is not moved or led away) that we deserve pain, blame, and wrath:

> I saw truly that God was never angry and never will be. . . . I saw that it is against the property of his power to be angry. . . . God is that goodness which cannot be angry. Our soul is united to him who is unchangeable goodness. And between God and our soul there is neither wrath nor forgiveness in his sight.[58]

A great popular favorite in the fifteenth century was the *Life of Christ* of Ludolph the Saxon (d. 1378), a Carthusian who compiled a book of meditations rather than a "life." He relied chiefly on Henry Suso's *Clock of Wisdom* and the *Meditations on the Life of Christ* attributed to Bonaventura, coupled with other sources. Like the author of the *Following of Christ,* he taught that imitating the Savior was the source of all perfection. The pious sister of Iñigo (Ignatius) of Loyola gave a copy of this book to the scion of the household, who was recovering in the family castle south of San Sebastián from a cannonball wound received in the siege of Pamplona.

Iñigo had asked for the romance *Amadis de Gaul* and was provided instead with this *Life of Christ.* Much moved by his reading of Ludolph, he then visited the Benedictine monastery at Montserrat and there in a cave near Manresa may have practiced the *Exercitatorio* of one of the monks, Garcia Jiménez de Cisneros. It too was a compilation. Once Ignatius (the saint's name he adopted) had been introduced to the *devotio moderna* of people like Gerard of Zutphen and Thomas of Kempen via the Catalán Benedictine Cisneros, he compiled his own *Spiritual Exercises.* They were a program of prayer extending over four weeks to be followed once in life with a view to a conversion of morals. The Manresa experience occurred in 1522. Ignatius called on the use of all five senses to meditate on "the mysteries of the life of our Lord." He suggested placing oneself, in imagination, in a gospel setting, seeing the persons in the gospel narrative, entering into their feelings, and ministering to their needs as if one were present there. In a

56. Ibid., 145.
57. Ibid., 216.
58. Ibid., 259. Cf. Marion Glascoe's *A Revelation of Love* (Univ. of Exeter, 1976) for the medieval text.

Note appended to the First Exercise of the First Week, he tells people following the *Exercises* to reflect on the enormity of sin as an act against Infinite Goodness, then to converse freely with Jesus:

> *Colloquy.* Imagine Christ our Lord before you, hanging upon the cross. Speak with Him of how, being the Creator, He then became man, and how, possessing life, He submitted to temporal death to die for our sins. . . . As I see Him in this condition, hanging on the cross, I shall meditate on the thoughts that come to my mind. The colloquy is made properly by speaking as one friend speaks to another, or as a servant speaks to his master.[59]

A Spanish mystic who was Ignatius's younger contemporary, the Carmelite reformer, Teresa of Jesus (d. 1582), confessed that she never had any success imagining Christ as a man, yet at times this darkness was pierced by a fleeting consciousness of the presence of God induced by reflection on "His Passion, with its grievous pains, and on his life, which was so full of afflictions."[60] Hers came to be a piety of the passion, like all of her time: "Let [the servant of God] help [Jesus] to bear the Cross and consider how he lived with it all His life long." She declared: "I desire to suffer, Lord, because Thou didst suffer."[61]

The Reformers Continue the Tradition

It should be no surprise that Martin Luther's theology drew heavily on his youthful piety, which in turn was nourished by some of the same sources as the Flemish, Italian, and Spanish mystics cataloged above. He was familiar with the thought of the Dominican Tauler and the anonymous *Theologia Germanica* (which he reedited), and also the "mystical marriage" doctrine as he found it in Bernard's commentary on the Song of Songs. Later in life he would reproach Bernardine thought for absorbing the cross into the heavenly glory, surpassing it, as it were, by a blessed union that anticipated the resurrection.

In his earliest development of a "theology of the cross" Luther identified as a marvelous discovery for himself the revelation of the hidden God in the cross alone.[62] His basic vision was authentically Christian and thoroughly

59. *The Spiritual Exercises of St. Ignatius,* trans. Anthony Mottola (New York: Doubleday, 1964), 56.

60. *Life,* vol. 1 of *The Complete Works of St. Teresa of Jesus,* trans. E. Allison Peers (New York: Sheed and Ward, 1946), 58.

61. Ibid., 67, 68.

62. It followed upon his "discovery" of the righteousness of God some time in 1515, understood as God's humiliation of humanity in order that by the same divine action it might be justified. This "humiliation" is not the "humility" of Catholic language, which Luther had begun to think of as a human work. If God is active in justifying, he thought, God must be active at every stage of the process, including humbling the human creature by making human-

traditional, but he came to deny to the cross anything but a manifestation of God's love for this sinful world. Any share of the divine holiness with humanity in this life seemed to him an arrogant anticipation of the glory that is reserved for the life of heaven. That may account for a piety marked by absorption with the sufferings of Christ to match anything known to the late Middle Ages, but without any element of transformative mystical union with God for the believer. God can and does impute the unique divine righteousness to the sinful creature *as if* it were the creature's own. Enjoying that righteousness as one's proper possession is reserved for the life of heaven. "His basic vision was man's personal relationship—on the sole basis of faith in Christ, God made man and crucified for man—with the God who reveals himself in the essential act of his transcendent love engraved for ever at the heart of our history."[63]

John Calvin's most important contribution to Protestant spirituality was his conception of God's glory, or better perhaps, God's glorification, as the ultimate purpose of Christianity. God's power had to be acknowledged as the only one that counts, the only one that is good, the only one that is real. A life wholly given over, in action as in prayer, to this acknowledgment is the only one that befits a Christian. Calvin's commitment to meditation on the mystery of Calvary yielded nothing to the intensity of that of his young Catholic manhood. He would not let it be represented, however, by any picture, statue, or crucifix lest such an intermediary device become an idol in which the notion of the true God and the divine love for humanity be lost. Calvin wrote of Christ crucified as a "singular mystery," developing it in Pauline terms as an accursed death that removed the curse under which humanity lay: "The Father destroyed the force of sin when the curse of sin

---

ity sinful. The sole means of receiving justification at God's hands is faith in the cross, again a work of God. "The CROSS alone is our theology," he wrote in his *Operationes in Psalmos* of 1519–21, capitalizing the word (*Werke,* 5.176.32–33 [Weimar, 1892]) and, "The cross puts everything to the test" (5.179.31). "All responsible Christian discourse about God must be based on the cross, and must be subject to criticism upon this basis. . . . God is revealed in the cross of Christ. Yet, as the Christian contemplates the appalling spectacle of Christ dying upon the cross, he is forced to concede that God does not appear to be revealed there at all. . . . For Luther, the cross mediates an indirect and hidden revelation of God" (Alister E. McGrath, *Luther's Theology of the Cross: Martin Luther's Theological Breakthrough* [Oxford: Basil Blackwell, 1985], 159, 161). There is some evidence that, by 1525, Luther had abandoned his earlier principle of deriving theology solely on the basis of the cross, as he came to acknowledge that the *hidden* God has dispositions unknown to us from the *revealed* God (McGrath, *Luther's Theology,* 166–67 with appropriate citations). In any event, Luther never ceased to preach Christ crucified to excite faith in the mystery of human redemption. Most often this was the *angefochtene Christus* (almost, but not quite, "tempted unto despair"), as a solace for human *Anfechtung,* our sorely tempted condition that has God as its ultimate source. This crisis of *Anfechtung* finds its solution "in the crucified Christ, who suffered precisely the same *Anfechtung* on our behalf, in order that his righteousness might become our righteousness" (McGrath, *Luther's Theology,* 173, citing *Werke* 5.607.32–37).

63. Louis Bouyer, *Orthodox Spirituality and Protestant and Anglican Spirituality,* trans. Barbara Wall (New York: Desclée Co., 1969), 70.

was transferred to Christ's flesh. . . . In taking the curse upon himself—he crushed, broke, and scattered its whole force. Hence faith apprehends an acquittal in the condemnation of Christ, a blessing in his curse."[64]

The German Pietist movement of the seventeenth century was thoroughly passion-and-cross centered. Its way was paved by the *True Christianity* (*Vom wahren Christentum*, 1609) of Johann Arndt, who died in 1621. Pietism's best-known expression was found in the hymns of Paul Gerhardt (d. 1676), one of which, *O Haupt voll Blut und Wunden,* was given tongue in music by J. S. Bach.[65] Jakob Spener (d. 1705) is credited as the founder of Pietism, to be followed by August Hermann Francke (d. 1727) at Halle and the distinguished exegete Johann Albrecht Bengel (d. 1752). All were passion centered. A peculiar brand of Pietism was that of Nikolaus-Ludwig Count von Zinzendorf (d. 1760), a native of Dresden. He wrote in one of his conferences about a spiritual experience in boyhood:

> What I believed, I wanted; what I thought, was hateful to me; and at that instant I made a firm resolution to use my reason in human things as far as it would go, and to instruct myself and make myself as cultivated as possible, but in spiritual things to remain sincerely attached to the truth as grasped by the heart, and in particular to the theology of the Cross and the blood of the Lamb of God, so that I might put it at the basis of all other truths and immediately reject all that I could not deduce from it. And so I have remained to this day.[66]

Zinzendorf was extremely influential on the piety of John and Charles Wesley, the former of whom brought the pietist spirit to the American frontier. Charles Wesley's hymns *were* Methodist theology, suffusing the American colonies with a "warmhearted piety" that is still an American legacy. A hymn on the mystery of redemption dated 1747, known by its first line, *Come, Sinners to the Gospel Feast,* contains this verse:

---

64. John Calvin, *Christianae religionis institutio,* 2.16.6. P. Barth and G. Niesel, eds., 1559 ed. (Munich, 1957), 489–91 (ET, F. L. Battles [Philadelphia: Westminster, 1960], 510–11). See also 17.1–6 on Christ's death as meriting our salvation.

65. Based on the "Salve, Caput Cruentatum" attributed to Bernard:

> O Sacred Head surrounded
> By crown of piercing thorn
> O bleeding Head, so wounded,
> Reviled and put to scorn,
> Our sins have marred the glory
> Of your most holy face,
> Yet angel hosts adore thee,
> And tremble as they gaze.
> (Trans. Henry Williams Baker)

66. *Reden,* vol. 1, *Vorrede* (preface), cited by Bouyer, *Orthodox Spirituality,* 178.

> See him set forth before your eyes,
> That precious, bleeding sacrifice!
> His offered benefits embrace,
> And freely now be saved by grace!

The first verse in a collection dated 1742 goes:

> Would Jesus have the sinner die?
>   Why hangs he then on yonder tree?
> What means that strange expiring cry?
>   (Sinners, he prays for you and me):
> "Forgive them, Father, Oh forgive,
> They know not that by me they live!". . .

> Those living, all-atoning Lamb,
>   Thee, by thy painful agony,
> Thy bloody sweat, thy grief and shame,
>   Thy cross and Passion on the tree,
> Thy precious death and life, I pray,
>   Take all, take all my sins away!

> Oh, let me kiss thy bleeding feet,
>   And bathe and wash them with my tears,
> The story of thy love repeat
>   In every drooping sinners ears;
> That all may hear the quick'ning sound,
>   If I, ev'n I, have mercy found.

And, lastly, there is this opening stanza in a hymn from a 1739 collection:

> And can it be that I should gain
>   An interest in the Savior's blood?
> Died he for me who caused his pain?
>   For me? Who him to death pursued?
> Amazing love, how can it be
> That thou, my God, shouldst die for me?[67]

67. Frank Whaling, ed., *John and Charles Wesley: Selected Prayers, Hymns, Journal Notes, Sermons, Letters and Treatises* (New York: Paulist Press, 1981), 179, 182, 197. Cf. G. Osborn, ed., *The Poetical Works of John and Charles Wesley* (London, 1868–72); J. E. Rattenbury, *The Eucharistic Hymns of John and Charles Wesley* (London, 1948).

CHAPTER SIX

Modern Soteriological Thinking: Cross, Creation and Universal Redemption

When Paul wrote that Jesus was handed over to death for our sins and was raised up for our justification (Rom. 4:25), he indicated, however unconsciously, that the death of Jesus had already become in his mind a fact to be believed in, and that God's response to that death was another, greater fact tending to wipe out the memory of the first. Paul was no doubt convinced that the death was real. It was no mere appearance of death as the Gnostics would later have it. Indeed, he probably added the phrase "death on a cross" for emphasis to a hymn he quoted in celebration of Jesus' death and resurrection in his Philippian letter (2:8). His description of those who claimed belief in the crucifixion yet were set upon the things of this world (3:18–19) was that they were "enemies of the cross of Christ." For him the ideal was to be committed to the cross, embracing it willingly. Still, the harshness of the way Jesus actually died seems to have eluded Paul's attention. He had translated "cross" into "death," humanity's last enemy to be destroyed (1 Cor. 15:26). Christ's resurrection had effectively accomplished that destruction, at least at root. Consequently, Paul did not in any extant letter stop to reflect on the horror of death by crucifixion.

He wrote of Jesus' offering of himself in sacrifice as life-giving for all under the legal figure of "justification," meaning acquittal at law. At other times he used the figures "reconciliation," "redemption," and "sanctification." Paul wrote that through Adam's sin all humanity was made subject to condemnation. Through another human being all were released from that sentence (see Rom. 5:19). It happened "at the appointed time" (v. 6), meaning that it was God's doing. The solidarity of the human race is essential to this mythic thought pattern, first under the headship of its progenitor in disobedience, Adam, then under the headship of one who by his obedience was the first of a new, figurative race of those released from sin. Paul consistently spoke of Jesus' death on the cross in this detached manner. It had become for him a deed of God with cosmic implications.

The Gospel writers, all of them, dwelt on the manner of Jesus' death at some length. They did nothing to hide its brutality, even if they did not indulge in much colorful language to describe it. Mark, who was apparently the first of them to reflect on the meaning of this event, put the opening verse of a psalm on Jesus' lips that had him cry, "My God, my God, why have you forsaken me?" (Ps. 22:2; see Mark 15:34). Whether Jesus actually recited it is of no consequence. What matters is that two early transmitters of the tradition—Matthew followed Mark in citing this psalm verse—were convinced that Jesus cried out against his dereliction by God. This was evidently the faith of the Markan and Matthean churches and became such for the entire church. Like the psalmist, the evangelists thought, he who had been supported by God throughout his brief career by signs of power had prayed a prayer of abandonment at the end. The commentators on the Gospels of the early centuries were at pains to show that, while Jesus in his humanity reacted to his sufferings as any human might, he was at no time literally abandoned by God. The conviction that he was uninterruptedly the Word of God in human flesh made such a literal abandonment unthinkable. Only with the late Middle Ages did Western piety begin to conceive of the man Jesus as totally bereft of divine consolation in his final hours.

Early Theorizing on How Jesus' Death Was Saving

If Jesus overcame sin and, ultimately, death for all by conforming himself perfectly to the divine will, it was this obedience of his that redeemed the human race, not the tortures of crucifixion as something positively willed by God. These were simply the result, the outcome in his case, of a life obediently lived. The church fathers and medieval theologians spoke of the proximity of total goodness to human evil, represented by the self-serving power classes of Rome and Judaea. In the contest, good overcame evil. Death and the devil were disarmed. God and God's creature the human race were victorious through the life, death, and resurrection of this one representative of all who both lived and faced death as humanity ought.

The early theories of a literal ransom price paid in the form of Christ's blood were largely deserted in favor of the earlier one featuring his obedience in death as expiatory: the voluntary offering to God and acceptance by God of a sacrificial victim who was at the same time a priestly mediator. The circumstances of his death were not forgotten. They were featured as indignities that all but passed belief, a cruel paradox that only a God brimming with love could allow an obedient servant to endure.

With the eleventh-century theorizing of Anselm, which was refined in the next century by Bernard and more clearly still by Thomas Aquinas, came the view that the divine mercy and the divine justice were fulfilled equally in a work of satisfaction that only God could make and only a human being should make. When Thomas, like all in the West who had preceded him, taught that Adam's sin and the sins of all were the reason for the incarnation (he softened it by calling sin "a certain—*quaedam*—cause") the "Subtle Doctor" Duns Scotus (d. 1309), a Franciscan friar, challenged Thomas's view by holding that the sin of Adam was *not* the cause of the predestination of Christ. If it were, he said, the supreme work of God—the Word enfleshed—would only be "occasioned." "Therefore I say that the fall was not the cause of the predestination of Christ. And even if [no one] had fallen . . ., even if no other beings than he were to be created . . . Christ would still have been predestined."[1] We shall return later to this opinion, taken up by several medieval mystics, that God achieved the incarnation of the Word as a way of being most intimately joined to the creation. This pointed the way to the ultimate design of God for the creation, not the mending, of some cosmic "fall."

The Scotist supremacy of the divine freedom unmotivated by any actions of creatures was congenial to the reformers of later centuries. William of Ockham (d. 1347?) had continued in the voluntarist line of thought of his fellow Franciscan with a distinction between the "absolute power" and the "ordained power" of God. This held that there were no constraints on the divine will except those that were self-imposed. Luther was a disciple of Ockham through his master in theology, Gabriel Biel, but he was no Scotist except in an unconscious way.

The speculation of the Scots friar John Duns led to the position that God had willed Christ into being as one in whom God would exercise a fitting human self-love and then as one who would love God perfectly. He was such without any relation to the rest of creation or a sinful human race.

A few texts in the Bible—our only source on why God acted to achieve redemption in Christ—lead to the conclusion that it all came about independently of human sinfulness. Among them are Paul's description of a "new creation" in which God reconciles "the world" to himself (2 Cor. 5:17–20). The context is human sin but the text is much broader. In another place Paul writes that no creature can "separate us from the love of God in Christ Jesus our Lord," and there his language is consciously cosmic (Rom. 5:38–39). A disciple who is utterly faithful to Paul's thought speaks of the redemption by Christ's blood for the forgiveness of transgressions but goes on to call this a part of God's "plan for the fullness of time, [namely] to sum up all

---

1. "God foresees a mediator coming to suffer and ransom the people, but he would not have come as mediator, to suffer and to ransom, had not someone previously sinned. . . . But if the fall were the cause of the predestination of Christ, it would follow that the supreme work of God would be only 'occasional'. . . . Therefore I say that the fall was not the cause of the predestination of Christ; indeed, even if no one, angel or human, had fallen, even if no other beings than he were to be created. . . . Christ would still have been predestined." (The sentences occur in reverse order in Scotus's text.) *In III Sent.*, D. VII, q. 4, schol. 2, n. 4 and 5 (Paris, 1894), 23.303, cited by Louis Richard, *The Mystery of the Redemption,* trans. J. Horn (Baltimore: Helicon, 1965), 202.

things in Christ, in heaven and on earth" (Eph. 1:7–10; cf. Col. 1:15–20, which also speaks of the primacy of Christ in creation). The thesis that God would have sent the Son to be one of us to manifest the perfection of creaturehood, human sinfulness quite apart, is therefore not without its scriptural support.

Luther and Calvin on the Efficacy of the Cross

Luther derived from Bernard his Anselmian theory of a redemption that resulted from God's love, achieved necessarily by one who was both human and divine. He did more than that. Taking on what he thought was the resurgent Pelagianism of his age—humanity as responsible for its own salvation through its deeds—he interpreted gratuitous salvation in Jesus Christ to be a matter of diametric opposition between the divine blessing and the divine curse (or "wrath"). Pure divine love (*agápē*) unadulterated by *érōs* (as Luther thought Augustine's *caritas* to be) gave the gift to humanity of a clear victory over evil. It did not involve the necessity of Christ's making any payment to God in return, as head of the new human race. Luther retained the Anselmian necessity of a God-man as the redeemer but saw in him a manifestation of the divine love, pure and simple. Humanity as such was in no sense a cause of the redemption. Christ was made as if a sinner on whom the divine wrath was visited, but he did not achieve expiation of sins as representative of a guilty human race.

The interior renewal of humanity by the Spirit of Christ, a Pauline teaching, was not part of Luther's program, so intent was he on seeing in Christ a substitutionary victim for our sins. He was convinced that God could not share the divine righteousness with sinners but only impute it to them, reckoning sinners "justified" or acquitted of their guilt while they in fact remained sinners. Similarly, God imputed all human sins to the sinless Jesus. The theology of imputation to creatures of what could be an attribute of God alone, and of guilt to one who was totally innocent, came from Luther's nominalist inheritance. Nothing was as it seemed in ontological reality; all was as it was denominated by language, which could not bridge the gap to existence or being.

Luther's difficulties were not consciously philosophical. He would have denied hotly that philosophy had any part to play in his exegetical reflections, saying that the gulf between the all-holy God and the sinful creature could be bridged by the incarnation from God's side only, not from the side of a humanity in solidarity with the redeeming Christ. Nothing that smacked of humanity's saving itself was acceptable to this zealous reformer. Above all, a fallen race had no active capacity for receiving the divine gift of redemption. Luther was sure that some of the scholastics like Thomas were wrong in denying that humanity had been permanently damaged in all its faculties by Adam's sin. Luther's teaching on the work of Christ in his Small Catechism had been:

> He has delivered, purchased, and won me, a lost and doomed creature, from all sins, from death, and from the power of the devil; not with gold or silver, but with his holy, precious blood and with his innocent suffering and death.[2]

And in his Large Catechism of the same year, 1529:

> Jesus Christ, the Lord of life and righteousness and every good and blessing. . . . has snatched us, poor lost creatures, from the jaws of hell, won us, made us free, and restored us to the Father's favor and grace. . . . He became man . . . that he might become Lord over sin; moreover, he suffered, died, and was buried that he might make satisfaction for me and pay what I owed . . . with his own precious blood. . . . The devil and all powers, therefore, must be subject to him and lie beneath his feet.[3]

This theology of God's power overcoming sin, death, and the curse, leaving Christ by his grace to rule in the hearts of the faithful, is by all means convinced of the efficacy of the sacrifice of the cross—but in history alone, not in sacramental symbol as a means of imparting its benefits. The cross conveyed the depth and breadth of God's love for the human creature, who offered God nothing in sacrifice from below. There was a solidarity in sin with Adam but there is no solidarity with Christ that is in any sense enabling. No sacrifice can go up to God to influence the divine will in a human direction. Luther would willingly affirm the exhortation of Ephesians to "live in love as Christ loved you and gave himself up on your behalf, an offering and sacrifice whose fragrance is pleasing to God" (5:2), provided that "on your behalf" was not read as if the faith of believers gave them any part with Christ in the offering of the sacrifice, only in the reception of its benefits by imputation.

The theology of this pioneer among the reformers is not our main interest, however. At least his major concern—how the grace of redemption is appropriated by a sinful humanity—is not. But his understanding of how Christ merited human redemption is of interest because it derives directly from the late medieval concentration on the physical punishments Jesus endured in his crucifixion. Luther wrote that the pure and innocent person of the God-man Jesus Christ was more than that. He was given

> to you by the Father to be bridge builder and redeemer, or better your slave, who, laying aside his innocence and holiness, puts on your sinful person that

2. Luther, *Werke* (WA) 30/1, 249; cf. 294, 296 (ET, *Dr. Luther's Small Catechism* [St. Louis: Concordia, 1943], 10).

3. Ibid., 186 (ET, Robert H. Fischer, trans. *The Large Catechism of Martin Luther* [Philadelphia: Fortress Press, 1959], 58).

he might bear your Sin, your Death and your Curse and become a victim and one accursed for you, in order to deliver you from the curse of the law.[4]

Such was the way Christ achieved satisfaction for us. God looked on him as a substitute for the guilty human race. Seeing us weighed down by the curse of the law (as Luther read Paul, seeing the law itself to be a curse, not failure to fulfill it, as Deuteronomy has it), God mercifully delivered us from it as we could not do by our own efforts.

> When the merciful Father saw us oppressed by the law and held bound by the curse, and in no way able to be freed from it, [God] sent his Son into the world and placed on him the sins of all, saying to him: "Be Peter that denier, Paul that persecutor. . . . David that adulterer; be that sinner who ate the fruit in Paradise. . . . in short be that person among all humanity who has committed the sins of all human beings [of all time]. See, therefore, that you pay and make satisfaction for them. The law then comes along and says: "I find this one a sinner, who has taken on himself the sins of all, and I see no sins other than those in him. Therefore he must die on the cross." At that point it pounces on him and puts him to death. That is how the world is purged and cleansed from all sins, and so delivered from death and all evils.[5]

That graphic language shares with Paul something of the mythic contest he framed between Christ, the new Adam, and *hamartía,* sin personified. But it misreads Paul, who never said that the law of Moses was humanity's enemy, *tout court.* What Paul did was fault those teachers who were forcing observance of portions of the law on pagans and on fellow-Jews on the assumption that faith in the cross and resurrection was not enough.

The reformer's vigorous prose does something else that Paul did not do. It interprets literally the apostle's statement about Christ: "God made him one with human sinfulness who was innocent of sin, so that in him we might be made one with the justice of God" (2 Cor. 5:21). The Lutheran understanding of substitutionary sacrifice sees Jesus absorbing in his own person all the punishments that the sins of the ages deserve (but not, strangely, the ultimate punishment of deprivation of the vision of God). In this outlook there is a solidarity of Christ with humanity in sin but not, as consistency would expect, a solidarity with him in holiness.

There is simply not enough evidence in the New Testament to say that Christ delivers humanity from the punishment its sins deserve by submitting to this torment in its place. God's "wrath" is a reality hanging over sinners for Paul, but this term, derived from Jewish apocalyptic, describes what the Bible thought would be God's fitting response to the deeds of the wicked on the last day. The word conjured up a choleric deity for late medieval Chris-

4. Ibid., 40/1, 448, 23–26 (ET, *A Commentary on St. Paul's Epistle to the Galatians,* "Middleton" ed., rev. and trans. P. S. Watson [London: J. Clarke, 1953], 279).
5. Ibid., 437–38, 20–27 and 12–15 (ET, Watson, 272).

tians and for many Christians since, right up to the present. But "sinners in the hands of an angry God," receiving physical punishment for their wrong-doing of the kind Jesus was subjected to, is hardly what Paul had in mind—either in Galatians or anywhere else. When he says (Gal. 3:13) that Jesus "became a curse for us," he is speaking in colorful terms of human deliverance from the power of sin by Jesus' death on the cross, that punishment cursed by God (Deut. 21:23). He is not speaking of a curse placed on Jesus by God as if he had committed every human sin. Luther is here betrayed by his literal interpretation of Paul's figurative speech. Paul warns, of course, of divine justice for the wicked at the final judgment: "There will be affliction and distress for every human being who is a wrongdoer" (Rom. 2:9). But to go from that threat of retribution, such as any Jew of the Bible might utter, to a Christ on the cross delivering humanity from sin, death, and the devil by accepting the blows that would more fittingly be directed at sinners is to take too large a leap.

Jesus suffered greatly. He delivered himself up freely for humanity's sake. In doing so he set sinners free from the end-time "wrath" that is their due. Paul teaches this clearly in Romans 5:9, while saying that the impenitent of heart can expect no such deliverance (2:5–6). But one has to deny that he proposes a Jesus who, on the cross, was himself a victim of the literal wrath of God. The message of Paul was that retribution at the final judgment will come upon all who spurn God's love. Right up to the end, Jesus has the same compassion for them that he has for all sinners. But he was never of their number. His solidarity with the wicked was not such as to make him deserving of their punishment, either on the cross or at the end of time.

Luther was probably repelled by the cool rationality (*nihil rationabilius,* "nothing more reasonable") of the Anselmian formula of satisfaction, basically a compromise between the demand for punishment and the remission of punishment. The clear dualism between the love of God and the curse or wrath that sins deserve suited his temperament better, and indeed the temper of the times. He saw the wrath of God operative in his own day rather than, as in the Bible, at the end of days. He trumpeted the traditional conviction that Christ had won the decisive victory over sin, death, and Satan, but his doctrine of satisfaction for sin by penal substitution made the more lasting impression.

John Calvin was a man of the same period who, not surprisingly, espoused this teaching. He expressed it in the following way, including a distinction that does not appear in Luther's more vigorous prose:

> Not only was Christ's body given as the price of our redemption, but he paid a greater and more excellent price in suffering *in spirit* [a later addition to Calvin's text] the terrible torments of a condemned and forsaken man. . . . Yet we do not suggest that God was ever inimical or angry toward his beloved Son, "in whom his heart reposed." How could Christ by his intercession appease

the Father toward others, if he were himself hateful to God? This is what we are saying: he bore the weight of divine severity, since he was "stricken and afflicted" by God's hand and experienced all the signs of a wrathful and avenging God.[6]

This is the orthodoxy into which Protestant theology passed as it took its lead from its founding giants. The intensity of Christ's afflictions were understood to be such that, in virtue of the dignity of the person on whom they were heaped, they surpassed by an infinity those of the damned. Thus did the figurative language of the Bible receive a literal interpretation in a period when cruel and public punishments were the norm for criminal infractions. The phrase "Christ in our place" is capable of a better Pauline understanding than this one given it, but such is the one it received: penal substitution, an action in the external realm. But this was precisely the opposite of the interior feelings of guilt and sorrow that the reformers hoped to induce.

One should observe that Catholic piety of this century and after much resembled Protestant. The prayers at various "stations" of the Way of the Cross—a seventeenth-century devotion of the Capuchin Franciscan friars—would say that the crown of thorns, the scourging, and the hammer blows "should more fittingly be imposed on me for my sins."

The liberal Protestantism of the nineteenth century modified this type of thinking to a large degree by presenting Jesus' sufferings and death as the most powerful call to repentance for sin humanity had ever experienced. His death on the cross came to be seen again as a free act of love revealing the heart of God that can impose the devotion of love as a condition of salvation and restoration.[7]

Who and What Were Redeemed by the Cross and Resurrection?

Catholics, meanwhile, had concerned themselves at Trent chiefly with the way the merits of Christ—which the council, like Thomas, placed before satisfaction—were made available to believers. It stated along the way the quite traditional doctrine that Christ (whom it calls our Lord and God) "offered himself to God the Father once on the altar of the cross, his death interceding, in order to accomplish an eternal redemption . . . that he might consummate and lead to perfection those who were consecrated [by his one offering] (Hebrews 10:14)."[8]

This leads to a brief but important inquiry into who was believed to have been redeemed by the death and resurrection of Christ. The short answer,

6. *Inst.* 2.16.10–11 (ET, 1.516–17).
7. See Auguste Sabatier, *The Doctrine of the Atonement and Its Historical Evolution*, trans. V. Leuliette (New York: G. P. Putnam's Sons, 1904), 131.
8. Session XXII, September, 1562, "Teaching on the Sacrifice of the Mass," DS, 1740.

going back to New Testament times, is the entire human race. Along with it, the whole creation for which it gives voice was thought to have been reconciled to God. Obviously humanity alone was alienated by its sin. It had been preceded in this state permanently by the rebellious angels. But since the earth had been given over to human care and the skies and the seas too (although the people of the Bible could not have foreseen how our race could ever be responsible for them), the universe itself was thought to be at odds with God.

Its visible free creatures had gone the way of disobedience and brought everything in their train. "On your account the earth will be cursed," Genesis had said. "You will get your food from it only by labor all the days of your life; it will yield thorns and thistles for you. You will eat the produce of the field, and only by the sweat of your brow will you win your bread until you return to the earth" (3:17c–19a). If humanity were to be reconciled, there had to be some sense in which all things visible would be restored to a right order with their Creator. The cosmos was thought to be in an undeveloped state, making its way toward some future unknown consummation at the "end of days." Humanity, above all, was obviously incomplete. It was not so much that God as creator had done an imperfect work that needed mending, in a second start labeled "redemption." It was simply that the whole cosmos was somehow in process and that the most mysterious divine work of all, the free human creature, seems to have perverted the gift of freedom from the start. This threatened to bring the whole edifice of human habitation tumbling down about its ears.

The earliest theology of redemption viewed this work of God as totally gratuitous, something God need not have done. But the entire creation was itself a gratuity. Redemption was not a second work of God after the first work, creation—although the sequence imposed by time gave it that appearance. All that God does outside divinity is but one work achieved by a single act of will, however manifold it seems to us. From our standpoint redemption appears to be distinct from creation. To it we add sanctification as a work of the Spirit. But this attribution of the works of God to persons in God is only a human way of conceiving things. In God there is no such multiplicity of action. Redemption like sanctification is an aspect of the one act of God that brought all into being. It is not the mending of the botched deed that initially resulted in the cosmos nor of a failed divine plan for the human race. Redemption is the ongoing development of creation that includes within it the gentle corrective of human folly. It provides a second chance at fulfilling our destiny as human in the world that is our home.

The Universality of Human Redemption

The announced subject of the present chapter is modern theological thought about what is included in salvation by the cross. First, one needs to ask who the subjects are of the divine gratuity known as "salvation" (being made safe) or "redemption" (being rescued, bought back), both of them figures of speech. Was the whole human race redeemed by the cross and resurrection or only those who would, in the event, freely avail themselves of it? Are its benefits confined to those who come to hear of Christ's sacrifice and acquire them by faith and the sacramental signs of faith? How can the whole cosmos and the planet earth be spoken of as redeemed, since they seem to have had no part in the sin of earth's inhabitants?

Paul, the first one we know to have reflected on the mystery of redemption's scope, declares its universality as regards the human race. He places Christ as a counterweight to that hypothetical *hā'ādām* ("the man") who with *ḥawwāh* ("life" or "Eve") begot the entire race. No one who has ever lived a human life falls outside this race, whatever the circumstances were of its origins. Death has reigned in it from the beginning, Paul observes, even over those who did not actually sin after the manner of Adam (Rom. 5:14). The gift God gave in Christ did not closely resemble Adam's transgression; it far outweighed it, "overflowing for the many" (v. 15). "The many" (*polloùs*) here is a Hebraism in Greek meaning "all." It has the same connotation in v. 19: "For just as through the disobedience of one person the many were made sinners, so through the obedience of one the many will be made just." Paul in that passage has no interest in who will or will not be among the saved on the last day. He is busy singling out the two individuals on whose actions the fate of everyone else depends. All who were sprung of Adam's seed were born prone to sin and fated to die. No one born after Christ has been relieved of the burden of mortality, but all are ultimately able to overcome it. Paul makes no exceptions in either case, that of Adam or that of Christ. He has in mind the whole human race. His image of the two progenitors is a way of dividing the race into the mortal and those destined for resurrection from the dead.

A disciple of Paul repeats the apostle's assumption. This writer of 1 Timothy identifies God as humanity's savior (2:3), immediately describing God as one "who wills everyone [*pántas anthrṓpous*] to find salvation and come to the truth" (v. 4). Jesus Christ, himself human, is humanity's one mediator with God; he "gave himself as a ransom for all" (*hypèr pántōn*, v. 6). The verb for "wills" in v. 4 means "desires" in Paul's usage and that of the times, and frequently designates a fixed will, while that with which v. 8 begins, "It is my wish, therefore," indicates a specific preference. The writer clearly puts God on record as willing universal human salvation. Augustine had a great problem with this text of 1 Timothy because of his conviction that God had predestined some to be reprobated. To the end of his life he interpreted it to mean that God willed those to be saved who would be saved. But the text does not say that. It says "all."

The first letter of John makes a similar declaration when it calls Jesus Christ "a sacrifice [*hilasmós*] to atone for our sins, and not ours only but the sins of the whole world" (2:2). It does not matter that the first-century writers had a restricted view of who the inhabitants of the globe were. What is important is that they did not say "believers in Jesus Christ" or, as one might have expected in 1 John, "all who know the truth" (see 2 John 1). They said "all," "the whole world." In the Johannine Gospel, which similarly has a restricted view of what correct faith in Christ is, we read: "The true light that gives light to everyone was even then coming into the world" (1:9). This Gospel will later state that some among this "everyone" will choose darkness over light by doing evil deeds, by not living in the truth (3:19–20). But initially the true light who is the Word come in the flesh is an enlightenment intended for all.

Laying Hold of the Benefits of Redemption

From the start those who evangelized imposed a condition on who would in fact be saved. That condition was right faith. It found its expression in the rite of baptism and regular participation in the community meal, the Lord's Supper. "Without faith it is impossible to please God," says the anonymous Epistle to the Hebrews (11:6). Paul writes in Romans 10:9 that faith in Christ raised from the dead is the condition of salvation. He goes on to say that calling on the name of the Lord Jesus by Jew and non-Jew alike is a possibility open only to believers. They have become such because they have heard of him. Proclaimers of the gospel are thus a necessity if there are to be any who believe in it. Belief without hearing is impossible (see vv. 10–15). This conviction was the reason for the spread of the gospel of the New Testament period, for the activity of the Celtic monks and the evangelizers of entire peoples like Cyril, Methodius, Willibrord, and Ansgar, for the spread of the gospel as far east as China by those committed to Nestorian Christology and in the Middle Ages by Franciscan friars. The conviction going back to apostolic times was that pagan peoples were at risk. The benefits of redemption might not be shared with them if believers in it did not bring the gospel to them. Thus the word of salvation was spread as a condition of professing the faith.

We have seen in chapter 3 that Christians of the patristic period and much beyond it thought that Jews possessed enough indication in their Scriptures that Jesus was Israel's Messiah to bring them to faith in him. This did not keep the men of the Middle Ages from private proselytizing efforts among Jews and public disputations with rabbis in city squares. It was much the same with Muslims. For long the latter were thought to be Christian heretics in the matter of the divinity of Christ—latter-day Arians, in fact—and, like the Jews, in a condition of bad faith as regards their failure to believe. Yet the teaching of Paul in Romans, which held that they could know the power and divinity of God by reflecting on the works of creation (1:19–20), was not without effect as regards pagans. In the next chapter of the same epistle "good pagans" were exculpated from their ignorance of Mosaic law by observing its prescriptions written in their hearts. "Their conscience bears witness and their conflicting thoughts will accuse or defend them on the day when ... God will judge people's hidden works through Christ Jesus" (2:14–16). The knowledge of Christ available to believers in the law will thus be open to others who never heard of the law or the gospel through their lives well lived. It is clearly a knowledge that will lead to salvation on the last day. Although Paul did not entertain the possibility at any length, he allowed as salutary the law-righteousness of Jews who had not heard the gospel preached (see Rom. 2:25, 29; 3:30; 4:12) if they had Abrahamic faith, even if that faith did not lead them to Christ as he thought it should.

Without question the Jews of the ages have never "heard" the gospel in any true sense. They have only had it shouted at them by their religious adversaries who were Christians in name.

If redemption was thought to be the heritage of those non-Christians who lived in the light—in other words, those who had faith in the Gospel, even if unknowingly, and did the deeds of justice—what is to be said of Cyprian's famous declaration that "outside the Church there is no salvation"?[9] It was framed, one should recall, against North African heretics whom Cyprian thought to be in bad faith, not against Jews or pagans. For the bishop of Carthage it meant that membership in the visible, true, or Catholic Church was a condition of being saved. Heretics like the Patripassians and five other groups he lists, all of whom denied the Trinity, could not expect it. This watchword was expanded in the fifth (or sixth) century with the *Quicumque vult* or Athanasian Creed, a prayer of the West not the East, which was stitched together from Augustine's treatise *On the Trinity*. "Whoever wishes to be saved," it begins, "must above all else hold the Catholic faith." This is defined as worship of the one God in trinity and trinity in unity, plus faithful belief in "the incarnation of our Lord Jesus Christ." This creed was chiefly a spelling out of the coeternity and coequality of the three persons in God without mention of the Greek terms of inner trinitarian life (begetting, proceeding, or sending). It ends with the warning that, besides faith, "all will have to give an account of their works."

Cyprian had taught the necessity of infant baptism lest babies who died be deprived of the blessed vision of God. Augustine followed him in this, using it as the chief building block of his theory of original sin transmitted

---

9. *Epistle (73.21².) to (Bishop) Jubaianus on Whether Heretics Should Be Baptized* (PL 3.1123A; ET, G. W. Clarke, trans. *The Letters of St. Cyprian of Carthage*, 4, ACW 47 [New York and Mahwah, N.J.: Newman, 1989], 66, 231). Cf. Epistle 4, n. 37. Cyprian maintains in this sentence that baptism would profit heretics nothing, nor would even public profession of faith by martyrdom, because salvation is available only in the church: "Baptism we conclude, cannot be common to us and to heretics, for we have in common with them neither God the Father nor Christ the Son nor the Holy Spirit nor faith nor Church itself" (21.3). For his list of heretics see 73.4.2.

by birth, which became a doctrine of the Western Church. Indeed, Augustine thought that the hereditary transmission of sin was accomplished by the sex act, which was sinful because reason never quite managed to overcome the force of passion. The Catholic Church did not follow him in this teaching, although as a popular assumption it came to be almost as widespread as the doctrine itself. So great was Augustine's influence in the West, both on the clear distinction between Catholics and heretics and on the necessary means of salvation—namely, faith, baptism, and a eucharistic life—that with the passage of time the Cyprianic watchword *Salus extra ecclesiam non est* came to be applied to all who did not live as Catholics in this life.

With something of that understanding it was incorporated into the legislation of the fourth Lateran Council in 1215 against the Albigenses or Cathari.[10] Theologians continued in later centuries to follow Paul in his teaching found in Romans 1 and 2 as they devised theories of "invincible ignorance" of the gospel. But there the conciliar teaching stood, beamed at heretics chiefly but also at Jews and Muslims. Peoples of the pagan world, whom thirteenth-century Europe was coming to discover in all their magnitude, were largely thought of as capable of being saved through observance of "the law written in their hearts" (Rom. 2:14–15). It was the professed heretics from Catholic Christianity who, the fathers of the fourth Lateran thought, did not stand a chance.

The Scope of "Redemption"

At this late stage it is important to ask exactly what the theologians who attended to the problem thought was meant by "redemption," the term so freely used but never defined by the church in council. Like "salvation," which began its career in Israel around the turn of the Common Era meaning deliverance from condemnation on the last day, "redemption"—literally a buying back—was conceived by the followers of Jesus to be a benefit given to sinners as a result of his expiatory action directed to a forgiving God. All human sin was forgiven from Adam's day to the end of time. There were no offenses so great that those who committed them could not identify them-

10. DS, 802: "Una vero est fidelium universalis Ecclesia, extra quam nullus omnino salvatur." Cf. DS, 3866–73, in which the Holy Office wrote a letter to the archbishop of Boston on August 8, 1949, reiterating the sentiment of Cyprian as a dogma but one that the ecclesiastical *magisterium*, not private judgment, needs to explain. The judgment of Father Leonard Feeney, S. J., that only Catholics could be saved was then repudiated in favor of the interpretation that an implicit desire (*votum*) to be of the church, if supernaturally motivated, suffices for salvation. Of course, God alone can determine when such conditions are met, even in the case of committed members of other faiths or those of no faith who maintain stoutly they have no such implicit desire. For a careful account of the history of Cyprian's watchword in patristic, conciliar, and papal teaching, triggered by the Feeney case, see Francis A. Sullivan, S. J., *Salvation Outside the Church* (New York/Mahwah, N.J.: Paulist Press, 1992). Cf. Louis Capéran, *Le Problème du Salut du Infidèle* (Toulouse, 1934).

selves with Jesus, their fellow human who had shed his blood in acceptable sacrifice, and be forgiven. The work of creation could thus proceed to its completion as divinely intended. The interruption constituted by sin was tragic by any reckoning. In holding out the possibility of human reconciliation God had simply proceeded with the creative intent, determined to see the promise of creation fulfilled.

If redemption was generally looked on in the patristic period as the restoration of a fallen world to the path on which it had initially been set, the medieval and subsequent ages began to see it as largely having its effect on a rescued humanity after this life was over. To be sure, the grace of Christ was the element or matrix in which the body of believers thought themselves to have their being. They saw themselves as a people redeemed. As for "salvation," it was something different, the life of heaven that came after life "in this vale of tears" as the medieval hymn *Salve Regina* put it. One might be "justified" or "given the life of grace" here. "Salvation" was hoped for hereafter. As a result of this hope for a blessed future, the present life was less and less thought of as being a redeemed condition. The power of sin and Satan was considered to be as strong as ever. People were led in their liturgies and in sermons to think of themselves as having been redeemed, but they acted as if its reality were something that lay ahead. The religious language of Christians spoke of redemption as a liberation from sin and the effects of sin. It seemed a distant prospect.

Redemption as Liberation

The Hebrews of the Bible experienced redemption at God's hands when they were liberated from Egyptian slavery and Babylonian captivity. Liberation connotes that which frees the poor and oppressed from the proximity of death and encourages them to live.[11] Those who are oppressed socioeconomically are near death and are likely to suffer a violent death when they work for their liberation. The liberating of the poor is central to the Jewish Scriptures, which Christians claim as their own. The same is true of the Synoptic Gospels if they are not read "spiritually" and, above all, of the Epistle of James. Yet, while relief of the poor was a theme of Christianity from the beginning, it found no echo in an understanding of redemption as the removal of the evils of society that create poverty. This silence was undoubtedly conditioned by the origins of the religion in a distinctly minority situation. When Christianity came to have influence and even a measure of power its bishops resisted the encroachments of political power upon spiritual power, but they left the affairs of state, by necessity, to emperors and kings.

11. For this definition see Jon Sobrino, S.J., "Eastern Religions and Liberation," *Horizons* 18/1 (Spring 1991): 79.

These Christian sovereigns were the ones who were expected to work justice. When they resorted to tyranny they were frequently condemned by the holders of spiritual office. The improvement of society was not, however, seen as a corollary of the redemption wrought by Christ. It was as if sin stood somehow in isolation from society: a moral evil in the lives of individuals only. Its effects in the form of widespread social injustices were not seen as part of it. Humanity in its sinfulness was thought to have been reconciled to God personally and individually but not as human society. To remedy the effects of sin in accepting the gift of redemption, no heavy price was expected to be paid beyond repentance. The damage to the race and to the world it dwelt in was not required to be reversed as a condition of forgiveness.

Redemption and Creation

This raises the question whether Christianity and the religion of Israel before it and contemporaneous with it are holistic religions. Do they see the cosmos as a whole and the earth within it as a created unity, not just the home of the human race? Christianity seems to have a quality that makes the holistic part of human experience difficult. On the ethical if not on the metaphysical plane there is a duality that favors a passionate taking of sides: grace vs. sin, life vs. death, God vs. moral evil.[12] The necessity of being *against* may interfere seriously with the need to be *for*—specifically, to be for the whole creation and not just the human race in relation to the creator God. Consulting the needs of the poor and the oppressed, if taken seriously, should mean caring for all subhuman life and nonlife as part of this concern. Often it does not. Sin inclines the human creature to be a predator of fellow humans and to plunder the earth with equal vigor. A correct understanding of the creation as a unity would know what the redemptive task is in response to the redemptive gift. Here Christianity has fallen short. It preaches living for others, but it does not specify the care of all creatures and their earthly habitat as the way God redeems the whole earth from its undeveloped state. The effects of sin are what keep that development from going forward.

Human unfulfillment—the result of sin and not just the fact of finitude— is as old as human life. In creating a race that was free God allowed the possibility from the start of a world in need of redemption from sin. Because God is God, the divine presence to the world has always been a reality. This makes for a redeemed world—the creation continually developed and a saved human race. For as long as there has been a planet earth populated by such a race, God has never been absent. God's work is to see the promise of creation fulfilled. The fullness of redemption in Christ may lie ahead—but there has always been redemption.

12. See Sobrino under "The Experience of Losing and Finding Oneself in the Whole," 84–86.

And it was there for all, not only for those to whom God was self-revealed, as to the Hebrews. The Jews . . . and the Christians . . . surely shortened God's arm by confining the divine graciousness to the self-disclosures that had been shared with them. God has never been bound by such necessity. The better truth . . . is that the redemptive grace of God is a reality of always and everywhere. There has not for an instant been an unredeemed world nor a person not called to fill the promise of creation, with or without a knowledge of Christ.[13]

What God did in the work of creation was well done, not imperfectly done. It is only humans and angels who have the tragic capacity to do badly what they are able to do well. Richard A. Norris, a theologian of the Episcopal Church, speaks perceptively when he says that the world is in need of, and has been offered, redemption:

The doctrine of creation is really the statement of a promise . . . which is ingrained in the very nature and structure of the world. . . . The world's createdness . . . is a pointer. It points to the possibility of the human world's becoming, in an open, explicit, and realized way, what it is already and in principle: God's world. . . . People talk about redemption, and about the need for redemption, because circumstances in the human world do not correspond with the promise of creation. . . . People are tied and bound in relations and attitudes which make them hostile to God and to one another. To actualize the promise of creation therefore means necessarily, to put right something which is wrong. . . . To speak of redemption . . . is to speak of the way God acts to fulfill the promise of creation. God does this by becoming present for people as his own Word, and so setting them free for life of a new quality—for a life fulfilled in love.[14]

Observe Norris's stress on the world as in need of redemption. Theologians generally speak of a human fall as requiring restoration, of human sin and death as requiring an overcoming at God's hands. This victory has been achieved by the death and resurrection of Christ, which opened to sinful humanity the possibility of a share in his victory. Of the need for redemption of the whole world, even the cosmos because both have had a share in humanity's shame, they are usually silent.

Can a cosmic or global alienation be simply a human conceit, puny human beings supposing that their fate governs the fate of the farthest star? Paul seems to have thought otherwise. He writes that creation itself has been made subject to futility but lives in the hope that it will be set free from its slavery to corruption "and share in the glorious freedom of the children of

---

13. Gerard S. Sloyan, *Jesus: Redeemer and Divine Word* (Wilmington, Del.: Michael Glazier, 1989).

14. Norris, *Understanding the Faith of the Church* (New York: Seabury, 1979), 71, 73.

God." What believers already possess is evidently something that the rest of creation does not. He follows that by saying: "We know that all creation is groaning in labor pains until now; and . . . we also groan within ourselves as we wait for adoption, the redemption of our bodies" (Rom. 8:20–24). His context is the hope he and other believers entertain as they await the general resurrection, but the underlying theme is that creation's period of gestation is far from over. The universe of things continues to be in the process of being redeemed.

The present century has revealed to us what we could not have previously known, namely, that we live in an evolving universe. Its tendency toward fulfillment of some sort, not just the entropy predicted for our small galaxy, is a hypothesis of some astrophysicists. Whether they are right or wrong, the evolutionary character of the universe and of all life on this planet cannot be doubted. This incontrovertible truth led the sometime paleontologist and full-time religious thinker Pierre Teilhard de Chardin to see Christ as central to evolution, as Paul had seen him as the end point of history. God has subjected everything to the Son, Paul says, and at the end of days the Son will be subjected to God "so that God may be all in all things that are" (1 Cor. 15:28). For Teilhard, Christ is the "Omega Point," the last term in the series that began with Alpha, the birth of the cosmos. But "while being the last term of its series it is *outside all series*. Not only does it crown but it closes."[15] As Gabriel Daly, an Irish Augustinian, sums up Teilhardian thought, "Omega embraces physics, chemistry, biology, anthropology, history, and eschatology. Teilhard quite simply identifies it with Jesus Christ."[16] The French Jesuit never loses sight of his commitment to the incarnation and the redemptive death of Christ: "To be alpha and omega [the terminology is from Rev. 22:13], Christ must, without losing his precise humanity, become co-extensive with the physical expanse of time and space."[17] Such a hypothesis may be said to have been contained in germ in Tertullian's speculation in *On the Resurrection of the Dead*: "The image of Christ, the man who was to be, was influencing every stage in the molding of the clay [at Adam's creation]; because what was at that moment happening to the earth's clay would happen again when the Word became flesh."[18]

Teilhard was not a theologian and did not presume to be. He never worked out theologies of the incarnation or redemption. But he did make some mid-twentieth-century theologians take seriously the thought of Paul on the intimate relation of creation and redemption and the cosmic outlook on Christ found in Colossians and Ephesians. Placing Christ at the focal

15. *The Phenomenon of Man*, trans. B. Wall (New York: Harper, 1969), 297. Italics in original.
16. Daly, *Creation and Redemption* (Wilmington, Del.: Michael Glazier, 1989), 77.
17. *Human Energy*, trans. J. M. Cohen (New York: Harcourt Brace Jovanovich, 1969), 61.
18. Chap. 6 (*PL* 2.802–3).

point of cosmic evolution, he forced them to see the historical event of the cross and resurrection as a stage on the road in the continuing story of creation-redemption.

Not all modern thinkers about the mystery of redemption conceive it in eschatological terms, although all have the problem of situating it within human history. The German theologian Karl Rahner wrestles with the question of how redemption as God's self-communication to a finite creature (which he takes it to be) can depend on the historical event of the cross. If that event is the manifestation in time of the eternal saving and redemptive will of God, that will must be the cause both of the event and the effect that flows from it. He answers his own question by identifying the cross as the efficacious sign of God's will to save, made irreversible by its appearance in the world in a historically tangible way. He sees in the cross "the real symbol . . . of God's definitive and victorious love for the world, [which] also implies in Jesus' obedience unto death the human acceptance of this offer on the part of the world."[19] God has no problem in making the historical reality of Calvary an effective symbol as it looks backward and forward over the whole sweep of time. For long concealed, God's will to redeem in this way was manifested at a particular point in time, as Ephesians says.

Rahner is so absorbed in the matter of the divine freedom as it is shared with the free creature that when he is asked to speak on the topic "Justification and World Development from a Catholic Viewpoint," he does not recognize it as an invitation to develop the idea of the ongoing redemption of the cosmos. Instead, he provides a bewildered audience with a discussion of the infused virtues of faith, hope, and love that are a concomitant of justification. Only at the end of a dozen pages does he speak of the way God's immediacy to the world is mediated by the existential decision of the Christian (in the singular) concerning an "intramundane goal as object of his choice . . . required as binding here and now."[20]

If Protestant and Catholic theologians may be said to be at present still largely absorbed with redemption by the cross as God's response to human sin, chiefly Adam's sin in the manner of Paul and Augustine, it should be said immediately that there is a growing concern in all the churches with redemption as the liberation of the poor and the oppressed. Among the oppressed are peoples of color and women everywhere on the globe. Some of this theological exploration does not go much deeper than disclosing the injustices done to these oppressed classes, which in itself is no little service. The direct application of the event of the cross and resurrection to all peoples everywhere, including non-Christians, is still in its infant stages. The applica-

19. Karl Rahner, S.J., "The Christian Understanding of Redemption," in *Theological Investigations*, vol. 21, *Science and Christian Faith*, trans. Hugh M. Riley (New York: Crossroad, 1988), 248, 251.

20. Idem, *Theological Investigations*, vol. 18, *God and Revelation*, trans. Edward Quinn (New York: Crossroad, 1983), 259–73.

tion of the meaning of this deed of God for an evolving universe *as a theological project* is only coming to birth.

There has been an inordinate fear of a "theology of liberation," up to this point, on the grounds that it may be Marxist-inspired, hence prone to a violent class warfare to achieve equity in a classless society, in the process denying both a right to private property and the God who ensures it. The proponents of such a theology have not been successful in maintaining that while they have had recourse to Marxist categories in their analysis of the problem of the world's poor and, inevitably, favored some of the same solutions, they have never derogated from human rights that can be demonstrated to be truly rights. The Protestant theologian Paul Lehmann has leveled a fairly harsh judgment at the opponents of the liberation of the oppressed. He speaks of:

> the self-justifying and polemical disavowal of liberation theology by those who have wittingly or unwittingly surrendered to the self-confidence, the achievements, and the temptations offered by the principalities and powers that have brought the "First World" into being, and keep it going.[21]

Endless arguments are possible about the moral aspects of restricted and unrestricted capitalism, about human labor as the first title to ownership, about the morality of state intervention in the distribution of property, goods, and services. These can be diversionary from the main question: Is humanity its brother's keeper? Put in Christian terms, is belief in universal redemption by the cross and resurrection of Jesus Christ compatible with political, military, and economic systems that produce obscene wealth for the few at the price of the dehumanization and death of the many?

The Latin American theologians, many of them trained in western Europe and taking the classical theology of the Bible and the church fathers as their foundation, are doing their theological work

> outside the great centers of imperial power. . . . They have been compelled by their faith to identify with the struggle of the dispossessed in their societies. As a result, *they speak of the great drama of redemption as the struggle for liberation on the part of the oppressed.* . . . If we take [the inhuman conditions in which oppressed people live their lives] seriously, we will no longer be content to say that God became human so that human beings can become divine. Rather we must affirm that God became a poor person so that those most dehumanized by exploitation and oppression can have a full human life. This is the goal of the divine intervention in history.[22]

Liberation theologians, rather than being a marginalized band speaking only for the marginalized, give evidence of being modern fathers and doctors

21. Paul Lehmann, "Foreword" to Richard Shaull, *Heralds of a New Reformation: The Poor of South and North America* (Maryknoll, N.Y.: Orbis, 1984), ix.
22. Shaull, *Heralds*, 68–69.

of the church. They have taken the well-worn phrasing about the conquest of sin, death, and the devil and made it specific. Far from denying the reality of a world to come, with which they are often charged, they are concerned to see whether any can believe in it among the millions who have so little evidence of a redeemed world that is *now*.[23]

23. The theological literature on the subject of human redemption in the persons of the world's poor and the earth that is theoretically theirs is immense. Much but not all of it comes from Latin America. This writing already begins to be joined by the work of theologians from Asia and Africa. One should observe that the focus of this theology on the oppressed and the marginalized, in light of the geometric rate of population growth of the present century, is a matter of most of the human beings who have ever lived on the earth. For theological discussions of human liberation as redemption, see in particular Gustavo Gutiérrez, *A Theology of Liberation* (Maryknoll, N.Y.: Orbis, 1971); *The True Church and the Poor* (Maryknoll, N.Y.: Orbis, 1984); George V. Pixley and Clodovis Boff, *The Bible, the Church and the Poor* (Maryknoll, N.Y.: Orbis, 1989); John O'Brien, *Theology and the Option for the Poor* (Collegeville, Minn.: Liturgical Press, 1992).

CHAPTER SEVEN

Piety Centered on Jesus' Sufferings

"Eccentric" means literally off center, and in the context of this chapter it denotes any departure from the more usual patterns of piety or devotion that have attended Christ's crucifixion and resurrection. One cannot speak of practices approved or disapproved by church authorities because this sort of approbation—or its denial—apart from the condemnation of heresy, tends to be quite modern. The refinements of church law and episcopal authority came long after centuries of popular devotion to the tomb of Jesus, his precious blood, and the instruments of his torture. Before examining the extraordinary or uncommon, we must explore briefly those expressions of faith and piety centered on Christ's death and resurrection that came to prevail. As to what was central to these mysteries and what was eccentric, it will be left to the readers to decide, though I caution them not to apply twentieth-century criteria to other ages.

Luke in his second volume, the book of Acts, contrasts the burial place of David in Jerusalem, which he takes to be a well-known contemporary site (traditionally on Mt. Zion in the old city), with the tomb in which Jesus' body does *not* lie. Acts has David prophesying Jesus' different fate from his own when Judah's king says in Psalm 16:10: "You will not abandon my soul to the nether world, nor will you suffer your faithful one to undergo corruption." Luke changes the possessive pronouns to "his," meaning Christ's, and goes on to have Peter say: "God raised this Jesus; of this we are all witnesses" (2:31–32).

Sites Connected with Jesus' Passion
in the Patristic Age

The next mention of Jesus' tomb is by the anonymous pilgrim of Bordeaux, whose journey to Palestine can be dated to 333 by his (her?) naming of the Roman consuls currently in office.[1] As observed in chapter 5 above, the bulk

1. See "The Pilgrim of Bordeaux," in *Egeria's Travels to the Holy Land*, ed. John Wilkinson, rev. ed. (Jerusalem: Ariel, 1971, Warminster: Aris & Phillips, 1981), 153–63. This transla-

of the pilgrim's account is in the form of listing the cities and towns where he (she?) changed modes of transportation. Naming among other sites Sarepta, Haifa (Sycaminos), Caesarea, Jezreel, and Scythopolis (Beth-shan), the pilgrim identifies them by incidents attached to them in the two Testaments of Scripture. In Jerusalem the author singles out two large pools that flank the temple site and the "twin pools with five porches called Bethsaida."[2] As to the sites connected with the passion of Christ, the pilgrim identifies the place where once the house of Caiaphas stood and says that "the column at which they fell on Christ and scourged him still remains there."[3] This pillar will have a long history as an authentic relic of the passion. It was brought from Constantinople to Rome by Cardinal Giovanni Colonna in 1223 and placed in a chapel in the Basilica of S. Prassede, whose protector he was. Some walls where Pontius Pilate once had his house are also mentioned by the pilgrim. So, too, is the praetorium of Jesus' trial, at a site unspecified except for the notation that "on the left is the hillock Golgotha where the Lord was crucified, and about a stone's throw from it the vault where they laid his body, and he rose again on the third day."[4]

The pilgrim speaks of a basilica (*dominicum*) on the site built at Constantine's order, beside which are cisterns—excavated in the twentieth century—and a baptistry. He or she identifies the declivity of the Brook Kidron with the Valley of Jehoshaphat and a vineyard on the Mount of Olives as being near the rock where Judas Iscariot betrayed Christ. This is probably the immense slab arising out of the earth within the modern Franciscan Church of All Nations. The only surprising feature of the account is the naming of a hillock near Mt. Olivet as the site of the transfiguration, which Cyril, bishop of Jerusalem, would shortly place on Galilee's Mt. Tabor. Nothing is said in the pilgrim's account about activities, liturgical or otherwise, at these places.

Eusebius, bishop of Caesarea, wrote a *Life of Constantine* in 337, the year of the emperor's death, which unlike the account of the Bordeaux pilgrim describes the cave that contains Christ's tomb ("the most holy memorial of the Savior's resurrection"), without any reference to the crucifixion as a separate event.[5] He speaks of a temple to Aphrodite, erected by pagans on this "divine memorial of immortality," that Constantine had demolished. Following the demolition, Eusebius writes, the removal of layer after layer

tion is based on *Itinerarium Burdigalense* (ed. P. Geyer and O. Cuntz in CChr, *Series Latina* 175 (Turnhout, 1965), 1–26. The CSEL version has been cited above, pp. 123, n. 7; 127.

2. Wilkinson notes that the temple remained in ruins until the Muslims cleared the site for reuse in the seventh century. Modern text-critical readings of the pool site are divided between Bethesda and Bethzatha.

3. Wilkinson, *Egeria's Travels*, 157; cf. the edition by A. Franceschini and R. Weber, CChr, Series Latina 175, 29–90.

4. Wilkinson, *Egeria's Travels*, 158.

5. Ibid., 164–71.

of subsoil revealed the cave he calls "the holy of holies." There is no mention of the outcropping of rock known as Golgotha. Constantine ordered a house of prayer to be built in the precincts of the cave site. This was evidently not a church since Egeria fifty years later would speak of only one called "the Great Church, the Martyrium."

The concentration on Jesus' resurrection and silence about his crucifixion is probably indicative of the way the mystery was being preached in the days the emperor was espousing the new religion. It will be interesting to see the near eclipse of the resurrection by the crucifixion after the year 1000. Eusebius goes on to speak of the emperor's having adorned the holy cave (the "most blessed place of the Lord's resurrection"), probably by building an open cloister to surround it. This was the Anastasis ("Resurrection"); to the east of it rose "a basilical church, a masterpiece." But again, as with the pilgrim of Bordeaux, nothing is said of the devotions practiced within these magnificent new structures.

That is left to Egeria, a woman pilgrim, probably a nun, who lived somewhere near the Atlantic Ocean and wrote a journal of her experiences in Jerusalem in 381.[6] The manuscript we have is incomplete but detailed and highly informative. Her report on the exercises of piety surrounding the places where Jesus died, was buried, and rose is exclusively liturgical. We learn from her the basic outlines of an early cathedral rite, namely Jerusalem's, and in that fabric the functions of a bishop, presbyters, deacons, monks and nuns, the other baptized, and catechumens. She informs us of how important the singing of the Psalter was to fourth-century Christians; the proclamation of the Gospel passages on the sufferings, death, and resurrection of Jesus on the presumed sites where they occurred; and the passages of the Hebrew Scriptures that spoke of an innocent sufferer, always assumed to be Jesus in type or figure. Of prayer to God through the medium of replicating the sufferings of Jesus in the bodies of individual believers or even the whole body, the church, she says nothing. The commemoration of the saving mysteries had evidently not yet taken that turn by the late fourth century. There was, however, much reflection on what Jesus had endured for love of his friends. The only form this took was that of meditation and sacramental memorial, of which preaching was an integral part.

Early Pieties Deriving from the Crucifixion

A devotional practice from the patristic period was the reproduction of the likeness of the cross in one's posture at prayer.[7] Ambrose, Tertullian, and

---

6. Ibid., 91–147, preceded by the valuable "Introduction," 3–88.
7. For this, see Louis Gougaud, "Attitudes of Prayer," in *Devotional and Ascetic Practices in the Middle Ages,* trans. G. C. Bateman (London: Burns & Oates, 1927), 1–43.

Augustine all proposed this practice. Maximus of Turin (d. after 465) wrote in a *Second Homily on the Cross of the Lord:*

> We are taught to [elevate and] stretch out our hands in prayer, for by such a position we show forth the Passion of the Lord. Our prayer accompanied by this attitude will be the more quickly answered, for, in this manner, while the soul speaks with Christ, the body imitates the Crucified.[8]

Maximus follows that with the observation, by his time a commonplace, that it is by this sign of the Lord that the sea is breasted (the mast and yard of a ship), the earth ploughed (with a single-handled implement), the heavens divided (into four cruciform compass points), and human beings rendered saved.

The practice of holding the arms extended in prayer is very old and continued, at least in private prayer among ascetics, well into the Middle Ages. Because it was tiring if sustained, it came to be adopted as a practice of mortification. As a regular penance in monasteries (e.g., for those who came late to exercises or broke the night silence), it was called "Going to the cross," a stretching out of the arms on an instrument used for the purpose. Without the actual cross the practice continues in convents and monasteries to this day. As indicated in chapter 5, all 150 psalms were sometimes recited (in Latin) in this posture as a penance, although supporting oneself on choir stalls or some other object has to be assumed to make these stories credible (consider Psalm 119 alone!). Sometimes the penance was performed on the floor or the ground, face downward. A special word was developed in Old Irish for the practice, *crossfigell,* from *crucis vigilia.*[9]

It is told of some saints, Ambrose among them, that they died lying prone in this position, and even of the Irish saint, Kevin of Glendalough, that his seven-year vigil with arms upwardly outstretched, resting against a plank, brought birds to nest in his motionless hands. The practice of holding the arms aloft continues among country folk to this day in places of pilgrimage like Lourdes and Czestochowa. One rite of penance at Lough Derg in Donegal is to stand with one's back to St. Brigid's Cross and recite with arms outstretched: "I renounce the world, the flesh, and the devil." The practice of uplifted arms even made its way into some Mass rites before Trent, as during the prayer after the major elevation, *Wherefore, mindful of his passion, death, and resurrection* (e.g., in the Carmelite rite), and throughout the canon or central eucharistic prayer for Carthusians.

From Cross to Crucifix

Images of the cross began to be displayed for public homage once the church was granted official status in the fourth century. At first the cross was either

---

8. *PL* 57.342–43.
9. Gougaud, "Attitudes of Prayer," 10–11.

bare or had five precious stones indicating Jesus' wounds to the head, hands, side, and feet (the last was represented by one gem, on the supposition that his feet were crossed at the ankles). Early attempts to show Jesus affixed to the cross were not very successful artistically. There is such a carving on a door in Rome's Church of St. Sabina (5th century) and an ivory with the same depiction from that century or the next in the British Museum. The crucifixion scene found on a page of the Syriac evangeliary of Rabula dating from 586 is, however, both naturalistic and quite successful.[10]

The Syrians are chiefly responsible for the diffusion of the crucifix in the West in the sixth and seventh centuries.[11] In the early Middle Ages there were few representations of Christ on the cross (see the counsel of the 12th-century Cistercian Ailred of Rievaulx to his sister, allowing her a crucifix only in her cell, p. 133 above). By the fourteenth and fifteenth centuries, which saw devastating wars and plagues, much spiritual strength was derived from viewing the tortures of Christ in the most realistic manner. These were the years of multiplied devotions to the passion of Jesus, his five wounds, and the outpouring of his blood. These developments I shall have to examine at length.

Devotion to the Five Wounds of Christ

It is fascinating to trace the concentration on the wounds of the Savior, how they came to be reckoned as five, and the way the devotion grew. Edmund of Canterbury (d. 1240), whose tomb at Bury St. Edmonds was long a center of pilgrimage, reportedly received the *Viaticum* on his deathbed and then washed with wine and water the five wounds of the crucifix he cherished in his last hours. He made the sign of the cross over these ablutions and drank them, having first quoted the prophet: "You shall draw water with joy at the fountain of salvation [or "of the Savior," as his Latin Bible read] (Isaiah 12:3)."[12] Peter Damiani (d. 1072) wrote in one of his minor works: "He [Jesus] is stripped of his clothing; he is beaten, bound, and spat upon; his flesh is pierced by a fivefold wound; so that we may be healed from the entry of vices, which reach us through the five senses."[13]

During the first thousand years of Western Christianity little attention was paid to the wounds of Christ aside from the early *crux gemmata* described above. The increasing popularity of the crucifix brought about the

10. Reproduced as fig. 3380 in H. Leclercq's article, "Croix et Crucifix," *DACL* 3/2 (Paris, 1914), 3075–76. The previous two cited above are figs. 3377 and 3376, respectively. The Rabula evangeliary is in the Laurentian Library, Florence.

11. Louis Gougaud, "The Beginnings of the Devotion to the Sacred Heart," in *Devotional and Ascetic Practices*, 76, citing Louis Bréhier, *Les Origines du Crucifix dans l'Art religieux* (Paris, 1904).

12. Ibid., 79, citing *Vita S. Edmundi* in Martène, Durand, *Thesaurus novus anecdotarum*, 3 (Paris, 1717), 1816.

13. *Opusculum* 43.5 (PL 145.683B).

change. The stigmata accorded to Francis contributed to the spread of the devotion. As early as 1139, a chronicler says, Alfonso Henriquez placed the emblem of the five wounds on his coat of arms as king of Portugal in thanks for a victory over five Moorish chieftains on the plain of Ourigue.[14] Important in this development was the emerging devotion to the wound from the spear thrust in Christ's side (from which ultimately came devotion to the Sacred Heart).

Popular prayer centered on the five wounds was known in Germany in the thirteenth century if not earlier. In the next century a feast of that title originated in the Benedictine monastery of Fritzlar on the Eder. It spread shortly to other monasteries and churches and by 1507 had made its way into the calendar of Mainz (the introit began *Humiliavit*, from Phil. 2:7). The feast was celebrated on the Friday after the octave of Corpus Christi.[15] The popular belief was that if this Mass were celebrated five times the release of a soul from purgatory was assured, while many graces and temporal favors would come to the living for whom the Mass was offered. Five candles were specified for the feast in a Dominican missal of 1519.

Many other pious practices surrounding the feast involved the number five. Among these was the custom of saying five Our Fathers and five Hail Marys at noon to the ringing of church bells in honor of the five wounds. The thirteenth century witnessed many private prayers composed to commemorate the wounds, among them one read at the request of the dying Clare of Assisi, according to her legend. She also had attributed to her a later prayer divided into five sections, each of them devoted to one of the wounds and beginning, "Praise and glory be to thee for thy most holy wound [of the hands, feet, side]." A *Pater* and an *Ave* followed each section, with the following versicle and response:

V.   The five wounds of God
    R.   Are my healing medicine.
V.   By [thy] five wounds
    R.   Deliver me, O Christ, from ruin.
V.   Grant peace, O Christ,
    R.   By thy five wounds.

A final concluding prayer read:

Almighty and eternal God, who hast redeemed the human race by the five wounds of thy Son our Lord Jesus Christ, grant thy suppliants that they who venerate these same wounds daily may, by His precious blood, deserve to be delivered from a sudden and an eternal death. This we ask through the same Jesus Christ our Lord.

14. Heinrich Schäffer, *Geschichte von Portugal*, 1 (Hamburg, 1836), 46–47, as cited by Gougaud, *Devotional and Ascetic Practices*, 16, n. 116.
15. Gougaud, *Devotional*, 82.

It was expected that, as indicated, the prayer would be recited daily. Gertrude of Helfta (d. 1302) said she knew of such a prayer in honor of the wounds of Christ. A briefer ejaculatory prayer was, "Let the five wounds of Christ be my medicine." Germany knew the wounds as *Minnezeichen* ("Signs of Love"). In the fifteenth century the wounds were sometimes described as "Fountains." Members of the religious order founded by Bridget of Sweden, both men and women (Bridgettines), wore an emblem of the five wounds on their habits. In England the wounds appeared on the banners of the Pilgrimage of Grace of 1536–37, the uprising of the Catholics of Yorkshire against Henry VIII led by Robert Aske.

One less-than-pious outcome of devotion to the five wounds was the blasphemous utterance common in medieval and Tudor England, "Zounds!" short for "God's wounds" (cognate with "'Sblood!" and "Odds bodkins," "God's [eucharistic] body"). Many superstitious promises came to be attached to the devotion to the wounds, which included doing all sorts of things in fives to be assured of spiritual effect.

The popular prayer *Anima Christi* is attributed to Pope John XXII (d. 1334) and goes, in a still popular English versification known to every former Catholic schoolchild above a certain age:

> Soul of Christ be my sanctification,
> Body of Christ be my salvation.
> *Blood of Christ fill all my veins,*
> *Water from Christ's side wash out my stains.*
> Passion of Christ my comfort be,
> O good Jesus, listen to me.
> *In thy wounds I feign would hide*
> *Ne'er to be parted from thy side.*
> Guard me should the foe assail me.
> Call me when my life shall fail me.
> Bid me come to thee above,
> With thy saints to sing thy love. Amen.

It occurs in the Roman missal as a prayer to be recited after communion, largely because of the devotion to it of Ignatius of Loyola, and is known to many as a hymn in the translation of Edward Caswall (d. 1878), "Soul of My Savior, sanctify my breast, / Body of Christ, be thou my saving guest."

If these prayers are thought of as *centered* on the sufferings of Jesus, the *eccentric* is typified by a revelation that Jesus supposedly made to Elizabeth of Hungary, Mechtild of Hackeborn, and Bridget of Sweden concerning the sufferings he underwent:

Be it known that the number of armed soldiers was 150; those who trailed me while I was bound were 23. The executioners of justice were 83; the blows received on my head were 150; those on my stomach 108; kicks on my shoulders, 80. I was led, bound with cords, by the hair, 24 times; spittings in the face were 180; I was beaten on the body 6,666 times; beaten on the head 110 times. I was roughly pushed and at 12 o'clock was lifted up by the hair; pricked with thorns and pulled by the beard 23 times; received 20 wounds on the head; thorns of marine junks [worn rope or cable], 72; pricks of thorns in the head, 110; mortal thorns in the forehead, 3. I was afterward flogged and dressed as a mocked king; wounds in the body, 1,000. The soldiers who led me to Calvary were 608; those who watched me were 3 and those who mocked me were 1,008; the drops of blood that I lost were 28,430.[16]

The Sacred Shoulder, Side, and Heart of Jesus

The collection from which the above is taken contains a prayer to the shoulder wound of Christ, which the Lord purportedly told Bernard of Clairvaux was his greatest unrecorded suffering. It reads: "O Loving Jesus . . . I salute and worship the most sacred wound of thy shoulder on which thou didst bear thy heavy cross, which so tore thy flesh and laid bare thy bones as to inflict on thee an anguish greater than any other wound of thy most blessed body."

The wound in the side of Christ came in for early veneration long before the other four were joined to it in the same devotion. The church fathers took their cue from John 19:34: "One of the soldiers thrust a lance into his side, and immediately blood and water flowed out." The following verse identifies this as the true testimony of an eyewitness. The evangelist calls it in vv. 36–37 a fulfillment of the Scripture passage (from Zech. 12:10): "They shall look on him whom they have pierced." The gloss of 1 John 5:6–8 on the passage reads as follows:

> This is he whose coming was with water and blood: Jesus Christ. He came, not by water alone, but both by the water and by the blood; and to this the Spirit bears witness, because the Spirit is truth. In fact there are three witnesses, the Spirit, the water, and the blood, and these three are in agreement.

The witness they are agreed on is presumably to Jesus' coming "in the flesh," to deny which is not to belong to God (4:2–3). In John 20:27, Jesus invites Thomas to place his hand in his side, the witness of the senses followed by the witness of faith: "My Lord and my God!" (v. 28). Belief in the Son of God is called by 1 John God's testimony on the Son's behalf, a testimony in the human heart concerning God's gift of eternal life found in the Son (5:10–12).

16. This prayer, surely medieval, bears the improbable tag, "Blessed by Pope Leo XIII, in Roma, 5 Aprile 1890" (*The Pietà Prayer Booklet* [Hickory Corners, Mich.: Miraculous Lady of the Roses, n.d.]). The booklet is published without the required ecclesiastical approval.

Nothing in the text of John's Gospel identifies which side of Jesus received the spear thrust, but patristic tradition from the third century onward assumed that it was the right, the side favored by the Bible and most ancient cultures. The soldier was called Longinus ("spear wielder"), although the Gospel gives him no name. Tradition conflated him with the centurion of Mark 15:39, whose testimony was: "Clearly this man was the Son of God." The wounded side shortly came to be viewed as a door of grace, the water and the blood as symbols of baptism and the Eucharist. Ezekiel 47:1 was influential in this interpretation: "I saw water flowing out from beneath the threshold of the temple toward the east." This became in the weekly *Asperges me* (Ps. 51:7; Vulgate, v. 9) that preceded the parish Mass a reminder to Christians of their baptism in Eastertide: *Vidi aquam egredientem de templo a latere dextro* ("I saw water flowing out of the temple from the right side"). The east had become the right side in the Latin Bible.

The door of the temple was on the right, said the Venerable Bede (1 Kings 6:8; Vulgate, 3 Kings); therefore it was the right side of Christ that was to be opened by the thrust of the lance.[17] The sixth-century Syriac evangeliary of Rabula depicts the scene in this right-side fashion, with the soldier's name printed over him as LONGINOS, the only identification in the picture. Later, medieval crucifixion scenes would show a figure to the right of Longinus representing the church, holding a chalice to receive the blood and water from the holy wound. The church itself was conceived as coming out of the right side of the recently dead Christ, even as Eve came from the side of the sleeping Adam.[18] The Benedictine abbot William of St. Thierry (d. 1148) addressed the wound in this way: "Lord, open the door in the side of thy ark, so that all those who enter may be saved from the deluge that threatens to flood the whole earth."[19]

The mystical experience of Gertrude the Great (d. ca. 1302) gave an impetus to devotion to the Sacred Heart of Jesus by her recorded visions of it, and when such a feast was instituted it was placed on the Friday after the octave of Corpus Christi, the traditional date of a feast of the wound in the side from the thirteenth-century Dominican liturgy. Already, toward the end of the thirteenth century, the change from the devotion to the side to the devotion to the heart was being accomplished, owing especially to the mystics of the Franciscan school. Thus Friar Ubertino da Casale (d. 1301) could write: "I drank from the water that flows from the open spring of his Heart."[20] And Blessed Angela of Foligno, a tertiary of the same order (d. 1309), writes that Jesus spoke to her, saying that he has suffered in

---

17. *Thirty Questions on the Books of Kings* 12 (PL 91.722). Gougaud says that exceptions were rare and cites two (*Devotional and Ascetic Practices*, 122, n. 69).

18. See Augustine *Tractate 120 on John* 2 (PL 35.1953).

19. *Meditatio 6* (PL 180.226).

20. Quoted in M. J. Bernadot, "Le développement historique de la dévotion au Sacré-Coeur," *La Vie spirituelle* 2 (1920): 193–215.

each member of his body for the sins of humans in all their members. In her case it was "for the sins of thy heart, sins of anger, of envy, of sadness, of guilty love, for the wicked love and bad desires, my very heart and my side have been transfixed by a sharp lance and a powerful remedy has come out, which is sufficient to heal all thy passions and all the sins of thy heart."[21] Many fourteenth- and fifteenth-century representations displayed the wound as wide open on the heart, or the pierced heart within either a diamond frame or a crown of thorns. Martin Luther's favored emblem of a heart set within a four-petaled white rose finds a place here.

The point of excess, not to say superstition, was reached in the fifteenth century when it was thought that the size (*mensura*) or the shape of the wound was known, with appropriate sketches provided.[22] Some of the directions accompanying these drawings say that Pope Innocent VIII (d. 1492) had granted an indulgence of seven years for simply looking at them or kissing them. True or not, the sketches prove the sorry ancient truth that the pathology of religion is the quantification of the sacred.

A Major Shift in Outlook

The fourteenth century marked a turning point in expressions of piety in Europe. A feverish intensity characterized the forms religious life took, even as the intellectual life of the era tended to extremes (e.g., the demand of the Franciscan Spirituals for total poverty, the freedom of God unrestricted by the divine nature or covenanted commitment posited by the nominalists, the political liberty claimed by some theorists of the state).[23]

> Christendom had long been familiar with penitential self-affliction, patient submission to suffering, absorption in Christ's passion, and states of spiritual bliss or excitation that one might call mystical, yet . . . all these forms of spiritual life [became] . . . more pronounced, more widespread, and (perhaps most importantly), more widely respected than before.[24]

But, as Richard Kieckhefer remarks, it is not enough to say that fourteenth-century saints were intense because their era was intense. A partial explanation lies in the sources available to us, that is, the kinds of writing that de-

21. *Visiones et instructiones*, ed. J. H. Lemmertz, chap. 35 (sixth vision), Bibliotheca mystica et ascetica 5 (Cologne, 1841), 140.

22. See Louis Gougaud, "La Prière de Charlemagne," *Revue d'Histoire ecclésiastique* 20 (1924): 223–27.

23. See David Knowles, "A Characteristic of the Mental Climate of the Fourteenth Century," in *Mélanges offerts à Etienne Gilson de L'Académie Française* (Toronto and Paris: Pontifical Institute of Medieval Studies, 1959), 315–25.

24. Richard Kieckhefer, *Unquiet Souls: Fourteenth-Century Saints and Their Religious Milieu* (Chicago and London: University of Chicago Press, 1984), 3.

scribe this intensity. Why did the saints' biographers represent them as they did? Local pride in the holy ones who lived in a particular district was part of it. To this were added attempts to convince the papal curia, with its recently refined canonization process, of the miracles that attended some extraordinary lives. But above all there was the pious public, literate and nonliterate, with its taste for the extreme and thirst for the miraculous. That fact must have colored the perceptions and recollections of those who wrote of the experiences of the penitents, and even of the mystics themselves.

Christ's patient response to adversity and suffering served as a cause for imitation. The pious, when afflicted with insults, rebuffs, or physical pain, turned to meditation on the Savior's wounds and injuries, telling themselves that if their adversaries were to beat them physically or pluck the hair from their beards (a most unlikely eventuality), they still would not suffer as much as Jesus did. Typical is the mentality that viewed the trials of a saint as something of an exchange. Christ appeared on the cross to Catherine of Siena at a particular point in her tribulations, bleeding as he did "when he entered the holy of holies through the shedding of his own blood." He spoke: "Catherine my daughter, you see how much I suffered for you? Do not be sad, then, that you must suffer for me."[25] A mind-set of reciprocity is at work here: Jesus endured much for sinners; they should in turn endure pain for him as the praise offering most acceptable to God.

Kieckhefer observes that the saints and their biographers of the fourteenth century could have taken all their experiences of healing or relief from affliction as an occasion to reflect on "how Christians share in the grace of Christ's resurrection even during earthly life," but they were not inclined that way.[26] They assumed—and in this Catherine of Siena is typical—that to share in Christ's passion while they were still on earth was the best and perhaps the only way to be united with him. The sins of humankind were even in the present thought to be causing him pain. It was as if his resurrection had not overcome it. The passion took precedence over all, not only the incarnation but even the resurrection.

Jesus' Sufferings Viewed Apart from His Exaltation

Jesus' upraising from the dead came to be viewed not as "the momentous event giving meaning to the antecedent suffering; instead, the suffering has meaning of its own and the 'resurrection' signals little more than that the mystical ordeal is over."[27] The infancy of Jesus, his "hidden life," and his active ministry were all overshadowed by attention to the mockery, oppro-

25. Kenelm Foster and Mary John Ronayne, eds., *I, Catherine: Selected Writings of St. Catherine of Siena* (London: Collins, 1980), 79.
26. Kieckhefer, *Unquiet Souls,* 96.
27. Ibid.

brium, scourging, torments, and death endured for the sake of sinners. Meditation on the passion alone could achieve unity with Christ and yield some share in the work of redemption he accomplished. Even when the reformers shied away from any "work" accomplished by sinners, saying that only faith made salvation available, this faith was in the saving passion and not the resurrection as an integral part of the mystery.

In art the motif of the "Man of Sorrows" dates to the twelfth century. By the fourteenth there were depictions of Christ risen from the dead but showing himself as the wounded and suffering Savior rather than in glory. Gertrud Schiller documents the large wall paintings of this motif found in South German churches in the years around 1300.[28] His risen state was no longer seen as his victory over sin and death but as the condition of one who still bore the emblems of their victory over him.

Catherine of Siena could insist that it was not suffering itself that God delights in but the love revealed by suffering. Despite her assertion, the spirit of the age seemed to insist that God accepted love manifested through suffering before that expressed in any other way. Once, experiencing intimacy with the Savior through entry into his wounded side, she "found . . . such knowledge of the divinity there that . . . you would marvel that my heart did not break."[29] The German Dominican Henry Suso has Eternal Wisdom respond to a servant of God who has sought Christ's divinity everywhere but found that only his humanity was revealed to him: "The higher one climbs without passing through My humanity, the deeper one falls. My humanity is the way by which one must go. My sufferings are the gate by which one must pass, if one would attain what thou seekest."[30] Surely this is an indication that what some call Luther's "breakthrough," namely, that one knows nothing of theology who has not meditated on the cross, had its origins a century and a half before. The suffering Christ as the sole revealer of the reality of God was for Luther the only true theology.

Some Exuberant Rhetoric and Practice

With such a mentality prevailing in the fourteenth and fifteenth centuries it is not surprising that excesses abounded. It has even been suggested that the definition of a popularly recognized saint is a person who goes to excess.

28. *Iconography of Christian Art* (London, 1971), 197–229. In the 13th and 14th centuries the depictions were solely of Christ on the cross. With the 15th century came the story in art of his successive torments leading up to it. See Grace Frank, "Popular Iconography of the Passion," *Publications of the Modern Language Association* 46 (1931): 333–40. She provides twelve plates from the *Codex Reginensis* 473, fol. 1r–18v, of the Vatican Library, dated ca. 1400, which depict in successive scenes from the canonical Gospels (and two apocryphal) the characters of the passion in clothing worn in medieval passion plays. There are empty tomb and appearances scenes.

29. Her *Life* by Raymond of Capua, 2.6.187 and 191, cited by Kieckhefer, *Unquiet Souls*, 218, n. 7.

30. Kieckhefer, *Unquiet Souls*, 116.

Exuberant love finds its expression in exuberant behavior. If greatness is to madness near allied, the truth of that epigram is certainly realized in some of God's servants. The much-referred-to Catherine Benincasa, that courageous daughter of a Sienese dyer who told vacillating popes what their next moves should be, spoke of Christians as plunged, drowned, bathed, clothed, and lost in "that sweet blood." Bridget of Sweden burned herself with candle wax every Friday to remind herself of Christ's wounds and ate bitter herbs to recall the gall (reminiscent of Jewish seder practice memorializing Egyptian slavery). Clare of Rimini had herself bound to a pillar in the piazza on Good Friday and beaten severely. Jeanne Marie of Maillé thrust a thorn into her head during Passion Week one year; it fell out on Holy Thursday without leaving a scar. Peter Olafsson wounded himself with hair cords and the briars and brambles on which he lay, adding to this self-flagellation.[31] It is easy to charge masochism in these cases, except that the saints took no pleasure in their pain. It revolted, disgusted them. But this is the way they thought it must have felt to their crucified Lord.

As one might expect, the Gospel data on Jesus' sufferings were enlarged and elaborated on in this period. Apocryphal works (like *The Gospel according to Nicodemus*) were consulted for details the four evangelists did not supply.[32] Thus in passion plays of the fourteenth and fifteenth centuries, Malchus, Longinus, Veronica (Greek for "bearer of victory"; she wiped Jesus' face with a cloth), and the devils pressing the band of soldiers to take Jesus captive all became major players. Jesus fell three times on the way to Calvary, it was maintained, probably as an extrapolation from Mark 14:35. The Gospel says he "fell to the ground" in Gethsemane and returned to his sleeping disciples three times (vv. 37–41). Similarly, Veronica became a concrete individual among the women who wept for Jesus along the way (Luke 23:27–31). Mary, the mother of Jesus, whom the Gospels portray as simply standing and looking on at Calvary, becomes a weeping figure transfixed with grief. His passion and her compassion for his sufferings are intertwined in art, and although in the *Pietà* of Michelangelo her features are composed, that is scarcely the case in the lamentation scenes of the previous two centuries. One had only to see the Oberammergau passion play in 1990 to hear the Virgin Mother wail distractedly, quite unlike the gospel account, "O mein Sohn, mein lieber Sohn!"

A Brief History of "The Discipline"

Whipping as a publicly administered punishment for monastic infractions occurs in several ancient rules, including St. Benedict's. As a self-imposed

31. Ibid., 119.
32. See Edgar Hennecke, *New Testament Apocrypha: Gospels and Related Writings,* ed. Wilhelm Schneemelcher, trans. R. M. Wilson, vol. 1 (rev. ed.; Louisville: Westminster/John Knox, 1990).

ascetic discipline it seems to have originated with Peter Damian, the eleventh-century Camaldolese prior of Fonte-Avellana in Umbria. From there it quickly spread to other houses of his order and to the Benedictine Monte Cassino. Rather than as a corrective penalty leveled by a civil or religious community for wrongdoing, flagellation was Peter's choice not so much as a means to obtain remission of sins or growth in merit but as a substitution for the martyrdom that was denied him.[33] He thought that no death to self could enable him to associate himself more closely with the passion of Christ than this one. Peter Damian's life of his eremetical confreres Rudolph, later bishop of Gubbio (d. 1061), and Dominic Loricatus (so named for the penitential breastplate worn next to his skin) tells of the latter's substitution of leather thongs for birch rods, evidently an innovation.[34] Men and women from among the nobility adopted the custom, Peter reports, hinting that in their cases the practice was penitential rather than purely ascetical as in the monasteries.

The saint spent his later years promoting the discipline in other monastic houses, defending it against adversaries as the fate of Jesus, the apostles, and the martyrs. Even if they received this corporal punishment passively, the devout should take it on voluntarily as they did fasting.[35] Self-flagellation came to be practiced in Lent and Advent especially, the latter season having by then taken on a penitential character ("St. Martin's Lent," going back to November 11). Bernard of Clairvaux speaks of the discipline in the twelfth century. By the thirteenth it had become a commonplace in religious houses and is recorded of Clare of Assisi by Thomas of Celano, the biographer of Francis. Knotted leather thongs gradually replaced birch rods, which had sometimes been interlaced with thorns. The discipline was not always self-administered. Fellow religious sometimes delivered the blows to each other and servants to their highborn mistresses and masters.

In the present age, when the practice is known only as a means of sexual or other pleasurable excitation, it is common to retroject such a view onto past ages. The medieval penitents and ascetics would have been horrified at the suggestion. They had in mind only their sins and the atoning passion of the Savior. A customary from the thirteenth-century monastery of St. James

33. These two motivations are cited, respectively, by Leo Marsicanus (*PL* 173.738) and Peter the Venerable (*PL* 189.1040). L. Gougaud cites R. Biron, *S Pierre Damien* (Paris, 1841), 19ff., as one of his sources in "The Discipline as an Instrument of Penance," *Devotional and Ascetic Practices,* 184–88.

34. Peter Damian, *Vita SS. Rodulphi et Dominici Loricati* 11 (*PL* 144.1019). One wonders if Rodolfo with his whip for bad boys and girls, who accompanies the gift-giving old woman Befana (Epiphany) in Italian folklore, derives from this figure. The same may be asked, seriously, of Rudolph the red-nosed reindeer if a lyricist familiar with Italian tradition had a hand in it.

35. More important than Peter Damian's doubtful reasoning on the point is his identification of the practice as "new and unheard of over the many centuries" up to his (*Letter 8; PL* 144.350B). Its absolute novelty may be questioned. Gougaud (see n. 36) cites the cases among others of the Celtic Kentigern (d. 603) and William of Gellone (d. 812), both of whom emulated "the sacrifice of the Lamb," the former during the paschal *triduum* until Easter morn.

in Liège is explicit in its description of alternating prescribed prayers and strokes (the latter fifteen in all), with the priests but not the brothers as administrators and the warning not to hit too hard.[36] Beginning in the twelfth century the nonpenal discipline accompanied by prayers like Psalm 51 and the *Confiteor* became a fixture in religious houses of men and women. It continues in some to this day in emulation of Jesus' passion, although increasingly less since the mid-twentieth century. In many congregations it was part of the rule, but in several, such as the Carthusians, authorization by the prior was required.

Penitential Practice Gone Wild

The fanaticism of some flagellants of the later Middle Ages casts a shadow on this carefully regulated practice but never eliminated it. Zealots such as these were the flagellant confraternities of lay folk in Italy.[37] Their whipping of themselves to atone for their sins spread all over northern Europe as an attempted means to check the Black Death (1347–49) and more generally ward off the wrath of God. They read letters that purportedly came from God threatening earthquakes, famine, and the devouring of people's children by wild beasts if they did not repent.[38] Besides the scourging, one chronicler reports, the ritual employed included lying on the ground in postures suggestive of the people's sins: a hand raised to heaven for cursing or false swearing; lying on back, stomach, or side to convey sexual sin; and so on.

Some mass outbursts had begun as early as 1260 in Italy, the date prophesied by the Cistercian abbot Joachim of Fiore (d. 1202) as the inaugural year of the third age of the world, that of the Holy Spirit, the contemplatives, or the freedom of the spiritual intellect (the *tertium regnum,* from which was derived the apocalyptic *dritte Reich* of National Socialism). R. W. Southern cites the chronicle of Bologna for that year, which was marked by the people of Perugia, Rome, then all Italy going barefoot and beating themselves with leather thongs through the night in all the fortified cities and towns.[39] This lasted throughout October, people then moving from city to city and crying out to God for mercy and peace. The Roman authorities declared a general amnesty in which imprisoned leading families were released, all in fear of the impending final age.

A chronicle of a quarter century later tells of a group of seventy-two men calling themselves the Apostles, followed some days later by twelve women,

36. Gougaud, *Devotional and Ascetic Practices,* 193–95, giving the *Liber Ordinarius S. Jacobi,* 113–14, as his source.

37. Documented in Paul Bailly, "Flagellants," *Dictionnaire de Spiritualité,* 5 (1964), 394.

38. See Richard Kieckhefer, "Radical Tendencies in the Flagellant Movement of the Mid-Fourteenth Century," *Journal of Medieval and Renaissance Studies* 4 (1974): 157–76.

39. R. W. Southern, *Western Society and the Church in the Middle Ages* (New York: Penguin, 1970), 275, quoting Corpus Chronicorum Bononiensium, ed. A. Sorbelli, 156–57.

going from Parma to Modena to meet their leader.[40] Gathered around him they chanted "Pater, pater, pater," stripped themselves of their clothes, and stood around naked until he told them to re-vest and go out to the four corners of Europe and across the seas. The Apostles' leader was burnt as a heretic in 1300 after years of toleration in Parma, apparently guilty of no charge more serious than offending public dignity. In 1349 in what is now Belgium a band of flagellants called the Red Knights of Christ, led by the preaching of a Dominican friar, declared themselves saved without need of papal indulgences or the impetration of the saints. Their shed blood, they maintained, was the noblest since that of the Savior himself. United with his, it would accomplish their salvation.

Between September 12 and October 10 an estimated crowd of thirty-five hundred, including assorted clergy, passed through Tournai. Reciting numerous *Paters* and *Aves* they flooded into the cathedral (while keeping their hats on even during the consecration) and in general terrified its residential canons—though through it all they did nothing wrong.[41] In Deventer that same year we read of a large band of flagellants being entertained by the town council at public expense.[42] There can be no doubt that the times were out of joint. The plague of 1347–49, poverty, and urban unemployment brought on spontaneous outbursts of emotion in many European cities. How else was the populace to express its fears and dreads but in the way it knew best? It called on the suffering Christ to absorb its sufferings in the blood of a self-designated few, so as to have God heal the many.

The mass hysteria of these years had some cruel concomitants, chiefly the persecution of Jews, especially in Germany. The mobs there, in seeking a scapegoat, accused the Jews in cities and towns of poisoning the well water. Pope Clement VI threatened these mad crowds with excommunication twice in 1348. He refused to receive a delegation that had come to him from Basel and offered the Jews of France refuge in his court at Avignon. The tide was running too strong, however, for any one person to stem it. In the next year the pope addressed a bulla to the bishops of Germany calling the practices of these simple folk unlawful and superstitious, while distinguishing their mob activity from legitimate penitential practice.

Chronicles of the time tell of bands of women baring their backs to each other for strokes of the rod while they uttered penitential prayers and cries.[43] There seems to have been much expression of sorrow for sin concomitant with the social protest of the dispossessed. Both spoke the language of Christ's passion.

40. Southern, *Western Society,* 276. The chronicler was the Franciscan Salimbene, who saw in this conduct a threat to the friars "who taught all to beg."
41. Ibid., 307–08.
42. Ibid., 333.
43. Bailly, "Flagellants," 397.

The activity of flagellant bands recurred in the Low Countries toward the end of the fourteenth and beginning of the fifteenth century. It often took a heretical turn, as in the case of Conrad Schmidt of Thuringia, who put himself forward as Enoch incarnate and led his followers under the title "Brothers of the Cross." They persisted for at least a century after his condemnation to death for heresy, teaching that baptism by water had been succeeded by a baptism by blood without which no one could gain heaven, indeed that all those who availed themselves of the church's sacraments sinned mortally.

Jean Gerson (d. 1429), chancellor of the University of Paris, wrote a letter in 1417 from Constance, the host city of a council in the planning of which he had an intimate part. In it he asked the popular preacher Vincent Ferrér (d. 1419) to reprove his followers for their adherence to the public practice of flagellation that popes and bishops had repudiated. The affair ended with Gerson's inviting the Spanish Dominican to the council (an invitation Ferrér refused) and praising him for his zeal in distinguishing between the company of flagellants he oversaw and the heretical turn that much of flagellant activity took. Jakob Gretser, a German Jesuit (d. 1625), defended the practice in a treatise of 1605 that arose out of a Good Friday procession in Augsburg. Flagellation has had an uninterrupted recurrent history. Czarist Russia knew the phenomenon as recently as the period before World War I, possibly with erotic overtones.

As early as the thirteenth century, however, devout penitents were domesticated by organizing them into confraternities, calculated to keep their zeal within the limits of Catholic orthodoxy. Organized as pious groups of *disciplinati* (or *battuti*), they have continued to emulate Jesus' sufferings down through the ages. The practice comes most to public notice when press dispatches and television bites are filed on Good Friday from the Philippines and Latin America, where the simulation of Jesus' crucifixion is likewise enacted. Behind the cloister doors of numerous religious institutes the practice of violent self-discipline has continued as a response of love to the Christ who endured it as proof of his love, though a sounder theology of the vowed life since the Second Vatican Council (1962–65) has diminished it notably.

This is no place for an excursus on late medieval heresy but the field for opportunity was rich and, as one might expect, there were predictable departures from Catholic faith and piety. For example, in the mid-fourteenth century at Würzburg, Berthold of Rohrbach abjured his errors that Christ doubted on the cross whether he was saved and that he uttered curses on both his mother and the ground that soaked up his blood.[44] John Hartmann, a devotee of the heresy of the Free Spirit, which held that perfection was achievable in this life, maintained in his trial at Erfurt that neither murder

44. Richard Kieckhefer, *Repression of Heresy in Medieval Germany* (Philadelphia: University of Pennsylvania Press, 1979), 31, 126, n. 58.

nor incest was sinful in one who possessed perfect freedom. His inquisitor asked whether Jesus and Mary Magdalene had had sexual relations after the resurrection, to which Hartmann responded that he knew but refused to divulge the answer.[45] This exchange establishes against Martin Scorsese and Tim Rice and Andrew Lloyd Webber that there is nothing new under the sun.

Far less clear is why the passion story underwent so many accretions and elaborations while the doctrine of the resurrection and the appearances of the risen Christ were the subject of relatively little concern. They came into their own in some of the mystery or miracle plays of medieval England. It is a commonplace to attribute the late medieval emphasis on suffering and death (and the concomitant disregard of Jesus' passage to a life of glory) to the angst and misery of the times. That, however, is an observation about two concurrent phenomena rather than an explanation.

The Origins of Embroidered Passion Accounts

An English professor of German literature, F. P. Pickering, stands almost alone in his denial that a "theology of suffering" (*Leidenstheologie*) or "late medieval realism" are givens that should pass without further exploration. In two publications a decade or so apart he examines the sources of the common lore of about 1200–1250 concerning the crucifixion.[46] He does not deny that there were great changes in the temper and tone of religious life in the twelfth and thirteenth centuries, but he says that the only scholarly way they can be accounted for is by textual evidence. The text that he calls a turning point in studies of Christ's passion is *The Works of the Trinity* by Rupert of Deutz (d. 1129).[47] This man of voluminous output generated a story of the passion never previously told by going beyond the narratives of the four evangelists (whom he called "simple and unlettered men") and writing a "Testament of the Spirit," the third part in his trinitarian framework, in which he presented the image (*spectaculum*) of a conflated Job-Christ.

There was nothing new about finding type and antitype in the two Testaments, but Rupert went beyond the familiar search for prophecy and fulfillment. He knew the text of the Vulgate thoroughly and substituted his

45. Ibid., 32; cf. Robert E. Lerner, *The Heresy of the Free Spirit in the Later Middle Ages* (Berkeley: University of California Press, 1972), 138.

46. "The Gothic Image of Christ: The Sources of Medieval Representations of the Crucifixion" and "Exegesis and Imagination: A Contribution to the Study of Rupert of Deutz," in F. P. Pickering, *Essays on Medieval and German Literature and Iconography* (Cambridge: Cambridge University Press, 1980), 3–45; "The Crucifixion," in *Literature and Art in the Middle Ages* (Coral Gables, Florida: University of Miami Press, 1970), 223–307, from the author's German original, 1966.

47. *PL* 167.197–1828. Pickering's essay "Exegesis and Imagination" is an exposition of Rupert's imaginative exegesis of Job as prefiguring the sufferings of Jesus. Hosea is dealt with in his *XXI Books of Commentaries on the Minor Prophets, PL* 168.9–836.

"spiritual exegesis" (the smallest detail in Job seen as an actual description of Jesus' sufferings) for the arguments from prophecy to which his predecessors of the last thousand years had confined themselves. He not only supplemented the Gospels from the Hebrew Scriptures, which was traditional patristic practice, but he also strove to displace them with his own "Testament." Rupert was a great hater of the Jews and hence found no difficulty in proving that the men in Caiaphas's court who mocked and tortured Jesus throughout the night were "sated and drunk with wine," as Hosea made clear to him (4:11b).[48] He regarded Hosea as a source of "historical" information, but when he came to Matthew's account he made it "the pretext for interminable spiritualizing interpretations."[49]

The evangelists are content to describe Jesus' being done to death by using a single verb, "they crucified him [Luke and John: there]." The preachers of the period 1200–1250 knew a second narrative tradition that they esteemed on a par with the Gospels. The witnesses in the train of Rupert of Deutz most quoted by medieval scholars are:

1. The so-called *Dialogue of St. Anselm and the Virgin.*
2. *The Meditations on the Life and Passion of Our Lord* ascribed to Bonaventura.
3. *Liber de Passione Christi*, etc., in the form of a lament of Mary, ascribed to Bernard.[50]

There were others, like the *Vita Rhythmica Salvatoris*, but these were the main ones, adapted time and again in the vernacular tongues. These are the writings that provide the alternatives, found in art, of Jesus raised by a ladder and nailed to an erect cross or nailed to a cross that lay on the ground. Jesus' body shown as twisted in the shape of an S or Z to simulate a serpent or a worm (the two words became conflated; John 3:14/Num. 21:8–9 and Ps. 22:6 [MT 7] are the sources, respectively) come from narratives such as these. There is a similar origin for his body pulled taut by the executioners' ropes like the strings on a harp, so that all his bones could be counted (Psalm 22:17 [MT 18]). Some of the typological fulfillment of prophecy was restrained, as in the manner of the New Testament and the fathers, but Rupert carried the day with his "Testament." It found the details of Jesus' last hours described with precision in a variety of places in "the law of Moses and the prophets and the psalms" (Luke 24:44).

One illustration of the way things developed up through the late Middle Ages should suffice. The Synoptic Gospels say that "They laid hands on Jesus" or "seized him" and "took him to the high priest." John writes: "The

48. See *Minor Prophets, PL* 168.106–11.
49. Pickering, *Essays,* 41.
50. *Pseudo-Anselm, PL* 159.271–90; *S. Bonaventurae Opera,* ed. Peltier (Paris, 1868), 12 (*Spuria*), 509–630; *PL* 182.1133–42.

troops with their commander, and the Jewish police, now arrested Jesus and secured him. They took him first to Annas" (18:12–13). A German prose tract of about 1350 says:

> Then they seized Christ with raving violent devilish gesticulations, one grasped his hair, a second his clothes, a third his beard. These three were as foul hounds as ever might cling to him . . . and so he was pulled away . . . with fierce blows of mailed hands and fists upon his neck . . . his back, on his head . . . on his throat, on his breast. . . . They tore his hair from his head . . . one pulled him back by the beard [twelve further lines of print]. So they dragged him down from the Mount. . . . [four lines]. And they hauled him to the gate of the town . . . until they brought him into Annas's house.[51]

Every word is to be found in some obscure place in the First Testament of the Bible.

How Did the Crucifixion Get Separated from the Resurrection?

As we leave this exploration of the piety centered on Jesus' sufferings, two large questions cry out for an answer. One is how the mystery of the cross got so completely separated from the mystery of the resurrection; the other, what happened to the declaration, so clear in the New Testament, that "Christ, once raised from the dead is never to die again: he is no longer under the dominion of death" (Rom. 6:9). The once-for-all character of Jesus' death is expressed more explicitly in another place: "He has entered heaven itself, to appear now before God on our behalf. . . . not to offer himself again and again [as the high priest does], for then he would have had to suffer repeatedly since the world was created. But as it is, he has appeared once for all at the climax of history to abolish sin by the sacrifice of himself" (Heb. 9:24b–26). Did the Christians of these ages of faith place no credence in their own Scriptures? Why did they seem to think that Jesus had to die again and again, even if only in his servants, to transmit the benefits of human redemption?

One can only offer speculative answers to these questions since the writings of the times do not supply them. One reasonable response is that the liturgies of the Christian East and the writings of the Syriac and Greek fathers that kept the mystery of human redemption the one, undivided mystery of cross and resurrection of the New Testament was not a legacy of the West. The Latin liturgy that did preserve it was not available to people on a weekly basis once that tongue was no longer the vernacular (increasingly after 600). A largely nonliterate population during the spread of the gospel over north-

51. Pickering, *Essays*, 3.

ern Europe from the seventh to the tenth century relied on a story of salvation, not on the Scriptures themselves. Augustine's version of the total Bible narrative was the one available to most people through vernacular homilies. It featured a primordial sin and its debilitating effects more successfully, it would appear, than the corrective supplied by the proclamation of the evangelists and Paul and his school that humanity was victorious in the risen Christ.

The Middle Ages in Europe were a time ravaged by wars, disease, and famine and hampered by the ignorance born of illiteracy. All of this meant that most of its Christian population lived lives that were, in Hobbes's phrase, "mean, nasty, brutish, and short." The specter of death was ever present. Sin and its brutal consequences were daily realities. Release from all this lay ahead in a risen life confined to the future. People's Christianity was real to them in the measure that they could conceive Jesus Christ as sharing their suffering. They did this best through imagining themselves as sharing his.

Did they truly not believe that Jesus, having died once for all, was freed of any power death might have had over him? They doubtless did believe it, but in their condition it gave them little comfort. A Savior in blissful repose with his Father and the Spirit, surrounded by the angels and saints, consoled them as a distant dream they aspired to, not as a present reality. But a crucified Savior who could not forget the agonies he had endured for love of them was a different matter. A Redeemer, the bitterness of whose passion could never be blotted out in his memory, was a living, heavenly presence with which they could identify.

And so they did. The end of that identification for the world's poor and oppressed is nowhere in sight.

CHAPTER EIGHT

A Variety of Responses to
a Crucified Redeemer

There are Christians in the late twentieth century to whom the mystery of Christ's death on a cross does not speak in any positive way. Quite the opposite: it repels them, saying to them only mindless violence. The message they derive from it is that the shedding of innocent blood is a perverted expression of the human spirit. Jesus' violent death should be expunged from memory rather than recalled forever, let alone, as they would put it, glorified. For these Christians (and former Christians) there is no parallel between the crucifixion and the eternal remembrance of an ancient wrong like the destruction of one's people by another people. In a case such as genocide the act has nothing good about it; no one praises it. All that is being recalled is the innocence of the victims and the horror visited on a people that lives on in its children. By contrast, some maintain that in the crucifixion thanks and praise are being devoted to the deed itself. It is even believed in as a deed of God, as genocide certainly is not. In this understanding of the crucifixion, God is supposed to have willed the death of Jesus, then accepted his blood in sacrifice and reckoned it satisfactory for the sins of the world. The death and its attendant violence are thus themselves counted as a good.

The outlook described above holds that one outcome of Christianity's concentration on this violent act as universally salutary is that its positive sanction of violence has multiplied violent behavior. Revenge, blood feuds, and wars have all received acceptance in a religion that has its roots in a death that evens the score, as it were, satisfying for the moral evil that preceded it and indeed all sins that would ever follow.

Not all who find themselves repelled or, less drastically, not attracted by the death of Jesus on the cross have arrived at a rationale like the above. For many it is not religiously symbolic in any sense. Their response to the crucifixes they encounter or verbal references to the event is simple: this death says nothing whatever, good, bad, or indifferent. Most people do not think of any death except when it is unavoidably thrust on them, as in the death of a relative or a work associate. It is a nonreality in their life experience.

Headlines and television news stories multiply deaths. Films, most of them violent, and television dramas wade in them. This tattoo on the senses makes little or no impact. Death in a cause such as the future of one's people or in sacrifice for another is not among the mental categories of many contemporaries. When the death of an individual is proposed to some as unique by the religion into which they were born, it does not affect them, either adversely or favorably. People are inured not so much to death as to the banal image of death that the culture has given them.

Suffering Accepted because of the Crucifixion?

Different entirely are those of sensibility, sometimes educated but often not, who struggle with the problem of how a God of love can be imaged—for God has been presented to them in no other way—as looking upon the sufferings of Jesus with complacency. In an essay that has as its main point the contention that women are the victims of Christian redemptive theology in a way that men are not, two women write:

> Classical views of the atonement have, in diverse ways, asserted that Jesus' suffering and death is fundamental to our salvation. Critical traditions have formulated the issue of redemption in different terms but still have not challenged the central problem of the atonement—Jesus' suffering and death and God's responsibility for that suffering and death. Why we [women] suffer is not a fundamentally different question than why Jesus suffered. It may be that this fundamental tenet of Christianity—Christ's suffering and dying for us— accepts actions and attitudes that accept, glorify, and even encourage suffering. Perhaps until we challenge and reject this idea we will never be liberated.[1]

The essay goes on to accuse various theories of atonement—the Christus Victor tradition, the satisfaction tradition, and the moral influence tradition—of accepting, each in its own way, the human necessity to suffer, and a God who demands satisfaction for his (sic) affronted honor. At the root of the last named theory, it is said, is the biblical idea of the power of blood sacrifice without a corresponding valuation of menstrual blood. In the theological theory made popular by Abelard, Jesus as victim should suffice for the moral edification of believers. In fact, however, the death of Jesus has provided Christians with a rationale for countless other victimizations.

Traditional interpretations like the three named above have been called in question, the writers say, by critical theologians who "have claimed that classical atonement theories have been used to maintain the status quo and

---

1. Joanne Carlson Brown and Rebecca Parker, "God So Loved the World?" in *Christianity, Patriarchy, and Abuse: A Feminist Critique,* ed. Joanne Carlson Brown and Carole R. Bohn (New York: Pilgrim, 1989), 4.

exonerate the purposes of a tyrannical God."[2] Cited are the proponents of a "suffering God," some but not all of whom see God as limited, and those who like Martin Luther King, Jr., believe that the undeserved suffering of African Americans is redemptive or with Archbishop Oscar Romero that Christ's letting himself be killed, like a seed going into the ground, resulted in a great harvest from which the oppressed should take heart.

A Mystique of Suffering Rather than Following Jesus

The liberation theologian Jon Sobrino radically critiques traditional views of the cross, saying they have spiritualized its impact and taken away the scandal. But even he sees in the cross a positive side:

> The Father suffers the death of his Son and takes upon himself all the sorrow and pain of history. This ultimate solidarity with humanity reveals God as a God of love in a real and credible way rather than in an idealistic way. From the ultimate depths of history's negative side, this God of love thereby opens up the possibility of hope and a future.[3]

Sobrino is by no means unaware of the way the cross has been mythicized, clouding the historical realities. It is often popular piety that has done this, but he does not absolve from complicity the purveyors of violence who subvert this piety for their own ends.

> There has been a tendency to isolate the cross from the historical course that led Jesus to it by virtue of his conflicts with those who held political religious power. In this way the cross has been turned into nothing more than a paradigm of the suffering to which all human beings are subject insofar as they are limited beings. This has given rise to a mystique of suffering rather than to a mystique of following Jesus, whose historical career led to a historical cross.[4]

This observation is valid once the minor correction is made that believers in Jesus Christ did not, from the beginning, memorialize a historical event in a merely historical way. By their faith in its effective power—something history could not know—they placed the historical crucifixion and the resurrection that followed it at the center of a religious *mýthos*. But the validity of Sobrino's analysis remains. To view Jesus' sufferings and death as a paradigm of the finite condition of all humanity is to miss the point. The disease and natural disaster, the ignorance and greed that from time immemorial have made suffering a concomitant of human life have served to obscure the

2. Ibid., 13–14.
3. Sobrino, *Christianity at the Crossroads* (Maryknoll, N.Y.: Orbis, 1978), 371, quoted in Brown and Parker, "God So Loved the World?" 23.
4. Sobrino, *Crossroads*, 373.

reality of Jesus' suffering for both the poor who suffer and the rich who cause their suffering. The former have been led to believe that their suffering is inevitable, the latter that the poverty of others is somehow part of the divine plan. The wretchedness of the poor and the oppression of people of color and women can find meaning in the cross, Sobrino is convinced, but not on the traditional terms:

> The whole question of God finds its ultimate concretion in the problem of suffering. The question rises out of the history of suffering in the world, but it finds its privileged moment on the cross: if the Son is innocent and yet put to death, then who or what exactly is God?[5]

The Central American Jesuit casts a critical eye on all interpretations of Calvary that rest at ease with the notion of Jesus' silent endurance of pain as the paradigm for all suffering viewed as the inevitable human lot. He asks the question that occurs to all thoughtful persons, whether Christian or not: Can a God be justified who allows the sinfulness of the world to kill the one the Christian Scriptures call "the beloved Son," "the only Son"? That is part of the larger question of how God can permit the wicked and the callously thoughtless to take human life, and of the still larger question of a human race able to choose evil without God's intervention to thwart the evil effects of a freedom once bestowed. A Christian woman delivers this thoughtful answer:

> God is not responsible for suffering; God is not pleased by people's suffering; God suffers with us and is present to us in the midst of pain and sexual and domestic violence; God does not abandon us even though everyone else may. . . . Just as God does not will people to suffer, God does not send suffering in order that people have an occasion for transformation. It is a fact of life that people do suffer. The real question is not, Why? but, What do people do with that suffering? Transformation is the alternative to endurance and passivity. . . . It is the faith that the way things are is not the way things have to be. . . . Transformation is the means by which, refusing to accept injustice and refusing to assist its victims to endure suffering any longer, people act.[6]

That is a traditional Christian approach to the insoluble problem of suffering, one to which many Jews and all Muslims would subscribe. At the same time it is not one to which all Christians are committed or in which most nonreligious people wish to have any part. For them the *only* question is, Why? There is but one thing to do with suffering and that is to eliminate it by any means possible. Transforming suffering means either of two things: coming to terms with it in some way other than avoiding it completely, or

5. Ibid., 224.
6. Marie F. Fortune, "The Transformation of Suffering: A Biblical and Theological Perspective," in Brown and Bohn, *Christianity, Patriarchy,* 146–47.

eliminating it in others at such cost to oneself that one cannot consider such transformation. Hence the idea of the transformation of suffering is inadmissible.

Justice, Love, and Liberation without the Cross

Many Christians ask, Why is the crucifixion necessary? Some put it this way: "Does God demand this suffering and death as payment for sin or even as a condition for the forgiveness of sin? Is not the question . . . Is God a sadist?" Joanne C. Brown and Rebecca Parker, the writers who pose the question in this way, are engaged in dialogue with an African American theologian who sees Jesus as a political messiah (their term) for black Christians.[7] They face him with this challenge: "Is the identification black people, particularly black women, felt with the suffering Jesus part of their oppression? . . . God's demand, the sacralizing of suffering is at issue and is not addressed by [William R.] Jones."[8] They say of a feminist theologian who views welcoming pain and death as a sign of faith that she is guilty of "theological masochism," that she fails to identify the traditional doctrine of the atonement as the central reason for the oppressiveness of Christianity.[9] She dissociates herself from a number of basic Christian doctrines but retains a doctrine of atonement in which Jesus redeems humanity by showing that salvation consists in an intimate, immediate loving relation with God. Since, however, this God who demands sacrifice is a patriarchal God and is the only one to be found in the biblical text, the woman theologian's project is judged to fail. She has cleared the God of the Bible of the charge of sadism by affirming that Jesus, in the prophetic tradition, despised sacrifice, human sacrifice above all, but regrettably—from the two writers' point of view— held on to the God upon whom the entire Christian tradition is built.

Brown and Parker conclude their plea for a Christianity that does not have a redemptive death at its core by envisioning a faith tradition that is essentially the "justice, radical love, and liberation" which Jesus' life exemplified. He chose to live in opposition to unjust, oppressive cultures, not making choice of the cross but choosing "integrity and faithfulness, refusing to change course because of threat." His death was the unjust act of men who chose to reject his way of life, seeking to silence him through death. The resurrection does nothing to redeem "the travesty of the suffering and death of Jesus" because "suffering is never redemptive, and cannot be redeemed."

7. Brown and Parker, "For God So Loved the World?" 25, putting questions to William R. Jones, *Is God a White Racist?* (New York: Anchor, 1973), 81.
8. Brown and Parker, "For God So Loved the World?" 25.
9. Ibid., 25–26, in dialogue with Carter Heyward, *The Redemption of God* (Washington, D.C.: University Press of America, 1982), 54–57.

Jesus was not an acceptable sacrifice for the sins of the whole world, because God does not need to be appeased and demands not sacrifice but justice. To know God is to do justice (Jer. 22:13–16). Peace was not made by the cross. "Woe to those who say Peace, Peace when there is no peace" (Jer. 6:14). No one was saved by the death of Jesus.

Suffering is never redemptive and cannot be redeemed.

The cross is a sign of tragedy. God's grief is revealed there and everywhere and every time life is thwarted by violence.[10]

How widespread this desire for Christianity without the cross is it is impossible to say. Adherents to the Christian tradition who misconceive the mystery of Calvary are certainly legion, probably because of the way it was presented to them in youth and continues to be preached in their adulthood. It may, again, have been proposed adequately but heard in a quite different spirit. Revulsion in the face of pain or violence marks the sensitive soul, but this is not the same thing as thinking that suffering is never redemptive and cannot be redeemed. Many of the goods asked for in a Christianity without the cross are already at the heart of various theologies of the atonement, but the writers do not seem aware of this. Their absorption with women's suffering at the hands of men is so great that they can only see in a drama of suffering a glorification of male-inflicted pain.

Is the resurrection of Christ in their outlook equally expendable? Strangely not, but here it is given a nineteenth-century rationalist twist of the kind recently revived in Hugh Schonfield's *The Passover Plot:*

Resurrection means that death is overcome . . . when human beings choose life, refusing the threat of death. Jesus climbed out of the grave in the Garden of Gethsemane when he refused to abandon his commitment to the truth even though his enemies threatened him with death.[11]

10. Brown and Parker, "For God So Loved the World?" 27; the above quotations are found in the same place. R. G. Hamerton-Kelly holds a similar view of the impropriety of any benign view of Jesus' death on the cross in Christianity. In *Sacred Violence: Paul's Hermeneutic of the Cross* (Minneapolis: Fortress Press, 1992), he acts as an interpreter of Paul's letters and career but depends largely on the French literary critic René Girard in doing so. Girard sees the sacred—the transcendental pole of primitive religion—as a mendacious representation of human violence. The prestige of kings, priests, and mythic heroes is institutionalized in sacrificial structures of violence. Hamerton-Kelly sees in Paul a Jew who had to leave his religion for a new one. The new religion abandoned the sacred violence of Judaism that required the death of Jesus. The book ends with its examination of the Pauline writings, giving only this clue to the author's view of Christianity's absorption with the cross: "The moment at which the church identified itself as the new Israel marks the moment at which it reveals its fall from grace and the deformation of its self-understanding as part of the new creation to a structure of sacred violence within the old. . . . [Paul's] attack on Judaism is the spearhead of his attack on the structures of this world" (pp. 187–88). Hamerton-Kelly sees in all interpretation of Paul's Letters a misconceived hermeneutic. He finds in Luther's theory the greatest power, elegance, and beauty up until now but hopes to propose his own (above) as not replacing it but as being of rival power, elegance, and beauty (pp. 5–6).

11. Brown and Parker, "For God So Loved the World?" 28.

Many a human being might choose life if they had the option of climbing out of the grave, but to say that is to obscure the issue. The issue is, Does the mystery of the cross have at its core a divinely decreed "appeasement of God" in response to the demand that Jesus' life be forfeited in bloody sacrifice? If such were the Christian doctrine, abjuring that doctrine would be a world well lost.

How significant is the incapacity to see in the incarnation any sharing of God in the pain of the human race? To see in the cross any symbolization of God's love for the human race? One wonders if the problem is peculiarly modern, confined to those exposed directly to little human suffering and even less to the traditional Christian response to it. For how many millions does a perfectly normal shrinking from violence translate into seeing the cross as a violent act, hence to be shrunk from as having any conceivable religious purpose?

Another View: Embracing the Cross Wholeheartedly

An inquiry into some expressions of piety as having a component of violence may be useful here. Deservedly or not, the Iberian peninsula and its daughter republics have long been thought of as wedding piety and violence. The northern countries, including our own, have for years indulged in feelings of superiority to lands that could be capable of such a deadly confusion. In the exploration that follows, one should remember that other Romance and some Slavic peoples have similar expressions of devotion to redemption by the cross.

To understand Spain and Portugal even in part, one must be familiar with the struggle various peoples have endured to exist on that ecologically inhospitable peninsula. Human groups there have developed over centuries what cultural anthropoligists and folklorists alike call "sociocentrism," a passionate regionalism in which inhabitants think their locale superior to all others. The phenomenon is by no means confined to the Hispanic and Lusitanian peoples. Mythic motifs have been developed in all the regions of the peninsula that have rationalized the violence previously visited on some groups by others. The result is that the violence continues. With the arrival of Christianity, local cults and images became part of the expression of this intense localism.

The extensive writings of Julio Caro Baroja over nearly forty years—a dozen books and as many articles—have laid bare this aspect of Spanish life.[12] He has disclosed that the forms taken by Spanish folklore with its mock persecutions and ritual scapegoats are hardly innocuous. They may

---

12. For a listing see Timothy Mitchell, *Violence and Piety in Spanish Folklore* (Philadelphia: University of Pennsylvania Press, 1988), 201–2.

account not only for unwonted expressions of cruelty in the Passion piety of the people but also, he thinks, catastrophes like the civil war of 1936–39. Spanish folk religion and Spanish fiestas are the same phenomenon, to the mind of anthropologist Lisón Tolosana, who calls the fiesta a "quintessential means of dramatizing, sublimating, and sacralizing [a community's] own social structure." [13]

Outstanding among the fiestas is the *romería* or small-scale pilgrimage of the people of a locality to the shrine of a saint or the Blessed Virgin, often set in a mountainous region of great beauty. Sometimes the two- or three-dimensional image of the saint or the Savior under some title will be brought home briefly to the village church, or else go in procession to the various hamlets under his or her special protection. The occasion of such a cult or pilgrimage will frequently have been a public vow made during a plague or natural disaster centuries ago. Reports from the 1960s to the present tell of increased rather than lessened participation in the *romería*. In places where tourism has replaced farming or the fishing industry, the celebration often takes the form of a homecoming for people who have migrated to the cities. A polluted harbor is likely to be the modern object of prayer rather than a cholera epidemic of centuries long past. Old rivalries between locales flourish as before. This is a report from only some thirty years ago:

> In the famous procession in Seville in Holy Week the escort of the Virgin from a poor parish would glare with ferocity at the Virgin from a rich church in a fashionable quarter. The Archbishop of Seville himself remarked that "these people would be ready to die for their local Virgin, but would burn that of their neighbors at the slightest provocation." [14]

The fiestas of Holy Week throughout Spain represent the betrayal, crucifixion, and resurrection of Christ and are marked by a certain ritual violence that the pilgrimage processions of the *romerías* and the feasts of Christmas, the Immaculate Conception (December 8), and the Assumption (August 15) do not share. Travelers in Spain of the last six centuries, particularly from the northern countries, have been horrified—but at times edified—at the sight of barefoot penitents flogging each other, dragging chains, and carrying huge crosses during Holy Week. Occasionally things get out of hand, as when some sixty years ago in the Burgos area a young man playing Judas was accidentally killed in the scapegoating practiced by overzealous townsfolk. [15] The popular theater of Passiontide contains elements that no one in the region can account for historically. Although the Gospel accounts are

13. Ibid., 31, citing Carmelo Lisón Tolosana, *Antropologia social y hermeneutica* (Madrid: Centro de Investigaciones Sociológicas, 1986), 77–79. See also Luis Maldonado, *Religiosidád popular* (Madrid, 1975), 193.

14. Hugh Thomas, *The Spanish Civil War* (New York: Harper Bros. Publ'rs., 1961), 36.

15. Julio Caro Baroja, *El Carnaval: Análisis histórico-cultural* (Madrid: Taurus, 1965), 132.

naturally at the heart of the portrayals, many of the most popular details of reenactment cannot be traced. Generic allusions by the learned to catharsis through mimetic victimization, persecution, and martyrdom to account for these expressions of piety abound, but the conscious—much less the unconscious—responses of the people to their participation go unrecorded.

Wooden statues of Christ called *pasos* having movable arms, which enable them to be placed at the figure's side as it is taken down from the cross, are the charge of various *confradías* (brotherhoods). The size of a village determines the number of *confradías* it can support and this in turn establishes how many moments of the passion can be represented, each featuring its own *paso* of Christ on a raised platform. For example, there can be the Prayer in the Garden (the name of a *confradía*), the Nailing, Jesus Fallen, *Ecce Homo,* and the Holy Sepulchre. These statues are up to four centuries old and will require, once mounted on a platform complete with gospel setting, anywhere from fifteen to fifty stalwarts to carry them. Jesus, the apostles, and the prophets all appear in these *tableaux vivants.* Judas is usually portrayed in demonic guise. On Good Friday morning in some towns, the Savior is nailed to the cross in effigy in a plaza not far from an image of the Sorrowful Mother, then taken down until nightfall, when a procession begins with his body carried in a glass coffin. The townspeople process solemnly carrying candles, as they go clothed in linen robes that will one day be their winding sheets. They conclude the exercise by reenacting the burial of Jesus.[16] Some Good Friday processions disintegrate into raucousness as their black-hooded figures play at dice to simulate the dicing for Jesus' garments and fortify themselves with strong local liquors against the predawn cold.

One may ask whether any dramatic representation of Jesus' resurrection in Spanish folklore matches that of his crucifixion. One unusual representation may be singled out, the encounter of mother and son on Easter morn, often reenacted in a town's plaza. Mary is no longer sorrowful. Jesus, for his part, is represented as an infant (to signify rebirth?). As the two reunite joyfully, flocks of doves are sent skyward. In some places, Jesus' image is hidden while the holy women who come to the tomb search for him throughout the day. An unexpected part of the Easter celebration is putting a torch to the effigy of Judas: the betrayer is overcome while risen life triumphs.

A researcher into popular festivals in the province of Castille, Consolación González Casarrubios, reports as recently as 1985 that living actors are increasing in popularity over statues.[17] There is no mention of increased pain

16. Carlos Blanco depicts one such scene from Bercianos de Aliste in Zamora, a town of a thousand people, in his *Las fiestas de aquí* (Valladolid, 1983), 43–46.

17. *Fiestas populares en Castilla-La Mancha* (Ciudad Real, 1985), 53–54. For the documented claims of eye movement in statues of the crucified Christ in Gandía in Valencia (1918), Limpias near Santander (1919), Piedramillera and Mañeru in Navarra (1920), and Melilla in North Africa (1922), see William A. Christian, Jr., *Moving Crucifixes in Modern Spain* (Princeton, N.J.: Princeton University Press, 1992). The author has garnered numerous testimo-

taken on by human beings, as in a village in Cáceres where men choose to have their arms roped to a wooden beam and wander the streets through the night to the encouragement of neighbors.[18] The underlying and unconscious motivations of the Holy Week reenactments have been identified as masochism, mass neuroticism, sadism, and oedipal parricide (Jesus killing God his Father out of envy at the attention paid to his mother).

Do These Depictions Reflect Redemptive Teaching?

Timothy Mitchell wisely remarks that "neurosis (or pathology or morbidity or excess) will remain in the eye of the beholder."[19] These passion processions are in any case psychodrama with more therapeutic value apparent than incitement to destruction.

> The genius of the Spanish cultural "style" lies not only in the ritual canalization of collective violence but also in the ritual dissolution of whatever guilt may attach to this violence. Those individuals who happen to have an above average amount of guilt for whatever reason simply use the existing cultural formats with greater intensity. Most penitents in a given procession will wear shoes; some will feel a need to go barefoot; a few will want to drag chains as well. If this is "masochism" it is of a benign, group-approved, abreactive variety.[20]

That cool outsider's view does not take a position on the cause of true guilt, which is sin, as contrasted with a variety of false or imagined guilts. It also attributes greater guilt to the more obviously self-inflicted penitents when an ardent nature might explain things better. In any case, a taking on of the sufferings of Christ by Christians in a spirit of repentance for sins and faults lies at the heart of these popular dramas. In times past all who partook in them were also to be found in their village churches participating in the ill-termed "Mass of the Presanctified." Basically a communion service on Good Friday with sacred hosts consecrated from the Holy Thursday preceding, this commemoration of Jesus' death was celebrated in funereal black vestments without organ or bells. Hosea 6:1–6 was read out in Spanish as well as Latin ("He has struck us but he will bind our wounds. . . . On the third day he will raise us up to live in his presence. . . . For it is love that I desire and not sacrifice. . ."), and John 18–19, the entire passion account.

There was a sermon on these two texts and silent veneration of the cross, usually with a *corpus* affixed, by the people approaching individually, either

---

nies from aged witnesses and tries to reconstruct for the reader the political, economic, and religious situation of northern Spain after World War I.

18. J. Pérez Gallego, "Semana Santa a la española. Desde la procesión de las palmas de Jerusalén a la desacralización de la fiesta," *El País,* March 9, 1986, 17–18.

19. Mitchell, *Violence,* 122.

20. Ibid., 123.

genuflecting three times or on their knees. Prayers followed for peoples of many classes and conditions, too lengthy because chanted by the presider at the liturgy and untranslated from the Latin. The Blessed Sacrament was retrieved from an altar of reposition decorated florally in the manner of a shrine, the people going in procession before it singing the doleful *Vexilla Regis Prodeunt* ("The Royal Banners Forward Flung").

This Good Friday liturgy was revised in 1951 and promulgated in 1955 for the entire Roman Rite. Its dramatic character came through more forcefully abetted by the vernacular languages, but it was a highly subdued drama, as it had always been, relative to the *Semana Santa a la española* of the ages. That liturgical change coincided with the rapid industrialization of Spain in the last years of the Franco era, a pace that has quickened remarkably under a succession of democratic governments. Popular religion is no longer what it was in city or town. Regular participation in the eucharistic liturgy is markedly down in Spain, although nothing like the rest of Europe, and in the *fiestas* as well, as people move to the cities in search of work. Some sociological questions have been explored that touch on these population shifts and the secularizing trends of culture (in which advertising, films, and television play a large part).

Not so readily the subject of an inquiry, even if religiously committed sociologists with theological training had the funds for it, would be the relative impact on people's faith of the Good Friday popular celebrations and the liturgical celebrations in the churches. One supposes that the populace would not be able to distinguish between them, not because of ignorance or inability to comprehend the question, but because there is no distinction in their minds. Does the crucifixion of Christ speak of God's love to them, and if so, specifically what does it say? Are they impelled to deeds of violence by participating in the scapegoating of Judas or by reenacting Jesus' passion in wooden images? Does the penitential aspect of the season achieve any reduction of backbiting or envy among neighbors, or is it lost entirely in renewed village rivalries? In short, we need to learn whether the popular mimesis of many centuries has captured the spirit of the various New Testament theologies of the redemption or distorted it beyond recognizable limits.

Denying That the Crucifixion Happened

The various gnostic religions abroad in the Roman Empire before Christianity are usually traced to the metaphysical dualism that marks Persian religion, although a minority of scholars of gnostic thought think them a corruption of the religion of Israel.[21] The problem may never be solved. What

21. See Kurt Rudolph, *Gnosis: The Nature and History of Gnosticism*, trans. P. W. Coxon, et al. (San Francisco: Harper and Row, 1983).

cannot be denied is that by the second century some Gnosticisms were using stories and names from the Hebrew Bible as vehicles for a spirit-versus-matter opposition that the Bible hardly sustains. The New Testament testifies to the threat posed by gnostic thinking and even some inroads made in passages that bespeak refutation like, "Every spirit that acknowledges Jesus Christ has come in the flesh belongs to God, and every spirit that does not acknowledge Jesus does not belong to God" (1 John 4:2–3). Some early believers were clearly holding to a discarnate Jesus Christ but not a fleshly one. A few verses later love is defined, not as humanly initiated love for God, but in response to the fact "that [God] loved us and sent his Son as expiation for our sins" (v. 10). This letter obviously maintains the reality of Jesus' death by crucifixion reported in the Johannine Gospel. More unequivocally than in the first letter, 2 John 7 says: "Many deceivers have gone out into the world, those who do not acknowledge Jesus Christ as coming in the flesh." Defining *this* as the teaching concerning the Christ, the epistle says that anyone who does not remain in it does not have God, neither the Father nor the Son (v. 9). A shunning technique is proposed for those who teach differently (vv. 10–11).

Paul speaks of angelic spirits, principalities, and powers as incapable of separating us from the love of Christ (Rom. 8:38) and refers to enslavement to the "elemental powers of the world" before believers had come of age in Christ (Gal. 4:3). The term "elemental powers" (*stoicheía*) is repeated in Colossians 2:8, 20 as if these were personal cosmic forces of the kind the gnostic systems dealt in. Ephesians, which seems to be the work of a Pauline disciple of a later generation, features the struggle of Christians with "the principalities, the powers, the world rulers of this present darkness, the evil spirits in the heavens" (6:12).

A Gnostic View Emergent and Reputed

Gnostic systems of a later time would feature the return of individual souls to the *plērōma* or fullness of spirit life from which they had fallen into entrapment in bodies, making their way upward through some kind of cosmic obstacle course. As for the dualistic outlook hinted at in the Johannine Epistles, it recurs in the letters of Ignatius of Antioch from shipboard: "Jesus Christ . . . was really born, ate, and drank . . . was really crucified and died. . . . And if, as some atheists (I mean unbelievers) say, his suffering was a sham . . . why, then, am I a prisoner?" (*Trall.* 9.1–10.1; cf. *Magn.* 9.1; *Smyrn.* 2; 6.7; Pol. *Phil.* 7). The accuracy of the detailed descriptions of the wedding of Christian thought with gnostic patterns provided by Irenaeus of Lyon in his *Five Books against Gnosis Falsely So Called (Adversus Haereses)* was doubted in some quarters (because not the work of an initiate) until the discovery of the Nag Hammadi library in 1945. This Upper Egypt find vindicated the Antiochian native, a bishop in Gaul, in his exposition of the teachings of Cerdon, Valentinus, and others by the close resemblance of the books the Coptic community lived by—rather than canonical Scripture, it would appear—to portions of his report.

Christian and Muslim Denials

This discussion of the gnostic outlook is preliminary to the presentation in the Holy Qur 'an of Jesus' last days. That book describes itself as the work of scribes who recorded the revelations made to Muhammad, the last of the prophets, "slowly, by degrees" (Qur 'an 17:106). The Qur 'an freely allows the inspired nature of the books of the Jews and the Christians, which it calls Tawrah (*Torah*) and Injil' Isās (*evangelium Iesu*). Later Islamic tradition would speak of both groups as having tampered with their Scriptures, eliminating references to the Prophet of Islam that the Qur 'an says are to be found there (3:81; 7:157; and 61:6). Another such instance of alleged alteration of the texts occurs in the following passage:

> And [the Jews were punished] because they said: "We killed the Christ, Jesus son of Mary, who was an apostle of God"; but they neither killed nor crucified him, though so it appeared to them. Those who disagree in the matter are only lost in doubt. They have no knowledge of it other than conjecture, for surely they did not kill him.[22]

The first recorded denial of the reality of the crucifixion by a Christian occurs in the Gnostic Valentinus, writing about 140 C.E., as quoted by Irenaeus:

> So Jesus did not suffer [on the cross], but a certain Simon of Cyrene was constrained to bear his cross for him, and it was Simon who was crucified in ignorance and error, since he had been transformed by Jesus to look like himself, so that people thought he was Jesus, while Jesus took on the appearance of Simon and stood by and mocked them.[23]

It is not possible to trace the exact influence gnostic Christian material exercised in seventh-century Arabia, but the Qur 'anic sura is clearly closer to the Valentinian than the canonical accounts of the passion. This is a puzzle because there is nothing whatever gnostic about the Qur 'an. Respect for 'Isā (Jesus) may account for the wish to deny a cruel death to him, cou-

---

22. *Al-Qur 'an*, trans. Ahmed Ali (Princeton, 1988), 4:157–58.
23. *Five Books against Gnosis (Against the Heresies)* 1.24.4. The same is found in the gnostic passion of the *Second Treatise of the Great Seth* VII, 55.19: "I did not die in reality but in appearance," in *The Nag Hammadi Library in English*, ed. James M. Robinson (San Francisco: HarperCollins, 1990), 365.

pled with the willingness to credit a popular Christian tradition that denies the authenticity of the Gospels on how Jesus died. A thirteenth-century commentator on the Qur 'an, al-Baydawi (d. 1286), attempts to tell what really happened:

> There is a story that a group of Jews insulted Jesus and his mother, whereupon he appealed to God against them. When God transformed those [who had insulted them] into monkeys and swine, the Jews took counsel to kill Jesus. Then God told Jesus that He would raise him up to heaven, and so Jesus said to his disciples: "Who among you will agree to take a form similar to mine and die [in my place] and be crucified and then go [straight] to paradise?" A man among them offered himself, so God changed him into a form resembling Jesus' and he was killed and crucified.
>
> Others say that a man pretended [to be a believer] in Jesus' presence but then went off and denounced him, whereupon God changed the man into a form similar to that of Jesus, and that he was seized and crucified.[24]

One should not think that there was but one gnostic view of Jesus' crucifixion, namely, that of Valentinus. Other allusions to his death in the texts from the Coptic library at Nag Hammadi will be given below. For now, however, some exploration of Islamic positions that differ from received interpretations like that of al-Baydawi are in order.

The death of Jesus is not denied in the Qur 'an but several times asserted (e.g., in 3:55; 5:117; 19:33). Whether he was crucified is the matter in question. The disputed phrase of 4:157 reads *wa lākin šubbiha lahum*, which is generally rendered, "it [or he] was made to appear so to them." In his exegesis of this phrase, the modern Shi'i scholar Mahmoud M. Ayoub acknowledges that, in their eagerness to confirm that Jesus was not crucified, Qur 'anic exegetes have generally interpreted the words *šubbiha lahum* to mean that another was made to bear his likeness (*šabah*) and die in his stead.[25] There are syntactical problems with this reading, but despite them the theories about who that substitute might have been continued over the centuries. Ayoub's main point is that the Qur 'an has a fully Islamic Christology "based not on borrowed distortions of early Christian heresies, but on the Islamic view of man and God. . . . Islam . . . does not admit of docetism in any form. . . . Thus any parallels that this [substitutionist] position may

24. Translation by F. E. Peters, *Judaism, Christianity, and Islam: The Classical Texts and Their Interpretation*, vol. 1, *From Covenant to Community*, chap. 3, no. 30 (Princeton: Princeton Univ. Press, 1990), 151.

25. "Towards an Islamic Christology, II: The Death of Jesus, Reality or Delusion (A Study of the Death of Jesus in Tafsir Literature)," *The Muslim World* 70/2 (April 1980): 95. Part I is subtitled "An Image of Jesus in Early Shi'i Muslim Literature," 66/3 (July 1976): 163–88, and presents the altogether sympathetic view of Jesus as a "slave of Allah" found in the Qur 'an (4:172) which Shi'i piety develops more than Sunni. There is no doubt in the Qur 'an that Jesus died. The question Ayoub attacks in his second article is how. For long this has been considered a settled question but, according to him, not in the Shi'i mind.

present with docetism can only be incidental."[26] The Qur'anic commentator al-Tabari (d. ca. 923) had quoted a number of traditions about the substitution theory. He said he received them from the Jewish convert Wahb b. Munabbih and various unnamed Christian converts, also a companion of the Prophet, Qatāda, who stressed that one associate of Jesus had Jesus' likeness cast on him voluntarily. Otherwise, God would have been guilty of causing an innocent man to die unjustly to save another.

Some elements of the Islamic tradition reflect a firsthand knowledge of the Gospel accounts of the passion. The story of substitution is related on the authority of the biographer of the Prophet Ibn Ishāq (d. ca. 768), which was supposedly told to him by a Christian convert. In this version the volunteer's name was Sergus. Jesus was seated in a house with the Twelve and offered a place with him in Paradise to whoever would bear his likeness and die in his stead. Sergus "took the seat of Jesus and the Master was taken up to heaven."[27] The stage that followed might be called a "punishment substitutionism." In it, a certain Titānūs was sent into a house to kill Jesus, who had taken refuge there, and he was turned by God into his likeness and killed in his place. The twelfth century saw the introduction of the tale of the calumny of Mary cited by al-Baydawi above. Judas Iscariot (Yutah Zechariah) was another of those who were crucified in place of Jesus.

Some modern Shi'i thinkers have allowed the possibility that Jesus died and that only his spirit was taken up to heaven; or that a spiritual and not a formal assumption of Jesus' body is meant, since the Exalted One has no place to receive bodies. Contemporary Sunni thinkers exhibit a fairly accurate knowledge of Christian primary sources but tend to look to nineteenth-century humanist attacks on religion as their means to discredit the Gospels. Muhammad 'Abduh, an early Arab modernist, is of this type, while Sayyid Qutb, founder of the Muslim Brothers, confesses he is agnostic about "the manner of [Jesus'] death and assumption" as the Qur'anic text presents them.

In general, Muslims think the Christian belief is irrational, namely, that the salvation of humanity depends on a crucifixion in which God allowed Christ, who had committed no sin deserving of this punishment, to suffer. Rather than reconciling the divine justice and mercy, it nullifies both. If belief in the crucifixion saves the believer, S. M. Rashid Ridā asks, no matter how grave his sins and evil his deeds, where would the justice of God and his mercy be? "The claim of the people of the Cross, therefore, that clemency and forgiveness are opposed to justice, is unacceptable."[28] The argumentation of contemporary Muslims on this point tends to be polemical and not grounded on serious inquiry into Christian theology.

26. Ayoub, "Islamic Christology, II," 94, 95, 96.

27. Ibid., 98.

28. Sayyid Muhammad Rashid Ridā, Tafsir al-Manar, 2d ed. (Cairo: Dār al-Manār, 1367/1948), VI, 23, as quoted by Ayoub, "Islamic Christology, II," 115.

Professor Ayoub is a distinct exception. He observes that Islam has often been thought of as having no place for the mystery of suffering, which in Christianity becomes the foundation for faith, hope, and love. This is far from the case, as the stories of the misfortunes of Abraham, Jacob, Job, John the Baptist, and the Prophet, told and retold to the pious throughout Islamic history, demonstrate. Since this is so, he asks, why does the Qur 'an deny the crucifixion of Christ in the face of all the evidence? He thinks that it does not, and that the pursuit of substitutionist theories by Islamic commentators is a mare's nest. For him, 4:157 is not in the realm of history but is theology in the broad sense. The Qur 'anic statement by the Jews, "We have surely killed Jesus the Christ, son of Mary, the apostle of God," is not explored historically but is intended to reproach the arrogance and folly that might be directed against God and his messengers.[29] For Ayoub the description of Jesus as the Christ in this passage is the more significant feature.

Jesus is not just a man but "the Word of God who was sent to earth and who returned to God. Thus the denial of the killing of Jesus is a denial of the power of men to vanquish and destroy the divine Word, which is forever victorious."[30] This means that the words "they did not kill him, nor did they crucify him," in which the opponents of Jesus stand in the place of all humanity, go deeper than into human history—penetrate the heart and conscience of the human race. "They did not slay him but it seemed so to them" indicates how vain is the imagining that thinks God's son can be overcome. "The words, *wa lākin shubbiha lahum*, do not disclose, therefore, a long-hidden secret of divine deception; rather they constitute an accusation or judgment against the human sin of pride and ignorance."[31]

When 4:157f. says, "They did not kill him, with certainty, rather God took him up to Himself, and God is mighty, and wise," human limitations are being contrasted with divine power and infinite wisdom. Humans may "wish to extinguish the light of God with their mouths," but God perfects this light—Christ the Word—in a judgment against human folly and pride. To interpret the Qur 'an thus is to do more than hold 'Īsā high among God's prophets and friends, as all Muslims do. It is to see him as the light of God shining with perfect splendor in human minds and hearts. The Shiite tradition speaks of Jesus in warmer terms of praise than the Sunni, and Sufism more honorifically still.[32] It is doubtful, however, if Professor Ayoub's plea to "let God be God" in the matter of his messenger Jesus will be hailed with enthusiasm by many of his fellow religionists, even by those who agree that

29. Ayoub, "Islamic Christology, II," 117.
30. Ibid.; cf. Qur 'an 3:45; 4:171. Elsewhere Ayoub speaks of the special place the Gospel of John holds in Shi'i and the allied Sufi thought and piety.
31. Ayoub, "Islamic Christology, II," 117.
32. Ayoub provides an appendix on the Christ of Sufism from Ismā'il Haqqi, *Tafsir Rūh al-Bayān* (Istanbul, 1130/1710), 2.318ff., which says that Jesus' departure from earthly existence was not through the gate of death. "He rather entered through the gate of power (*qudra*) and departed through the gate of majesty (*'izza*)."

God's taking him up to himself does not require that no crucifixion shall have preceded this assumption to heaven.

The earlier reference to Valentinus's teaching as reported by Irenaeus could give the impression that gnostic Christians of the second century generally denied that Jesus died by crucifixion. That is not true. Some denied it and some did not. Among the former should perhaps be listed the *Gospel of Thomas,* the 114 sayings attributed to Jesus that do not dwell on the crucifixion (except obliquely in 55 = Luke 14:26–27 par. Matt. 10:37–38) or the resurrection. More clearly among the denials of the crucifixion is the teaching of Basilides of Alexandria, reported by Irenaeus (ca. 180) but possibly based on a lost work of Justin (ca. 150):

> The ungendered . . . sent its first-born, the intellect, called Christ. . . . And . . . it appeared on earth as a man, and he performed deeds of power. Hence he did not suffer. Rather, a certain Simon of Cyrene was forced to bear his cross for him, and it was he who was ignorantly and erroneously crucified, being transformed by the other, so that he was taken for Jesus; while Jesus, for his part, assumed the form of Simon and stood by, laughing at them.[33]

In the chapter in Irenaeus's *Adversus Haereses* that follows immediately on his treatment of the Christian Gnostics and that perhaps should be part of it, some unidentified "others" are said to teach that the anointed (Christ), combined with wisdom (Sophia), descended into Jesus enabling him to perform miracles, heal, proclaim the unrecognizable (or unknown) parent, and openly confess himself to the child of the first human being. "The rulers and the parent of Jesus [Ialdabaōth, ruler of heaven, who impregnated Mary] were angry at this, and worked to have him killed. And while he was being led away (to death)—they say—the anointed (Christ) himself, along with wisdom (Sophia), departed for the incorruptible realm, but Jesus was crucified."[34]

The version of the gnostic myth attributed to Ptolemy, a disciple of Valentinus, by Irenaeus held that when the impassible anointed (or Christ) was brought before Pilate, the spirit that had been deposited in him was taken away.

> What suffered, therefore, was what they consider to be the animate anointed (Christ) [or lower Jesus, born of Mary], who was mysteriously constructed . . . so that through him the mother might display a representation [symbol] of the

---

33. Irenaeus *Against Heresies* 1.24.4, in Bentley Layton, trans., *The Gnostic Scriptures* (Garden City, N.Y.: Doubleday, 1987), 423. See the *Second Treatise of the Great Seth* VII, 2.56.4–25: "Yes, they saw me, they punished me. It was another . . . who drank the gall . . . it was not I. . . . They struck me with the reed. . . . It was another on whom they placed the crown of thorns. . . . And I was laughing at their ignorance. . . . For I was altering my shapes, changing from form to form" (Robinson, *Nag Hammadi,* 365).

34. Irenaeus *Adversus Haereses* 1.7.2; in Layton, pp. 295–96.

superior anointed (Christ) [the savior or higher Jesus], who had stretched out along the cross. . . . For all these things—they say—are representations of ones in that other (realm).[35]

A Valentinian anthology known as *Gospel of Philip* contains some one hundred short excerpts from other works: sermons, treatises, and collected aphorisms. One is of particular interest to the question of Jesus' crucifixion: "'[My] God, my God, why O Lord hast thou forsaken me?' He spoke these words from the cross; for he [had] withdrawn from that place."[36] A sentiment cognate to the one from Ptolemy above appears next in the collection: "[. . .] born from [. . .] by God. The [. . .] from the dead [. . .] exist(s), but [. . .] is perfect [. . .] flesh, but [. . .] one."[37]

These citations indicate the early shrinking from the thought that the Christ was passible in a wing of Hellenic Christianity, which spread to Upper Egypt, Syria, and Mesopotamia. Jesus was a material being, having been produced by a Craftsman (*demioúrgos*) and Mary, and hence could suffer. The spirit Christ could not. Some gnostic strains denied suffering even of the human Jesus and adopted the substitution theories here reported on. Others feature his victory over the corruptible world without taking a position on how he exited it.[38]

Gnosticism as a mythology lived on in some form until the eighth century. It continued to influence orthodox Christianity, however, by inserting the gnawing doubt that a human Sufferer could himself redeem those who suffered, or that suffering could be predicated of a divine person. So much in all this depends on the metaphysical starting point. Is created spirit the only good and is matter evil? Are corruption of the flesh and death unmitigated evils without any place in the divine purpose? Is redemption by suffering an obscenity, not to say a blasphemy? Christianity emerged with one set of answers to this age-old debate, the gnostic systems with another.

Not all the gnostic evidence, one should note, goes in the direction of denial of the crucifixion. Some extant documents show themselves to be in accord with the Gospel evidence. Some scholars, though not all, classify the *Apocryphon of James* from the third century or earlier in Egypt as sympathetic to the Valentinian position because of its emphasis on knowledge and the use of themes like sleep, drunkenness, and sickness. It says:

Scorn death, therefore, and take thought for life! Remember my cross and my death, and you will live.

35. Ibid.
36. This damaged manuscript is found in the Nag Hammadi collection only and is in the Cairo Coptic Museum; Layton, *Gnostic Scriptures*, 342.
37. Ibid.
38. Thus the "Treatise on the Resurrection" addressed to Rheginus: "The savior swallowed death. . . . laying aside the corruptible world, he exchanged it for an incorruptible eternal realm" (ibid., 321).

But I answered and said to him, "Lord, do not mention to us the cross and death, for they are far from you."

The Lord answered and said, "Verily I say unto you, none will be saved unless they believe in my cross. But those who have believed in my cross, theirs is the kingdom of God." [39]

In the same vein is the *Gospel of Truth*, hypothetically attributed to Valentinus:

For this reason [the hiddenness of the will of the Father of the all] Jesus appeared; he put on that book [of the living, written in the thought and mind of the Father]; he was nailed to a tree; he published the edict of the Father on the cross. O! such great teaching! He draws himself down to death though life eternal clothes him. [40]

The *Tripartite Tractate* has a *plērōma* made up of a triad of Father, Son, and Church, an innovation that Tertullian attributes to the Sicilian Gnostic Heracleon. It contains no reference to the crucifixion but speaks of the Savior's taking on himself the death of those whom he thought to save, conceived and born as an infant as he was, in body and soul. [41] The one who appeared in flesh is the Son of the unknown God, the firstborn Son of the Totality who was incarnate and gave redemption to humans and angels, having first received it from the Logos who descended on him. [42] Finally, the *Sophia of Jesus Christ,* a Christianized version of the religio-philosophical epistle *Eugnostos the Blessed,* says in its opening lines: "After he rose from the dead, his twelve disciples and seven women followed him (and) went to Galilee onto the mountain." There, in his risen state, "the Savior" shared all sorts of metaphysical speculation with his disciples, but at least, in conformity with the Gospels, he was credited with having undergone death. [43]

It is not because of any queasiness over blood or violence that many of the gnostic writings tread lightly before the mystery of Calvary or avoid it altogether. Corporeality itself is the problem. The professedly Christian adherents to gnosis of whose teachings we have a record are committed to the total superiority of spirit to matter. Hence the redemption of angels or humans by a spirit who is embodied is either mildly repugnant to the gnostic mentality or quite unthinkable. The Son's ascent to the heavenly realm is something they are thoroughly at home with, but not when it entails coming

39. *Apocryphon of James* 5.30–6.7 (trans. F. E. Williams, in Robinson, *Nag Hammadi,* 32).

40. *Gospel of Truth* (I,3 and XII,2) 20.23–30 (trans. George W. MacRae in Robinson, *Nag Hammadi,* 42).

41. *Tripartite Tractate* 115 (trans. H. W. Attridge and D. Mueller in Robinson, *Nag Hammadi,* 92- 93).

42. Ibid., 133, 125 (ET, 101, 97–98).

43. *Sophia of Jesus Christ* III, 90.15 (trans. D. M. Parrott in Robinson, *Nag Hammadi,* 222).

forth as a recent corpse from the tomb that held it. The way the life of Jesus ended is not what gives pause. It is his enfleshed condition in the first instance. The Christ of Christian Gnostics is not only an immortal eon (Coptic *ain*) but an incorruptible one, powerful among those who emerge from the One (or All) because of his incapacity to change like the creatures he saves.

Hindu, Buddhist, and Confucian Views of the Cross

The composition of the 108 books known as Upanishads, which interpret philosophically the hymns and ritual texts called Vedas, are dated by Western scholars between 1000 and 600 B.C.E. Hindu savants tend to have little interest in their age. They think of them as timeless because they heighten the awareness of what is everlasting. These texts derive their importance from the fact that they provide a window on the timeless. The force behind and above all gods that makes possible every sacrifice, every ritual, and all creation is called the Brahman and is the foundation of the Vedas and the Upanishads. The Vedas are the Brahman's first manifestation, its "word," while visible creation is the externalization of the word. Vedanta means literally the "end of the Vedas" or the final scriptures of the Vedic literature. Somewhat like "Metaphysics," the name given to the treatise that came after (*metá*) Aristotle's treatment of the physical world, Vedanta came to mean not only the culmination of the previous writings, especially the later ones, but of all knowledge (*veda*) which is relative with respect to it. The school of Shankara (ca. 800) is called Advaita Vedanta, meaning "not-two" or nonduality. There is only one reality, the Brahman, and all multiplicity is merely illusion (*maya*). *Atman* in this philosophical system is the indestructible real self behind the superficial personality and is an expression of the Brahman.

Many Westerners take Advaitan philosophy to be synonymous with the Hindu tradition, but this is a mistake. It might even be said to be a minority position held by intellectuals. Western thinkers tend to consider it the most attractive form of Hindu thought, especially if their own grasp of theism is weak. For the majority of Hindus their religion is much more theistic than nontheistic. Vishnu is the highest god of the triad (*trimurti*)—*not* trinity—Brahma, Vishnu, and Shiva. Vishnu becomes incarnate as Rama and Krishna. Ishvara is the personal god as Creator, Preserver, and Destroyer. Kali is the best-known name of the mother goddess.

The legendary dramas that most Hindus live by, played out annually in their villages, are the Mahabharata (Great Epic) and the Ramayana (Adventures of Rama). The Bhagavad Gita is a tiny fragment of the Mahabharata but is immensely influential in the lives of ordinary Hindus, who view it as direct divine revelation. In this legend the hero, Arjuna, is addressed by the divine figure Shri Krishna, who takes him beyond the immediate problem of the war between the Pandavas and the Kauvaras into a discussion of the ethics of battle and with it all struggle, the true nature of humanity, and the indestructibility of the individual self. Krishna comforts Arjuna with the assurance that, as cosmic Lord, he defeated the enemy long ago, "that Arjuna is only performing the deed on the stage of history in the dimension of space and time as an instrument of God, to whom it is also proper to dedicate the fruits of his action."[44]

How does Hinduism, which calls itself *sanatana dharma*, "eternal religion," conceive a faith that has at its center a crucified and risen redeemer who is both divine and human? Better put, how might it be if the bulk of India's 800 millions had ever heard of Christianity and its teaching? The learned who have had contact with the West, chiefly through India's colonial domination by the Portuguese, then the British, are prone to say that the Hindu tradition can accommodate all the world's religions (except for Buddhism and Jainism, which broke off from it), hence it has no problem finding a place for the more transcendent aspects of Christianity. The admiration of India's holy men like Shri Ramakrishna (d. 1886), Swami Vivekenanda (1902), Shri Auribindo (d. 1950), and its political liberator Mohandas K. Gandhi ("the Mahatma") for the teachings of Jesus is well known. The Gospel of John is a particular favorite of Indian thinkers, with its theme of a man come from heaven to which he must return. What they might think of redemption from sin and death by faith in his cross and resurrection is not well documented. In the Vedantic understanding,

> what really matters is *re-remembering* one's original unity with the divine. After a . . . journey through the finite maya-worlds [appearance; diversity hiding the *one*] where it plays this or that role, the infinite finds it way back to itself—to discover at the moment of enlightenment that it has actually never left, because it knows neither time, nor space, nor causality, neither a before nor an after.[45]

This describes the reflective Vedantin well enough, if not the ordinary Hindu devotee of one or other god (actually, an *avatar* or manifestation of the divine).

44. Hans Torwesten, *Vedanta: Heart of Hinduism,* adapted by Loly Rosset from a translation from the German by John Phillips (New York: Grove Atlantic, 1991), 83.
45. Ibid., 201; Kathleen Healy's *Christ as Common Ground: A Study of Christianity and Hinduism* (Pittsburgh: Duquesne University Press, 1990) confirms this Vedantic understanding, taking it to be representative of Hinduism in its entirety. Having made clear, on the testimony of numerous Indian scholars, that the tradition is xenophobic, suspicioning any religious thought that does not originate in India, Healy quotes many of the country's thinkers who say the tradition can easily accept a timeless, transcendent Christ—much as Christian gnosticism was able to do—and the compassionate teacher, Jesus, but that it balks at a man of history of whom it is claimed that he is the unique redeemer, and at a redemption that rejects reincarnation in other forms. Of Jesus' death or the suffering that accompanied it as redemptive, neither the author nor any Hindu or Christian she quotes has anything nonformulaic to say.

One should remember that Vedanta is but one of six major viewpoints represented in Hindu thought.[46] A person committed to Vedanta and above all its Advaitan branch—represented modernly by Vivekenanda and Ramana Maharshi (d. 1950)—will have a problem with any religion like Judaism or Christianity that is rooted in events that take place in time. If human finiteness is absorbed in a timeless "now," all events in time for which an eternal significance is claimed will create a problem. It is as if the peasantry of fourteenth-century Erfurt were viewed as conceiving its Christian faith in identical terms with the Dominican prior of the town, Meister Eckhart. But such was not the case, nor is it so in modern India. The people of that vast subcontinent would be quite able to take in the figure of Jesus as central in the Christian epic, even though viewing him as the unique *avatar* ("descent") of deity would come hard. It is the claim of uniqueness that causes the problem, not that he might be an expression of deity in human form. The category of history is not readily available to those familiar for centuries with saga only, yet the biblical narratives partake of that character more than post-Enlightenment Christians realize or like to admit. Moreover, the Upanishads feature few personages who could be considered historical individuals. As to Christ as a god experiencing every human emotion and response to adversity, there is again no problem.

To come down to the crucifixion and resurrection, devotees of Hindu religion certainly know suffering well enough to recognize it in a great teacher, a *guru*. They would find it easy to compassionate him in his pain and welcome his compassion with their suffering. As to violence and bloodshed, the Hindu mind has neither more nor less affinity for it than any people but is as familiar with both phenomena as any, especially when they are visited upon innocence. The sacred books tell of such occurrences, though not in a framework of the redemptive power of a death.

In sum, the story of the death of Christ as compensatory for the sins of many would strike the normal Hindu devotee as novel. Some would resonate to his death in sacrifice. Many would find it incomprehensible. It would constitute the same scandal or folly to Hindus as to Paul's Jews and pagans—for him the whole of humanity—in his day. But it is not correct to view the cross, as many Western philosophers of Indian religion do, as too gross or too time-bound for that culture to accept. Most Indians, to be sure, classify

---

46. "The Vedas, the Upanisads, and the Bagavadgitā, along with one extreme Vedāntin Sankara, have dominated the Western picture of Indian philosophy, but they do not constitute anything like the whole or the essence or even, as so often contended, the basic spirit of the almost infinite variety of philosophical concepts, methods and attitudes that make up the Indian philosophical tradition. Instead, if these are taken as the whole or the essence—as, to be sure, even many Indians would have us believe, there would be a narrowness and a limitation of significant philosophy that would well warrant the neglect that Western philosophers have shown toward that tradition. But they are not the whole" (Charles A. Moore, ed., *The Indian Mind* [Honolulu: University Press of Hawaii, 1967], 10, cited by Balbis Singh in *Foundations of Indian Philosophy* [New Delhi, 1971], 258).

Christianity as the religion of the white West. Those are the only terms on which most have encountered it. Others as fully Indian, however, if not Hindu, have lived by faith in a crucified and risen Lord for centuries—going back to the apostolic age with the arrival of the apostle Thomas in their own recounting, or whenever Syriac Christianity arrived. These believers are as fully Indian as any others. They have not for centuries been philosophically or religiously Hindu. Culturally they have never stopped being such because it is impossible.

As he meditated on human misery and suffering, Gautama, "the Buddha," concluded that it was not the rational but the irrational self that caused them. Thus one must conquer this self if misery and suffering are to be eliminated. Once suffering is conquered, what lies beyond it will be possessed. For this thinker, the ideal of *nirvāna* is the ideal individual in possession of self. "Ignorance and desires are cut at their roots and the source of all misery and suffering vanishes once and for all."[47] How they are to cope who do not achieve *nirvāna* and yet continue to suffer is not spelled out, beyond the teaching that they must continue to strive. The early Buddhas eliminated God and the soul from their religion, leaving almost nothing that could be a source of solace and inspiration for the sufferer. It is thus that the bulk of Hindus refused to follow their native son Gautama, seeing in his appeal to persist in the strenuous path and unswerving faith in the moral law a "mere abstract and mechanical way of life."[48]

Those who continue in this path are called Hināyāna (or "smaller vehicle") Buddhists. They are people for whom the Buddha is but a historical person, a great teacher. They hope to cut the knot of ignorance or bondage and thereby attain enlightenment (*arhatship;* for Hindus, *jivanmukti*). Achieving it extinguishes all sorrow and suffering in the Hināyānist view. For many Buddhists this outlook was seen to be selfish at root and to find no traditional place for God and the soul. The Mahāyāna school ("greater vehicle") arose in response, proposing as the ideal the *bodhisattva* (lit., "knower of reality"), one who seeks not enlightenment for the self alone but the salvation of all sentient beings through active participation in the life of society. For the Mahāyānist, Buddha incarnated himself to inspire others to relieve the multitudes of their sufferings. "So long as there is suffering in the world the spiritual aspirant cannot claim salvation for himself. It is only the . . . constant concern for the welfare and happiness of others that can make one *bodhisattva* or knower of reality."[49] D. T. Suzuki writes:

Therefore all Bodhisattvas, in order to emancipate sentient beings from misery, are inspired with great spiritual energy and mingle themselves with the filth of birth and death. Though they thus make themselves subject to the laws of birth

47. Singh, *Foundations,* 328.
48. Ibid.
49. Ibid., 230.

and death, their hearts are free from sins and attachments. They are like . . .
those immaculate, not contaminated by it.[50]

From what has been said, it is clear that the Hinayāna tradition, which is
an ethic rather than a religion, would be sympathetic to the teachings of
Jesus and to those Christian bodies that are conscious of the need for striv-
ing, under the divine impulse, to be free of the bondage imposed by ignorance. The notion that another can gain merit for the individual is beyond
the ken of the normal Hinayānist. Each person must become detached from
all sorrow and suffering by dint of personal effort. Similarly, the concept of
concentrating on the sufferings of Jesus, who did nothing to avoid or tran-
scend them, would puzzle if not repel this type of Buddhist. The flaw observed in Christianity is that it has as its role model one who, unlike the
Buddha, has led millions to accept their sufferings. The majority of Christians even assume that such acceptance has some sort of redemptive value if
joined to the sufferings of Jesus. The Hinayānist is not so naive as to think
that all grief and pain can be avoided but considers the failure to keep striv-
ing for enlightenment in spite of them a refusal to walk on the noble path.

Mahāyāna Buddhism knows something of the redemptive principle at the
heart of Christianity, hence it is not dismayed by a teaching about the cross
and what faith in it may accomplish. One of the core convictions of the
Mahāyāna tradition is that

a *bodhisattva,* pure and perfect, takes upon himself the sins of others in exchange for his own noble deeds (*parivarta*) and willingly suffers its unpleasant
consequences. *Parivarta* is the "turning over" of one's virtuous deeds toward
the uplifting of the suffering masses, a transfer of merits of a kind unknown
to primitive Buddhism.[51]

It is hard to say that there was no Christian influence on the phrasing of
the Indian scholar who wrote that, in light of the effect the British religion
of the last century had upon Hinduism to remind it of its strong theistic
strain. The Anglican claims made for Jesus and his redemptive death have
simply been placed before Hindu culture for two centuries, perhaps serving
to repel as much as to attract because they are the religion of the oppressor.
The same is true, although not as forcefully, in those lands where Mahāyāna
Buddhism prevails.

The Catholic and the Nestorian Christian presence is a matter of much
longer standing in India and China. It is correctly said of China that all
its billion people are endemically Confucian, whether Buddhist, Muslim,
or Christian. But Confucius was a guide to administrative protocol and a

50. *Outlines of Mahāyāna Buddhism* (London, 1936), 293–94.
51. See Daisetz Teitaro Suzuki, *Outlines of Mahayana Buddhism* (New York: Schocken
Books, 1963), 282–86.

philosopher rather than a man of religion. He had the respect for "heaven," a verbal symbol for nature and the deity behind it, that marks all the Chinese. The same is true for veneration of ancestors. But one does not find Confucius concerned with questions like sin and forgiveness or eternal salvation. Virtue, yes. Confucius was solidly committed to the virtuous life, but his ethic was uninfluenced by any reference to heaven—even though most Chinese incorporate into their ethic a future in paradise for the spirits of the good. It is even less fitting to ask what the Chinese soul rather than the Hinayāna Buddhist might make of Jesus' painful death and resurrection in the flesh. One does not normally get philosophical answers to fit religious questions with any precision.

The eminent modern philosopher Fung Yu-Lan describes the introduction of religious Taoism as a nationalistic reaction to the alien faith, Buddhism. Similarly, in the nineteenth century with growing Western influence in the military, commercial, and industrial spheres, there came a strong Christian missionary presence. One response was the movement, toward the end of the century, in favor of a native Confucian religion to counteract its impact, led by the statesman and reformer K'ang Yu-wei (d. 1927). He attempted to restore the thought of the Han dynasty scholars (206 B.C.E.–220 C.E.), finding in that school enough material to establish Confucianism as an organized religion in the proper sense.[52] The movement for a Confucian religion suffered an early death, however, with the overthrow of the Ch'ing dynasty and its replacement by the Republic. K'ang's friend T'an Ssu-t'ung (d. 1898 at the age of thirty-three) wrote an important treatise entitled *The Science of Jen* (human-heartedness), proposing that one read certain books before turning to it, including the New Testament. Western contributions to mathematics, the sciences, and sociology have been more influential in China up to now than anything philosophical or religious.

It is extremely chancy to estimate how the doctrine of a crucified Messiah, an intermediary with God who is himself divine-human, might be received by the billions of Asians who have never been confronted with him or know him only through the lens of colonialism. The speculation engaged in here is entirely hypothetical. It asks what the probable tolerance of these three worldviews might be for an idea foreign to them. Their classical texts, the work of intellectuals, are taken to reveal to us the innermost thoughts of many, the majority illiterate, in these three traditions. Even the simplest persons are no doubt influenced by the centuries-long circulation of the ideas behind these writings. At the same time, the intellectual West tends to have no awareness of the popular religious practices of the peoples of India, China, and southeast Asia to which much in oldest Christianity is cognate. It deduces instead that the classic books and commentaries on them by the

---

52. See Fung Yu-lan, *A Short History of Chinese Philosophy* (New York: Macmillan, 1948), 322–25.

learned *are* the religions of these peoples. Modern expositors of the Asian religious spirit from those countries do not hesitate to speak for millions with whom they are in no close touch. They tend to think the populace ignorant and superstitious relative to the advances in the realm of the spirit made by the great figures of the past who authored the classic texts.

But the problems that the peoples of Asia face daily and the solutions they seek are quite like those of the rest of the globe. Why is life a backbreaking struggle with so little reward, as Qohelet put it eloquently when their cultures were already old? What becomes of the dead? What is the meaning of disease and typhoon and failed harvest? Why do our holy books preach compassion when life's only problem seems to be coping with violence? In brief, does heaven care or is the universe mute on all these questions?

It is a still unanswered question what a man who died cruelly, out of love, might mean to all these millions.

Conclusion

What can one reasonably conclude of all that has been written, prayed, and experienced over the course of two millennia about Jesus' death on the cross? Only a small portion of all that is possible has been reported in the pages above. Have I learned anything in the process or am I still left, as Robert Hamerton-Kelly says of the English author of a book about Paul entitled *The Mythmaker,* with "the courage of his concoctions"? I have the religious faith I began with. Otherwise my reports on the theology of that faith should not be trusted. I have learned much Christian history in the process, Eastern and Western: how people have prayed this mystery, been consoled and occasionally terrified by it, and how they have made it part of the fabric of their lives.

We should start with the fact that Jesus' crucifixion—an event in history—was mythicized within fifty years. It did not stop being an event in history, but it was mythicized history from the first we hear of it. The proof is that the crucifixion was coupled with Jesus' resurrection as a single happening from the start. The occurrences of a particular Friday in the Passover season are reportable as history. Jesus' glorified state as risen can only be called metahistory, that is, events having taken place beyond space and time. The faith response of believers to what they saw and heard could be reported historically but not the career of the new denizen of heaven.

An important fact is hidden beneath this observation. Death and resurrection are the one mystery of Christ from the first we learn of it. It is a single divine-human reality in the midst of human lives. Later, the four evangelists, all of whom adopted a narrative mode in their writing, would provide details on Jesus' arrest through to the point of his imperviousness to all human restraint. They fleshed out the original myth of faith with historical reminiscences, fulfillments of biblical prophecy, and theological convictions. The chief of these was that, by the power of this deed of God, all human sin and sinfulness were remitted to any who would believe in it. What was awry in human life was set aright. The baleful forces aligned against God and those who serve God were stripped of their power. All creation sang with joy the morning Jesus stepped forth from the tomb. Such is the essence of myth: a truth too large for ordinary discourse to handle, however much of history might reside at its core.

The writers of the Gospels and the Acts of the Apostles traded more in the details of Jesus' death than the writers of epistles and other literary genres. They reported that Jesus died through a miscarriage of Roman justice, but they featured the villainy of the temple priesthood and the Jewish "elders" even more. Whether because it was a well-remembered fact in their Jewish minds or because of subsequent antipathy between the residual power class in Palestine and the believers in Jesus for whom the evangelists spoke, we cannot say. In cool retrospect we may call this account of his condemnation an indifferent matter and one only to be expected. Collusion among the powerful who are otherwise opposed to each other is the first law of power: "That same day Herod and Pilate became friends; before that they had been enemies" (Luke 23:12). Antipas, son of Herod the Great, was no representative Jew any more than Caiaphas and Annas were. Jewish history is clear on that. But by adding in the jeering mobs with their cries, "We have no king but Caesar," "His blood be on us and on our children," and "Crucify him!" the Gospel writers outdid themselves. They might have added these colorful touches simply because that is the way mobs acted. Unhappily, since there were none but Jews in Jerusalem besides the occupying army for the pilgrimage feast, the executioners—who were the pagan prefect and soldiery of fact—became "the Jews" of imagination. The tragedy of those colorful accounts is that they have haunted Christians ever since and worked horror upon Jews.

At the beginning it was not so. For almost a century that we know of, Jesus' death was reported as a death by judicial sentence, its details not featured in the recounting. It would have taken a century after the crucifixion for the four Gospel narratives to have circulated widely. Mid-second-century antipathies between the two communities of believers put an end to the unadorned faith proclamation of Christ as dead and risen. As in all tensions described by historians and journalists as "sectarian violence," this one was ethnic and economic at root. The Jesus people had become a largely though not exclusively gentile group, and the two groups lived too close to each other everywhere. The one religious factor was the vying of burgeoning Judaism and emergent Christianity for the pagans and the Gnostics who began to show interest in this Middle Eastern phenomenon of the religion of Israel with a difference. To them it was all the one religion of that archaic people "the Hebrews." The similarities between the two religions heightened the bitterness.

At the turn of the third century an ugly development raised its head. In North Africa, where the strongest Latin culture was found, and in Alexandria and Antioch, the strongholds of Greek culture, some learned Christians and later monks and bishops began to manufacture a surrogate enemy, "the

Jews." The alleged cause was the death of Jesus at their hands, even though the central public prayer of Christians, the Eucharist, made no mention of this. All that in the earliest creed and all later creeds said was "suffered under Pontius Pilate, was crucified, died, and was buried." But the stigma against the Jews caught on, thanks no little to the rhetorical power of Melito of Sardis, Tertullian, Origen, and Clement of Alexandria. A new and debased myth was born that has cast a shadow on the nobler myth of death and resurrection ever since: Jesus had been put to death by the same Jews who had proved so hard-hearted throughout the biblical period and who would not accept him as their Messiah even to this day. Such is the form it took.

While this myth was in formation, Christian Greek-language intellectuals were at work on a theology of how the life and teaching, death and resurrection of Jesus had profited the human race. Their sources were the inspired books of the two Testaments of the Bible, which they had in Greek. The theological pattern that emerged was one of an entire race healed of its wounded condition by its solidarity in humanity with Jesus Christ. From the moment the Word of God took human flesh it rendered that flesh immortal. He could die on the cross because he chose to share the universal human lot of mortality, but his upraising by God established the deathlessness that was essentially his. Whoever expressed faith in Christ risen was able to share in his incorruption, even though as members of a sinful race they first had to undergo corruptibility. Their belief in the resurrection of Christ accomplished a *théōsis* or divinization in them. Human by nature, they received a share in the divine, even as in the incarnation divinity had had a full share in humanity.

Latin or Western theology went another route in exploring the redemptive mystery. It showed more interest in the damaging effects of sin on the human soul and spirit than on the body rendering it corruptible. For the Latins, whose theology of redemption peaked with Augustine, faith in the cross and resurrection largely but not entirely reversed the darkening of intellect and weakening of will caused by Adam's sin. An infusion of grace came with baptismal faith, but it was not as unqualified as the *théōsis* of the East. Hereditary sin and guilt left a deeper stamp on the human psyche than in the East. The victory over sin achieved by Christ was, from the human side, never quite complete.

While all this was going on, the sufferings endured by Jesus out of love for fellow humans continued to be featured in East and West. When they were spoken of it was in familiar formulas, as much from Isaiah 53 as from the Gospels. There was little elaboration, certainly not at homily length, in the form of imaginative word pictures of his physical and mental anguish. The patristic era saw Christ more as Word made flesh than as flesh united with Word. He was believed in as the risen Messiah and Lord far more than as the prepaschal victim of human cruelty. Even when "the Jews" were blamed for Jesus' death, as they were with regularity, it was always in the same formulaic fashion—well-worn and packaged phrases without much fictional reconstruction.

With the age of Gregory the Great, the "dawn of the Middle Ages," Western thinkers begin to separate the crucifixion from the resurrection. After the Carolingian era, descriptions of Jesus' cruel treatment at human hands begin to proliferate. They are distinct from the word pictures of his risen state. The resurrection begins to be treated as proof of his divinity more than as vindication of his innocence at God's hands as previously.

The turn of the millennium in Europe signals a new approach to Jesus' sufferings and death. There the stages of his passion begin to be distinguished: the indignities he endured before the chief priests and Pilate; his mockery, scourging, and crowning with thorns; the hammer blows, his cries from the cross, and his ultimate expiration. The tide of this rhetoric is slow in rising. By the fourteenth century it has come to the full.

In the eleventh century a Western theology was developed of the way humanity was redeemed by the cross and its sins expiated. Anselm's theory held that the divine justice could be satisfied only by the God-man, who could achieve it in his double role as a member of the sinful race and one who was equal to the God who had been infinitely offended. Abelard countered this theory of perfect satisfaction with one that said that God had displayed an infinite love and forgiveness in the person of Jesus Christ, who died to heal humanity's wounds. Through this example the onlooking believers have the opportunity of being filled with compunction at the horror of their wrongs and accept the reconciliation held out to them.

Thomas Aquinas accepted the propriety of Christ's death as satisfaction for the sins of all and concurred that human beings could see in this death how much God loved them, hence be moved to love in return. He went on to lodge the final efficacy of this death not in Jesus' sufferings but in his obedience to God's command. For Thomas, the fact that it happened in history meant that it was eternally decreed, since nothing escaped the divine will. I would put this another way: that Jesus willingly accepted the inevitable, whether comprehending why God was allowing it the record does not show. As to the cruelty of the death, Thomas proposed that, by Jesus' acceptance of the extremes of torture, the just might face the most painful death with equanimity. The point is that Jesus' sufferings were not primary in achieving human redemption. His obedient spirit was. It won for humanity the possibility of being similarly obedient to the divine command. The sufferings were but outward signs of the trial of his spirit. Thomas also says, when responding to his own question on whether there was good reason for Christ to die, that he could die because he was a human being but it is as God that he is the source of life to us. He suffered a death that came to him from without and submitted to it willingly to show that his death was deliberate. We were saved by a freely chosen death and must freely choose to accept its beneficent effects.

The extravagant embroidering of New Testament passion narratives came with Rupert of Deutz, a Belgian who died as an abbot in Germany. In the early twelfth century he mined the Bible in a typological exercise gone wild. A legion of visionaries took their lead from his writings. Others of a more sober cast who attempted to replicate the sufferings of the Savior in their bodies followed in the train of Peter Damiani. In a twist of history it is Bernard of Clairvaux a century later who, because of his literary output, is credited as the pioneer in passion piety. Many a male and female mystic and indeed ordinary Christian in those centuries imitated Jesus' passion or took on in their bodies the extreme torments to which he was subjected. The practices were in part penitential but more largely mimetic, in a desire to return love for love. They took on Christ's sufferings, as the Epistle to the Colossians says, "for the sake of Christ's body, the church, . . . completing what still remains for Christ to suffer in [their] own person[s]" (1:24).

The reformers relinquished nothing of their Catholic commitment to Jesus' passion and death as having achieved human salvation. They did not, however, countenance any response to this deed of God as fitting other than one of faith. All attempts to imitate Jesus in his sufferings and any claim of having received divine gifts in the order of ecstasy or the stigmata were repudiated as human "works." But Christian redemptive piety centered on Calvary continued in Protestant circles unabated.

The extreme personalism that marked the age of the Reform was equally prevalent in the Catholic post-Reformation era. This means that only lately has either the Roman Church or the family of Protestant churches been able to conceive of the mystery of the cross as either one mystery with the resurrection or as having achieved the reconciliation of humanity and the cosmos to God in any but a personalized way. If for centuries Christians, even those with a strong ecclesial sense, have thought of themselves as "on their own" before God in their sinful and redeemed condition, it will take some time for them to think of themselves as a redeemed church or human race. A conviction of solidarity in the body that has Christ as its head comes slowly. That Christ died "for the many," in the Semitic phrase of Jesus' words at the supper table, does not mean "for large numbers" but "for all"; and not for each singly but for the totality of humanity, as in the biblical phrase "all Israel." It will not be easy for a fragmented Western mentality to take in this comprehensiveness. Africans and Asians, who have a strong sense of peoplehood, absorb the idea of the comprehensiveness of redemption better. Even they, however, like all the peoples on the globe, have to struggle to accept the idea that their inclusion does not thereby mean the exclusion of others, notably of their hated enemy.

If the universally beneficent effect of Christ's death and resurrection is hard for Christians to take in—and no peoples but Christians need concur in what is a fact of faith for them—it will be harder still to accept the idea of the reconciliation of the subhuman cosmos to God. This begins with the human acceptance of responsibility for the earth, the seas, and the air, claiming all for God as a redeemed creation. Belief in the human race as the primary object of divine concern does not make Jews, Christians, and Muslims wickedly anthropocentric, as some ecologists like to claim. It simply means that humans alone can care for the whales and the threatened species because no subhuman species can care for them.

The cruel and inhuman way Jesus died has had a paradoxical twofold effect ever since. It has caused revulsion in some, making it in Paul's words a stumbling block or scandal. It has been strangely consolatory for others. Both the wretched of the earth and the more comfortable in their time of extremity—war, famine, illness, separation, death—have taken comfort from their faith that deity itself was acquainted with injustice, abandonment by friends, physical pain, and mental anguish. It is not likely that the Christian masses will soon desert a God who has experienced their pain. Christianity without the cross is conceivable among some race other than the present population of the earth. With this one, so beset by natural catastrophe and the evident effects of human sin, it is unthinkable.

Index of MT, LXX, and Vulgate Canons

Index of Authors

Index of Subjects and Persons